Green Gold

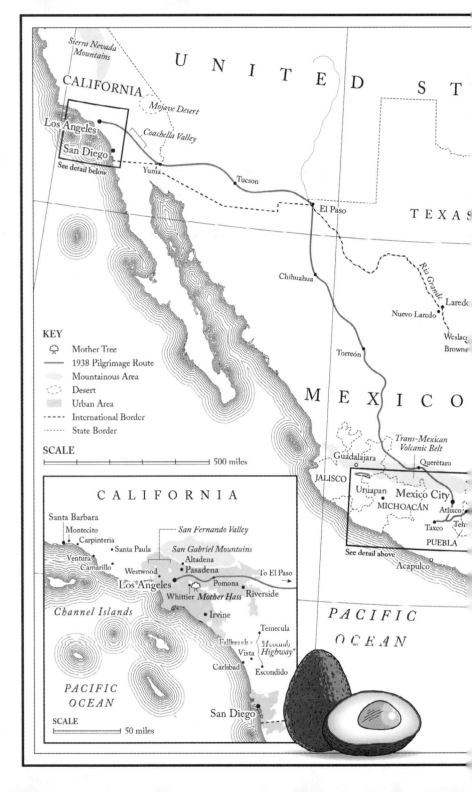

KEY

🌳 Mother Tree
— 1938 Pilgrimage Route
Mountainous Area
Desert
Urban Area
--- International Border
····· State Border

SCALE
|———|———|———|———| 500 miles

UNITED STATES

Sierra Nevada Mountains

CALIFORNIA

Mojave Desert

Coachella Valley

Los Angeles

San Diego

See detail below

Yuma

Tucson

El Paso

TEXAS

Chihuahua

Rio Grande

Laredo

Nuevo Laredo

Weslaco

Browns

Torreón

MEXICO

Trans-Mexican Volcanic Belt

Guadalajara

Querétaro

JALISCO

Uruapan

Mexico City

MICHOACÁN

Atlixco

Taxco

Teh

PUEBLA

See detail above

Acapulco

CALIFORNIA

Santa Barbara

Montecito

Carpinteria

Santa Paula

San Fernando Valley

San Gabriel Mountains

Altadena

Pasadena

To El Paso

Ventura

Camarillo

Westwood

Pomona

Los Angeles

Whittier *Mother Hass*

Riverside

Channel Islands

Irvine

Temecula

Fallbrook

"Avocado Highway"

Vista

Carlsbad

Escondido

PACIFIC OCEAN

PACIFIC OCEAN

San Diego

SCALE
|———| 50 miles

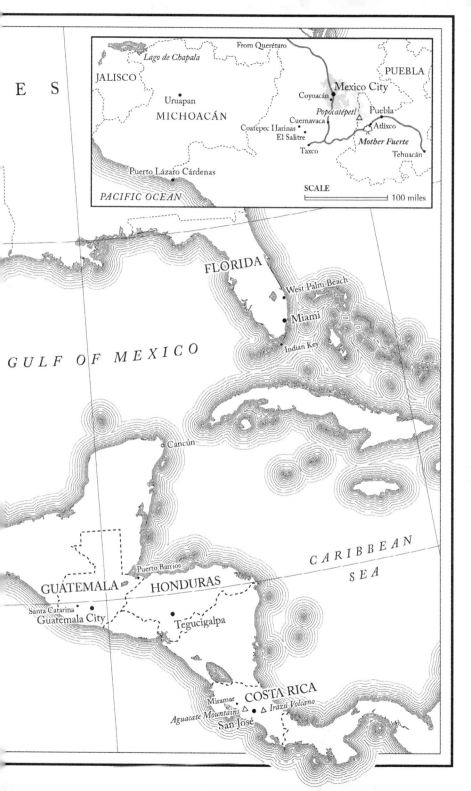

Green Gold

The Avocado's
Remarkable Journey
from Humble Superfood
to Toast *of a* Nation

Sarah Allaback *and*
Monique F. Parsons

GREEN GOLD

This is a work of nonfiction. However, some names and identifying details of individuals have been changed to protect their privacy, correspondence has been shortened for clarity, and dialogue has been reconstructed from memory.

Copyright © 2025 by Sarah Allaback and Monique F. Parsons

First Counterpoint edition: 2025

ISBN: 978-1-64009-676-9

The Library of Congress Cataloging-in-Publication data is available.

Jacket design by Farjana Yasmin
Jacket image © iStock / UlaBezryk
Book design by tracy danes
Interior images: avocado skin © Adobe Stock / Jevanto Protography; avocado icon © Adobe Stock / pandavector; paper texture © Adobe Stock / Anlomaja

Map by Mike Hall, www.thisismikehall.com

COUNTERPOINT
Los Angeles and San Francisco, CA
www.counterpointpress.com

Printed in the United States of America

1 3 5 7 9 10 8 6 4 2

For Marion—S.A.

For Teddy, Ruth, and Jules—M.F.P.

Contents

Introduction

WHY ARE AVOCADOS EVERYWHERE?

As childhood friends growing up in Carpinteria, California, in the 1970s and '80s, we saw avocados every day. They were just as much a part of the "Carp" landscape as the beach town's famous surf break. We assumed it had always been that way. Orchards blanketed the hillsides behind town, and significant hours of our childhoods were spent exploring the Parsons' avocado farm—crunching through the fallen leaves, playing beneath shady canopies, and climbing among smooth branches. It was only after leaving home and heading east for college that we recognized just how much we had taken for granted. Avocados were part of what we left behind.

Even in the 1980s, many Americans had never seen an avocado, much less tasted one. Over the decades, the fruit gradually became more common in supermarkets nationwide. Seemingly overnight, they went from occupying a small display in the "exotic" section at specialty markets to being everywhere. They appeared in New York City bodegas, midwestern megastores, health food stores, and delis. Nearly every grocery store in the United States sold avocados, almost always the Hass variety, with its black pebbly skin, rich flavor, and medium-sized pit. Hass avocados are now on the menus of Mexican restaurants, sushi bars, Korean coffee shops, pricey gourmet restaurants, and fast-food chains. Avocado toast has appeared at Dunkin' Donuts and mom-and-pop restaurants in all fifty states. Before Cinco de Mayo 2020, in the early days of a deadly pandemic, a social media campaign promoting Mexican avocados generated 6 billion impressions.[1] In 2023, Americans ate close to 3 billion pounds of avocados, tying a record set in 2021. Some analysts predict that by 2030, the average American will eat more than eleven pounds of avocados a year.[2]

Strikingly, Americans' obsession with the avocado goes beyond food or nutrition. Avocado merchandise is sold everywhere, too—from museum gift shops and highway rest stops to Etsy and Neiman Marcus. Products feature avocados in many guises: friendly-looking cartoons, often of half avocados with round or heart-shaped pits, some transformed into cats, or Santa Claus, or breasts. They grin. They pose. They wear sunglasses, tiny hats, wide sombreros, or sweatbands. Some smoke and hold beers. Several wrap their arms around toast. Many sport mottos like "let's avocuddle" and "avocado addict." Those suffering from that affliction can buy avocados shipped directly from California farms or find thousands of avocado-themed items to satisfy cravings. Among the most unusual is a Taco Tuesday baby set with a lemon-lime plastic teether and an avocado-shaped rattle. One online store sells a T-shirt with an image of the Virgin Mary, her face replaced by a severed avocado. The caption reads: "Our Lady of Guacamole."

Carpinteria rode the wave and capitalized on the avocado's fame. In 1987, our hometown launched the California Avocado Festival. The event draws tens of thousands annually to shop, eat, and celebrate avocados while strolling down palm tree–lined avenues. The festival brings the community together: the high school cheer squad makes vats of guacamole, community clubs sell avocado sandwiches, and local businesses offer avocado-chocolate truffles and avocado ice cream. Farmers from across the region come to town to demonstrate grafting and sell rare avocado varieties. The organizers mount a historical display with photographs from the early days and use profits to fund civic programs. With three stages featuring a rotating lineup of performers, it's evolved into the largest free public music festival in the state, all in honor of the avocado.

Despite its festive image, the avocado's fame has a sinister side. Images of decaying, bloody, and bullet-ridden avocados, avocados reimagined as grenades, and avocados on arid landscapes or deforested mountainsides appear on media sites. These images often illustrate articles about the 200,000 American-made guns that make their way into Mexican drug cartels' arsenals each year.[3] Sometimes the message is about the climate crisis, corrupt or inept politicians, or Americans' insatiable greed. Bruised and browning avocados become stand-ins for lost youth, poverty, deception, or death.

How did a regional staple from Latin America come to occupy such a central spot in American culture? Why has the avocado become a meme—outshining popular fruits like grapes and bananas—representing individuality and healthy living? And why is it also used as a symbol for all that's gone wrong? These questions led us to wonder about the people behind the product, those who propelled the avocado into our diets and our consciousnesses and who made it an international icon.

The story goes back more than a hundred years. To track it down, we visited nurseries and laboratories, walked through acres of orchards, and spoke with people from six continents. We discovered a history of avocado frenzies that paved a way for our own, spurred on by a tight-knit group of avocado pioneers—midwesterners, Californians, and Mexicans—who fought (sometimes with one another) to get an industry off the ground. Among them were explorers and spies, entrepreneurs and scientists, university professors and railroad tycoons, marketing geniuses and savvy salesmen. Their passionate quest for the perfect avocado and the ensuing battle for its marketplace depended on the branches of two trees that launched the avocado industry: the Fuerte and the Hass. Across borders, decades, drought, pestilence, the Mexican

Revolution, and two World Wars, the Fuerte made the avocado an affordable, nationally known fruit. In time, Hass eclipsed it in spectacular fashion. *Green Gold* is the story of two trees and the people who nurtured them, for money and love.

Part I

The Fuerte Mother Tree

(born c. 1884, Atlixco, Mexico)

Alejandro Le Blanc, left, and Wilson Popenoe with the Fuerte
mother tree, Atlixco, Mexico, 1938. California Avocado Association
Yearbook, 1938. *(From the collection of the Lenhardt Library of
the Chicago Botanic Garden)*

Agua Cate Salad (Cuba)

Cut three ripe aguacates in halves,
take out the stone or seed, and scoop
the pulp from the skin. Add three
tomatoes, first removing the skin and
core, and half a green pepper pod
cut in fine shreds. Crush and pound
the whole to a smooth mixture, then
drain off the liquid. To the pulp add
a teaspoonful or more of onion juice,
a generous teaspoonful of salt, and
about a tablespoonful of lemon juice
or vinegar. Mix thoroughly and serve
at once.

--Janet M. Hill, "Seasonal
Recipes," *The Boston Cooking-
School Magazine*, October 1904

1 · **Dreamers**

FREDERICK POPENOE WAS ONE OF TOPEKA'S RICHEST men in 1896, when he invested in a Costa Rican gold mine. For the past fifteen years he had worked tirelessly, first as a stenographer and then as a member of a loan company. When Popenoe struck out on his own to open the Accounting Trust Company, his creativity and charismatic personality earned him support from regional businessmen. An established civic leader by 1900, he bought a controlling interest in *The Topeka Daily Capital* and devised an unusual plan to boost circulation. He hired the pastor of Central Congregational Church to produce a paper virtuous enough to satisfy Jesus. Reverend Charles Sheldon had become one of the region's most influential preachers through the publication of *In His Steps*, which coined the question "What would Jesus do?"[1] Although Sheldon's edition skyrocketed newspaper sales for a week, Fred's decision to continue the paper as a Christian enterprise failed dramatically. By the end of the year, he was deeply in debt and facing a public scandal. Leaving a trustee to sort out his finances, Popenoe escaped with his wife, Marion, and three young sons to Costa Rica.[2]

The family traveled from Kansas to New York, boarded a steamship of the Atlas Line, and spent two weeks at sea before reaching Porto Limón, Costa Rica. At the dock, they gaped at the magnificent loads of bananas setting off to America, a precious few destined for Topeka. The Popenoes' journey continued by rail to San José, the country's capital, and then on to Alajuela, a city at the base of the Aguacate Mountains. Great grass-covered cones and domes poked out of the tropical flora, the result of the region's volcanic origins. Fred was a seasoned traveler along these routes. A few years earlier, he had mapped out an itinerary through the rugged terrain that divided the sixty-mile journey into four stages, each terminating in a small town. His two-seated buck-board, drawn by a pair of American mules and often driven by a roughrider from Arizona, was waiting to meet them. Confront-ing the Monte del Aguacate range, the family boarded the buck-board and headed off on the first fifteen-mile pull. When they finally reached Miramar, in Puntarenas province, a distant view of the Pacific Ocean greeted them. This was the Montes de Oro district, known for its ore veined with gold. Popenoe managed a gold mine for the Bella Vista Mining and Milling Company, an enterprise supported by a settlement of more than 1,200 residents, comprised of three to four hundred Italian and Jamaican laborers and their families.[3] The "community under Popenoe's care," also included Americans, primarily from Topeka and Colorado, who served as managers and supervisors.[4]

The tropics did little to relieve Fred's anxieties or to assuage Marion, now caring for the children with no servants, friends, or relatives for support in a foreign country. Naturally optimistic, Fred feigned confidence in the mine's ability to restore the fam-ily's wealth and status but privately struggled with feelings of des-peration as he watched his fortunes wane. His nine-year-old son, Wilson, saw things differently.* For him, Costa Rica might as well have been the Land of Oz, and coming from Kansas made him feel like a character in L. Frank Baum's new book. This land of moist warmth, lush, enveloping fern forests, brilliantly colored birds, and flowering vines invited exploration. Wilson befriended the lo-cals, learned their language, chattered with monkeys, chased wild hogs, marveled at palm fronds sixty to eighty feet long, picked

---

* Born Frederick Wilson Popenoe, Wilson used his middle name from a young age and was known as Wilt to his friends and family.

orchids, and tasted all sorts of tempting delicacies: cherimoyas, loquats, dense breadfruit, and a savory fruit with a smooth, thick skin known as aguacate. Shaped like pears and hard as rocks until ripe, avocados grew wild in this magical place. The experience would shape his life and the future of the avocado itself.[5]

Three years after arriving in Costa Rica, Fred Popenoe gave up on the gold mine and moved his family to Los Angeles, eager to make a fresh start. He hoped the dry climate would alleviate his nagging health problems but mostly sought freedom from the anxieties plaguing him over the last few years. On the strength of his newspaper experience, he was hired in 1905 as the California manager of *The Pacific Monthly*, a magazine "of education and progress," later known as *Sunset*. Among the magazine's featured articles were two by nurseryman D. W. Coolidge, whose rich descriptions of a city dedicated to health and bountiful harvests (a single avocado tree produced eighty-five dollars' worth of fruit in a season, more than $3,000 in 2024) may have inspired Fred to move his family from Los Angeles to Altadena, a suburb of Pasadena.[6] Following the death of his father, Fred came into an inheritance that allowed him to buy a rustic Craftsman-style house designed by the prominent architectural firm Greene and Greene.

The Popenoes' new California hacienda at the northwest corner of Santa Anita Avenue and East Calaveras Street stood in the foothills of the San Gabriel Mountains.[7] For a family accustomed to Topeka's grasslands and harsh winters, this dry, temperate landscape within walking distance of an ocean view offered a new outlook on life. Here the formalities of the family estate, run by servants and accompanied by an unspoken etiquette, were forgotten, as Fred took on the rugged, can-do attitude of a California rancher.[8] Wilson and his older brother, Paul, slept in a storehouse on the property (they called it "the shack") alongside a chicken coop and accompanying corral, and tended an adjacent garden.[9] Wilson's horticultural education, shaped by his experience in Costa Rica, rapidly progressed in this hospitable, subtropical environment.

Pasadena was already a recognized center of gardening, its tradition dating back to the first Tournament of Roses in 1890.[10] Growing unusual species of flowers and exotic plants was a status symbol. Twice a year, the Pasadena Horticultural Society hosted the Pasadena Flower Show, a gathering of elaborate plant displays that attracted the most celebrated plant enthusiasts in the region. These included railroad tycoon Henry Huntington and German-born horticulturalist William Hertrich, the nurseryman planning and building Huntington's lavish estate gardens. Through the flower shows, the Popenoes would meet local plant lovers and nurserymen, novices and experts alike.[11] Fred enjoyed sharing memories of the family farm and of his father, Willis, who had exhibited apples at the Philadelphia Centennial Exhibition, America's first world's fair.[12]

The Owens River project coincided with the family's first year in Pasadena. The ambitious engineering endeavor sought to irrigate Southern California. From its source deep in the Sierra Nevada Mountains, the new aqueduct stretched more than 230 miles and crossed the vast Mojave Desert before plunging into the city with tributaries to quench the thirst of Los Angeles County and surrounding regions. Led by publisher Harrison Gray Otis, the *Los Angeles Times* championed the project in ways that impressed Fred, who appreciated a bold effort.

California could not grow without water, but once it arrived, the possibilities for progress seemed limitless. Local papers were full of news about the region's unique offerings: the latest fruit varieties, bargains on flowers, and acres of land where orchard trees flourished. Fred knew a city as new and promising as Los Angeles needed not only designers to plan the city and water to sustain it but also the horticultural wherewithal to develop its burgeoning fruit and vegetable industries. Ohio native John Henry Reed, founder of the Riverside Horticultural Club, recognized the importance of expert intervention and encouraged members to petition the state legislature and the University of California system in support of scientific research related to issues plaguing the citrus industry— from improving fertilization to combating the ever-changing pests preying on both trees and fruit. After many years of lobbying, backed up by the increasingly powerful California Fruit Growers Exchange (later known as Sunkist), his dream came true. In 1906, commissioners representing the university signed off on a plan for a pathological laboratory in Whittier and an experiment station in Riverside, about fifty miles east on a twenty-three-acre site at the base of Mount Rubidoux. On Valentine's Day 1907, the Citrus Experiment Station was formally opened, ushering in a new era in scientific fruit analysis.[13]

Horticultural journalist Ernest Braunton recalled coming to Los Angeles in 1887 and seeing more tropical fruit trees than residents. Most of the "old settlers" along San Pedro Street tended an avocado tree or two from Mexico, often in the company of cherimoyas and sapotes. Braunton considered the avocado "one of the most ornamental of all fruit trees, handsome in form and foliage."[14] A member of the Lauraceae family, the avocado shares a lineage with cinnamon, camphor, sassafras, and laurel. The leaves of the latter, formed into wreaths, have crowned victors since Roman times. Despite this august pedigree, the avocados in turn-of-the-century Los Angeles hardly resembled the lauded modern variety. Small, with large seeds and little flesh, they were not considered worthy of a potential commercial industry. These dooryard avocado trees shared the street with nurseries offering tropical and semitropical plants and fruit trees, primarily of the citrus variety.[15] As downtown Los Angeles developed, they were razed.

Fred immediately recognized the potential of exotics thriving in the native landscape. In 1907, he purchased two seedling avocado trees at Coolidge's flower shop. The new additions to the property sparked Wilson's interest.[16] For some time, he'd been earning money growing rosebushes from cuttings—Maman Cochets, Papa Gontiers, or Ulrich Brunners, varieties coveted by wealthy neighbors from the East. After school, he frequently dug up a dozen and delivered them by wheelbarrow, bringing home $1.50 with little effort.[17] In 1908, when Easter lilies were all the rage, the government promoted the craze by distributing seeds derived from scientific studies. George W. Oliver, expert propagator at the U.S. Department of Agriculture (USDA), sent seeds to sixteen-year-old Wilson, who proudly recorded their progress in a notebook page later pasted in his scrapbook.[18] By this time, the teenager was corresponding with horticultural experts in the West Indies and other British colonies regarding his efforts to propagate new plants. Late at night, he pored over free catalogs and seed lists from nurseries and botanic gardens in tropical countries. He sent to Florida for a young mango tree, a frangipani, and a few other tropical plants and, despite their failure to flourish, boldly posted a sign at the end of his garden plot advertising "West India Gardens."[19] His efforts to replicate the tropics in Altadena inspired his father's next venture—a fully equipped nursery just down the block.

California was experiencing a horticultural golden age when the Popenoes arrived.[20] Nurseries abounded from San Diego to San Francisco. Nurserymen had developed a network for plant distribution throughout the state, and owners were becoming promoters of the industry nationwide. Fred Popenoe had learned from Coolidge, now one of the celebrated pioneers in the field, and recognized that success depended on finding his own niche in the rapidly expanding nursery business. The avocado would become his specialty. Founded in 1909 at the foot of the San Gabriel Mountains overlooking Pasadena, West India Gardens offered a wide range of tropical and subtropical species but concentrated on the avocado, an "exotic" with unlimited potential. Fred relied on his intuition—his years in the tropics had given him the kind of experience necessary to succeed—and saw encouraging signs of prosperity in the region, a requirement for marketing the luxuries he planned to propagate. The time was right to champion the miracle fruit that would restore his name, support his family, and lead to a life of ease.

The year Fred joined the ranks of nurserymen, a seamstress named Jennie C. Gano moved from Westlake to Whittier, where she and her husband purchased a run-down farm with a few straggly avocado trees. Gano had come to Los Angeles from Greensboro, Indiana, in 1907 seeking to improve her health. Her new farmhouse was so dilapidated that the couple initially slept in the barn, but Gano immediately perceived the richness of the soil, the climatic blessings, and the potential to grow a livelihood. She made ends meet by trudging to markets twice a week with a suitcase full of avocados. While Fred promoted his business, Gano diligently worked at improving methods of fertilization, pest control, and fruit handling as an independent grower. The two new California residents represented the range of opportunities for avocado enthusiasts in these early years.[21] As to success—only time would tell.

The first avocados planted in the continental United States came to Florida in 1833, courtesy of Henry Perrine, the American consul in Campeche, Mexico. Perrine was responding to a request from President John Quincy Adams for government officials to assist in identifying and shipping seeds of useful tropical plants to America. In addition to selecting those that might boost industries—like rubber, dye, and timber—Perrine chose avocados for their nutritional value. He also chose Indian Key as his home base, despite tensions with the surrounding Seminole people in that region of the Florida Keys. His experiments with avocado growing ended in 1840, when he and his family were killed by the Indigenous people and his property burned.[22] Perrine went down in history for his avocado introduction, but more than fifty years would pass before Florida nurserymen organized themselves as the Florida State Horticultural Society, a group devoted to the state's tropical plants. By then, "mangoes, avocado pears and guava trees shaded almost every door yard" in regions like the Pinellas Peninsula. Locals considered avocados more valuable than citrus.[23]

The Lincoln administration formalized the federal government's role in American agriculture in 1862 with the establishment of the Department of Agriculture and passed the Morrill Land-Grant College Act, giving new states the authority to establish colleges within largely rural communities. In the midst of the Civil War, Kansas State Agricultural College led the way as the first land grant college and from its founding in 1863 focused on training students in agricultural professions. Five years later, federal funding supported the establishment of the University of California, Berkeley, when a public agricultural, mining, and mechanical arts college was merged with a private college in Oakland. In the meantime, the USDA made training farmers and dispersing seeds integral to its mission of education and economic development. After the war, USDA chief botanist William Saunders ventured into plant importation by requesting a variety of navel orange from the U.S. consulate in Brazil. Passage of the Hatch Act of 1887 supercharged funding for agricultural experiment stations at land grant colleges throughout the nation. The stations were a welcome contribution to local economies, and within ten years, more than fifty were actively growing and testing new plants gathered from around the world. By this time, the USDA had been elevated to cabinet status.[24]

One beneficiary of this new federal mission was plant explorer David Fairchild, who began his career working without pay for the Office of Seed and Plant Introduction, a government department he led from its founding in 1898. Fairchild's deep interest in plants did not go unnoticed.[25] Barbour Lathrop, a wealthy amateur botanist, knew that USDA funding for foreign expeditions would not be forthcoming. He offered to sponsor Fairchild as a government "special agent" and accompany him on travels around the world dedicated to discovering, importing, and distributing plants of potential value to the U.S. economy.[26] During the first leg of the trip, the travelers stopped in the coastal town of Santa Barbara, California, to meet the famous Italian plantsman Dr. Francesco Franceschi and tour his nursery on State Steet. Here they encountered numerous imported species, including the avocado, and admired an unusual Italian vegetable called the zucchini. Fairchild was so impressed with the nurseryman's efforts, achieved on a slim budget, that he contacted his new office in Washington and arranged to have Franceschi made a "collaborator" and receive plants appropriate for testing in the region.[27]

The globe-trotting plant expedition included stops in Jamaica, Barbados, Trinidad, Venezuela, Panama, and Peru. In 1899, Lathrop and Fairchild arrived in Santiago, Chile, and discovered a hardy avocado alleged to have survived snow and temperatures as low as twenty-three degrees Fahrenheit. Fairchild immediately recognized the value of this attribute for trees in Southern California. He carefully selected and packed a bushel of the "small, black-fruited avocado, at times a little stringy" in boxes and shipped them to the USDA.[28] The first officially registered avocados were opened by plant scientist Orator F. Cook, who found them rotten but managed to salvage seeds.[29]

Before the founding of the Bureau of Plant Industry in 1901, no system existed for recording plant shipments, but the government significantly increased its efforts to bring new plant immigrants to America and to advertise their arrival.[30] During the first few years of the new century, Cook led an expedition to Mexico, Central America, and the West Indies in search of coffee, rubber, and other lucrative products. His assistant, botanist Guy N.

Collins, noticed the different varieties of avocados in each region, studied them, and soon became enamored of their flavor, not to mention potential for expanding the U.S. diet. For those prescient enough to imagine an avocado industry, he provided a comprehensive USDA bulletin on the topic.[31]

Collins's report, *The Avocado, a Salad Fruit from the Tropics*, was distributed to the public on request and included a salad endorsed by Janet M. Hill, founder of *The Boston Cooking-School Magazine*. Arguably the first published American recipe for guacamole (tortilla chips not included), the dish she described had long been a popular staple in Mexico.[32] She used Cuban avocados, the most accessible to eastern housewives, noting that the fruit grew wild in Mexico and locations of a similar latitude. Passengers on the steamers running between these countries and New York could order aguacate salad as an accompaniment to any meal. Having recently completed a banana recipe book for the United Fruit Company, Hill was immersed in the versatility of tropical fruit and its potential for expanding the nation's diet. She considered the aquacate equal to the banana when it came to carrying flavors pleasant to the American palate and predicted a taste for it would be easily acquired. Aguacate salad fit the bill for breakfast, lunch, or dinner.[33]

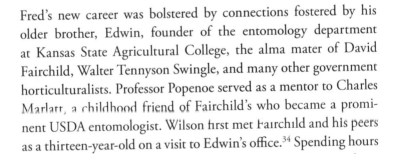

Fred's new career was bolstered by connections fostered by his older brother, Edwin, founder of the entomology department at Kansas State Agricultural College, the alma mater of David Fairchild, Walter Tennyson Swingle, and many other government horticulturalists. Professor Popenoe served as a mentor to Charles Marlatt, a childhood friend of Fairchild's who became a prominent USDA entomologist. Wilson first met Fairchild and his peers as a thirteen-year-old on a visit to Edwin's office.[34] Spending hours squinting at insects under microscopes seemed tedious to him, but his father pointed out that Kansas State had done much to support the country's agriculture. Uncle Edwin and his colleagues were helping to keep agricultural pests at bay, and thanks to this fortuitous relationship, West India Gardens had been identified by the USDA as an experimental testing site. The Popenoes were now exchanging letters with Fairchild, as well as with the most accomplished avocado growers in Florida.[35] West India Gardens would look beyond citrus to rare fruits that could flourish in California: the feijoa, the cherimoya, the white sapote, and most of all, the avocado.[36]

While Fred navigated the expanding social network of Southern California horticulture, Wilson learned how to grow subtropical plants. He tracked down promising avocado trees, often with his high school friend Knowles Ryerson, and secured propagating rights for the family nursery.[37] The two explored the gardens of Pasadena on bicycles, vascula (oblong metal carrying cases) slung over their shoulders to securely transport fragile botanical specimens. Knowles knew all about avocados from his work at Coolidge's Rare Plant Gardens, where he was introduced to the latest varieties and shown how to light orchard heaters for frost protection. Coolidge let the boys follow as he wandered through the nursery, checking on the progress of his plants. An expert at grafting citrus fruit, he had recently turned to budding as the most efficient way of achieving desired avocado varieties. This new obsession became a delight he enjoyed sharing with Knowles and Wilson, whose enthusiasm brought back memories of introducing his daughter, Roma, to the mysteries of the plant world.[38]

On one visit, as the trio walked past the lathhouse, the boys asked about strangely wrapped sticks stuck into the open ground.[39] Coolidge explained that these newly budded seedlings would grow into hardy trees, if he was lucky. He took them over to another section of the nursery, where shorter plants were growing—seeds he had planted to serve as rootstalks from trees that exhibited particular qualities he hoped to encourage, like disease resistance and abundant bearing. Together, the three hunted for budwood in the orchard, looking for flexible, well-matured wood from the previous season. Coolidge bent one cutting and, when it snapped, explained that it was too hard. Choosing the proper scion was essential. To the boys, the scion had almost supernatural qualities. It allowed the nurseryman to replicate any tree he chose by attaching it to the rootstock of a compatible tree. After an assortment of more pliant branches with plump buds were collected, the three gathered around a seedling grown from a choice seed of Mexican origin. Now that the diameter of this tiny tree was slightly larger than a lead pencil and its sap flowed freely, the budding process could begin.[40]

Wilson and Knowles followed Coolidge's every move as he turned to the stalk and, with his razor-sharp knife, deftly made a vertical cut three inches above the soil. This was followed by a perpendicular incision across the top of the first, creating a T shape that caused the loose bark to fall open and form a pocket. He then turned to the scion and sliced off a thin two-inch shield of bark with the bud attached. Working quickly, he gently slipped the freshly cut side of the shield into the stalk's pocket, taking care to see that the fit was uniform, smooth, and straight.[41] Next, he wrapped the budded stalk, beginning from the top and leaving a space for the bud's "eye."[42] He used thin strips of waxed cloth, prepared earlier, to bind the bud to the stalk. The skilled nurseryman rapidly budded several more trees as he proselytized on the technique, the intimate knowledge of avocado varieties required, and the propensity for failure. Before leaving for the day, the boys were reminded to return in about six weeks to remove the wrappings.[43] Back at West India Gardens, they tried slicing branches with pocketknives and soon realized the skill involved. It would take them years and much practice to master the ancient craft.[44]

The boys also learned from nurseryman C. P. Taft, one of the first to introduce a new avocado variety in California. Like Coolidge, Taft had recently adjusted his method of grafting and was now an expert in budding avocados. To reach his ranch, Wilson and Knowles traveled to Santa Ana on the Pacific Electric Railway and then continued to Orange on the "dummy," a steam-powered streetcar with wheels set so close that shifting their weight made it rock. For the last leg of the journey, they hired bicycles and rode through the dust.[45] It was a long trip but worth the effort. Taft was famous for his eponymous avocado variety grown from Guatemalan seed, and the boys never failed to check on its parent tree, planted in 1900. This successful variety deserved expert care, but they were puzzled by Taft's thoughtful tending of an unimpressive tree with small purple fruits, until the nurseryman explained these were ancestors of the first Chilean avocados Fairchild had shipped to America. Although the fruits were "fibrous," Taft maintained the tree as a token of his "first helpful experience with the avocado," its seed a gift from the USDA.[46] In exchange, he did his part to expand avocado cultivation by passing on seedlings to his fellow plantsmen in the region, including Joseph Sexton, who planted a Mexican variety at his home grounds in Goleta.[47] Taft's ranch would eventually boast more than six hundred avocado trees. Despite earning honors as one of the first to market avocados commercially, Taft was still looking for his "ideal fruit."[48]

Rambling throughout the Pasadena region in search of hardy avocado trees, the boys soon acquired knowledge of all the productive nurseries. They routinely rode the three miles between Wilson's house and the Coolidge gardens, not far from Henry Huntington's magnificent estate and grounds, searching for promising new trees. Huntington had become smitten with the avocado in 1905, after developing a taste for the fruit at the Jonathan Club. The private men's club in Los Angeles occupied the top two floors of the Huntington Building, the new Pacific Electric terminal for the city's electric railway system.[49] As president of the club and owner of the Pacific Electric Railway Company, Huntington occupied a sixth-floor office and enjoyed the convenient proximity of the club dining room. Once accustomed to the fruit's buttery flavor, he couldn't get enough. He obtained an "alligator pear" seed through the club's chef and, after Hertrich corrected the misnomer, requested his help in growing avocados.[50] For several months, the two collected seeds, Huntington from his club and Hertrich from plantsmen throughout the area. The seeds were planted in pots and, after about two years, transplanted into orchard fields, twenty-five feet apart. Now Hertrich was faced with the challenge of budding the trees.

During these years, quality budwood was scarce and the grafting process proved difficult, but Hertrich persevered.[51] By the time the boys were learning to bud, his successful husbandry had resulted in the first commercial orchard in California—seven acres covered with about four hundred trees.[52] Huntington kept Hertrich busy. Construction never stopped, as Huntington poured his fortune into glorifying the land around his vast estate. More than 15,000 plants were growing on the grounds, including redwoods, Himalayan cedars, Canary Island date palms, and pepper trees. He soon incorporated lily ponds, lined with concrete and heated by a plumbing system. Wilson and Knowles watched in awe as giant trees were moved to the property and lowered into the ground, multiple reservoirs constructed, and a small village of cottages, barns, and storage buildings completed to house the property's many workers and their equipment. By 1908, Hertrich was developing a new cactus garden, but he always stopped what he was doing to show the boys his orchard of young avocado trees.[53]

Although Wilson enjoyed nursery work, his goals for the future were more far reaching. He read accounts of the mutiny on the *Bounty*, Lieutenant Bligh's infamous experience transporting the breadfruit tree from Tahiti to the West Indies, and of the explorers Hasskarl, Markham, and Spruce, who cured malaria with their discovery of "superior varieties of the quinine-yielding cinchona trees."[54] His living heroes were government plant explorers Ernest H. Wilson and Frank N. Meyer (namesake of the lemon), then scouring distant corners of China. Their discoveries in foreign lands would not only contribute to the national economy but also offer new delicacies for Americans to enjoy.

Wilson's imagination ascended to even greater heights when West India Gardens received an unusual letter from Mexico. "Riordan," a lumberman, had been shown an Aztec pictograph by his neighborhood Jesuit priest. It seemed to represent an avocado tree, and Riordan had enclosed a rough sketch in the hope that the American avocado experts could tell him more. A primitive trunk issuing from a bed of roots sprouted three branches with bushy leaves. Thrilled by the query (which made him feel like a seasoned plantsman), Wilson resolved to track down the origins of the image, most likely by traveling to the village one day and seeking out other pictographs for clues. In the meantime, he filed it away with other important papers and vowed to learn all he could about avocados from Mexico.[55]

While Wilson was still in high school, David Fairchild and Palemon H. Dorsett, leaders of the USDA's Office of Seed and Plant Introduction, arrived in Pasadena to inspect plants the bureau had sent to Coolidge, the Popenoes, and others carrying out experimental work for the government. Fairchild and Dorsett hoped to jump-start the California avocado industry. They predicted the fruit would soon "rank as one of the most important . . . grown" in the region.[56] Wilson imagined an even more illustrious achievement: the avocado would surpass citrus as the state's most important fruit. He soon became one of the first, and certainly the youngest, serious competitors in the race to discover the avocado best suited to California.

A steadfast admirer of Fairchild and his crew of adventurers, Wilson was surprised to learn of an equally accomplished plant explorer closer to home. Charles Fuller Baker, an entomologist and professor of botany at nearby Pomona College, once served as chief of the department of botany at the Cuban Experiment Station in Santiago de las Vegas and curator of the herbarium and botanical garden at the Museu Paraense Emílio Goeldi in Brazil.[57] By 1909, Baker had amassed a personal collection of more than 100,000 specimens from distant lands that now formed the core of the Pomona's new herbarium. Federal officials from the USDA, attracted by the possibility of building on this research opportunity, encouraged Baker to establish a program of "plant life" as part of Pomona College's biological department.[58] The program added a professional component to the college curriculum. Wilson enrolled in the fall of 1910.

Wilson's year of intense study included work in the college's botanical laboratory, where rare and exotic fruits and plants were exhibited, and an invitation from Professor Baker to write for the first volume of the *Pomona College Journal of Economic Botany*. The new publication was intended to reach beyond academia and appeal to "growers, planters, amateur fanciers, greenhouse-men, nursery-men, seed-men, importers, experimenters and botanists."[59] Baker pushed his star pupil to "circulate around among the gardens, parks, private places, orchards, greenhouses, and nurseries" as much as possible and to keep his "eyes open, constantly writing up at the end of each day just as full notes as possible."[60] Wilson rose to the challenge, authoring "The Avocado in Southern California," a groundbreaking article in which the nineteen-year-old boldly predicted the future of the California avocado industry and provided tips on how readers might ride the wave of its success.[61]

With all the bravado of an undergraduate, Wilson threw down the gauntlet to his fellow avocado entrepreneurs, urging them to exercise self-restraint and rely on science to further their enterprises. He isolated the central problem limiting the growth of the avocado market—the lack of standardization in varieties—and challenged his peers to join forces in reining in the spread of "mere chance seedlings" by developing industry standards for the fruit. "At our very door lies a boundless experimental garden," he proclaimed, "where countless varieties have originated, and where now are growing hundreds of thousands of trees from among which we have only to select the best."[62]

Wilson's article came out at a perfect time. The month before, in the *California Cultivator*, produce importer William D. Stephens described avocados he had encountered in Atlixco, Mexico, and predicted a breakthrough in the industry. Stephens offered his news with a spirit of goodwill, suggesting the "promise of enlarged horticultural possibilities" for all, but he also let it be known that his nursery would soon receive supplies of wood for use in budding the seedling stock.[63] The Popenoes read his article with excitement tinged by jealousy. Stephens had traveled extensively in Mexico and, like Fred, was a former miner who recognized the potential value of avocados upon moving to California. But Stephens had only recently established a partnership with Dan Clower of Monrovia in the hope of importing superior avocados from Mexico. During his travels, he came upon delicious thin-skinned avocados in the Atlixco region and met Gabriel Fuentes, an exporter who grew up in the United States and was now exporting fruit for Wells Fargo. Stephens selected some promising seedlings, and Fuentes agreed to ship him five chosen varieties. Based on his hopes of success, Stephens wrote up his discovery in the *California Cultivator*.[64] When a severe frost in Monrovia caused Clower to bow out, Stephens made a deal with Albert Rideout, a successful nurseryman in Whittier. It was here, at the A. R. Rideout Magnolia Nursery, that Stephens would receive his first Wells Fargo shipment.[65]

The reputation of Atlixco, a southern highlands village in the state of Puebla, as the birthplace of elite avocados was known to a few Californians by 1890, when native fruits were first imported to Los Angeles. Juan Murrieta, a former sheriff of the city, is credited with growing and distributing the earliest seeds from Atlixco. Spanish-born Murrieta was introduced to Mexican avocados through J. C. Harvey, a Standard Oil Company official who shared a seedling acquired during his travels.[66] Impressed by the fruit's unusual nutty flavor, Murietta wrote to Wells Fargo for information about how to acquire additional trees. In 1893, Fuentes shipped him a variety of different fruits, both thin- and thick-skinned. Murrieta planted the seeds, and before long, his robust trees were attracting attention. Although he never engaged in a formal nursery business, preferring to give or sell seeds and buds to friends, Murietta generously distributed the Mexican avocados that would inspire the California industry. Recipients of his largesse included the Popenoes, Taft, and William Spinks of Los Angeles. Stephens and other entrepreneurs were retracing not only Murrieta's route to Atlixco but the path of many outsiders who viewed Mexico as a site of natural riches worthy of plunder. At this exceptional time in California's horticultural history, growers, scientists, nurserymen, and enthusiasts mingled their resources. Wilson would benefit from them all.[67]

Upon completing his year of study at Pomona, Wilson justifiably considered himself a California avocado expert. Now he felt equipped to apply his knowledge to the field—to formally enter the competition to engineer the ideal avocado. Emphasizing the "widening horticultural horizon," a field of exploration including "the tropics and subtropics of the whole world," and reasserting his belief in the avocado's potential to "outstrip the orange" as a commercial product, Wilson wrote to Fairchild announcing that West India Gardens had sent a man to Mexico, at its own expense, to collect budwood and seeds from some "exceptionally fine" avocado trees, winter bearers of first-class quality weighing one to two pounds, varying from oval to bottlenecked, with exceptionally thick and tough skins, and a small seed tight in the cavity.[68] Wilson and Fred hoped their gamble would yield a variety that could withstand shipment, a quality not seen in the Mexican varieties to date. Stephens banked on the same as he contemplated his own investment.[69] Reading between the lines, Wilson was setting up West India Gardens to discover the next big avocado. He and his father mapped out a strategy and had a man for the job. Only the Mexican Revolution stood in their way.

Hawaiian Sandwich

Remove skin and seed from one
avocado. Mash the flesh, add salt
and pepper, and a dash of vinegar or
lime juice, and spread liberally on
lettuce leaf between thin slices of
buttered bread. This is a dainty way
of serving the avocado, and a most
delicious one.

> --*The Avocado*, West India
> Gardens brochure, 1912

2 · The Survivor

DURING HIS EARLY DAYS RUNNING THE TOPEKA NEWS-
paper, Fred Popenoe spent time with Ernest Schmidt, a Washburn
University classmate who worked as a local agent for the Atchison,
Topeka and Santa Fe Railway. When the Mexican Revolution
broke out in 1910, the Schmidts fled their home in Mexico, and
the Popenoes took them in. The boys enjoyed the company of
Carl Schmidt, who had left Cornell University to join his family.
They listened, riveted, as he told stories of the revolutionaries, his
eyes flashing with desire to fight under General Pancho Villa.[1] His
parents were less enthusiastic. Fred saw an opportunity to benefit
everyone. He would hire Carl as West India Gardens' representative in Mexico, charged with ferreting out the country's best
avocados. Although yearning to join Carl, who was just his age,
Wilson knew his skills were better employed at the nursery, grafting budwood.[2]

Carl set out in the summer of 1911. His first stop was San Luis
Potosí, where he found promising fruits, but it was a little farther
south in Mexico City's Merced Market that he chanced upon
the most delicious avocado he had ever tasted. The fruit's savory
flavor—*nutty* was the word that came to mind—left him craving
more. Now the hunt for its origins began. In conversation with
merchants, Carl learned that the fruit was grown in Atlixco, further confirming this town's prestige as a source of exceptional avocados. A narrow-gauge railway carried him into the mountains. In
Atlixco, he encountered avocados that seemed to fit every criterion:
they were flavorful and hardy and could survive shipping. One of

the locals directed him to the residence of Matildi Dion. A tree
outside his home seemed lacking, but once Carl stepped into the
courtyard, he gazed in amazement. The thirty-foot tree was broad,
strong, and loaded with avocados. Dion described it as twenty-five
years old and bearing in October and November. Its fruit displayed
all the attributes stipulated by West India Gardens. Over the next
several months, Carl collected samples from nearly thirty trees,
identifying each by numbered copper tags and shipping them to
the Altadena nursery. Meanwhile, the Popenoes prepared young
seedlings in the lathhouse. Wilson and Fred reviewed the shipments and requested budwood from trees that showed promise.[3]

Carl's samples were accompanied by the names and addresses
of growers; elevations, ages, and dimensions of trees; and the bearing seasons, often with additional comments such as "prolific,"
"buttery," or "vigorous." His sketches showed the location of each
tree in relation to nearby streets, buildings, or natural landmarks.
In addition to numbers, some of the specimens were named. Two
fall varieties from Atlixco—no. 13, grown by Vicente Pineda,
and Matildi Dion's no. 15—were known locally as "ahuacate de
China" and stood out as particularly promising.[4] Wilson budded
the trees as quickly as possible to increase the chances of a successful graft. Now all they could do was wait to see how the trees
would respond to the soil and climate of their transplanted country.
The Popenoes' competitors were also waiting. An advertisement
in the *California Cultivator* touted A. R. Rideout's Lyon variety
as the best in Southern California and the Rideout-Stephens partnership as controlling "the finest and largest varieties that Old
Mexico can produce."[5] The race was on.

In his spare time, Wilson applied himself to academic writing.
As part of his ongoing contribution to the Pomona journal, he
observed a variety of other fruits—the mango and feijoa among
them—as the first step in developing a grand Southern California Horticultural Calendar of Operations. For now, Wilson
traced the origins of the white sapote, a gift to California from

the "Franciscan fathers" who established the missions more than a hundred years earlier. The publication included a photograph of an aged sapote tree in Santa Barbara, respected as the first tropical fruit tree planted in the state and a horticultural landmark.[6] Wilson also repurposed part of his scholarly analysis of the avocado for the popular *Rural Californian*, further demonstrating his practical bent with an article on the fruit's commercial potential.[7] The teenager's three articles for the journal that year contributed to a body of writing that led to his election as a fellow of the British Royal Horticultural Society and the offer of a four-year scholarship to Cornell University.[8]

During the summer, Wilson enjoyed the company of his Pomona College friend Ralph Cornell, who was working at the nursery to help pay for his education. The young men made trips up the coast to Santa Barbara, where they stayed in a hotel on State Street and visited Francesco Franceschi at his home and nursery on Mission Ridge Road. The famous plantsman met them at the old mission, the end of the streetcar line, and, crowded together in his "tiny phaeton" pulled by an elderly sorrel horse, they made their way up a winding road to the Riviera. Montarioso covered forty acres—ten of which were a cultivated wonderland of plant introductions.[9] When Franceschi left Italy with his family in 1891, he spent two years in Los Angeles before choosing Santa Barbara as the destination most similar to his native land and most likely to support a range of species. Inspired by the region's seemingly endless potential for nurturing semitropical fruits, Franceschi founded the Southern California Acclimatizing Association, an international plant business specializing in raising "from seed rare and beautiful plants from every country of the globe." He was soon a voice for the nascent avocado industry, announcing in the *Rural Cultivator* that "in the culture of the ahuacate, Santa Barbara takes the lead in California," and including the *Persea gratissima* from Mexico (the well-known ahuacate, or alligator pear) in the Southern California Acclimatizing Association's 1894 catalog.[10]

Franceschi spoke with pride of Santa Barbara's role in avocado history as the home of the oldest avocado tree in the state.[11] Judge Robert B. Ord, the local police justice, is said to have brought the first avocado plants from Mexico in 1871.[12] He passed on one of his trees to his old friend Silas Bond, who planted it in Montecito, just east of Santa Barbara. The tree became well known as a resident of the E. H. Sawyer estate. Mrs. Sawyer hosted the Santa Barbara Historical Society's meeting in 1885, the year it began bearing fruit.[13] Three years later, H. C. Ford, president of the society, introduced the tree to a national audience, describing it as twenty feet in height with smooth bark, oblong leaves, and purple fruit similar to "the delicate rich taste of a peach" in his presentation to the National Horticultural Society in Riverside.[14] Over thirty feet tall when Franceschi visited it in 1894, the famous tree was then said to bear as many as five hundred avocados a year.[15] Its hardy seedlings were eventually distributed throughout the region. One lucky recipient, the British-born nurseryman Kinton Stevens, planted the state's first avocado orchard at Tanglewood, his home and nursery, in 1895. His grove was lost during the drought of 1897, but the property would continue to display botanical prowess two generations later, as Lotusland, the estate of Ganna Walska.[16]

By the time Wilson and Cornell visited Montarioso in 1911, Franceschi was operating his nursery from his home, a property featuring more than two hundred plants he introduced to the state, more than any other California nurseryman. Here the young men gawked at the gigantic spiked agave and its sinuous relative the *Agave attenuata*, both reaching magnificent dimensions; the rare Montezuma cypress, or ironwood, Franceschi had obtained from Santa Cruz Island; his popular *Lippia repens*; and his most famous introduction, the pineapple guava. The *Persea gratissima*, later known as *Persea americana*, was coming to him from tropical America and selling for fifty cents as a potted seedling. Franceschi not only inspired Wilson but also helped West India Gardens develop into a highly regarded regional nursery by sharing plants, knowledge, and camaraderie. The two soon witnessed the fruits of their labors at the fall Pasadena Flower Show.[17]

The biannual exhibition had long outgrown its location, the tennis court of the Maryland Hotel covered with a canvas tent, and this year's rainy weather brought urgency to plans for a horticultural hall. Franceschi's exhibit of rare plants demonstrated the diversity of this "flower" show. Although none of the thirty specimens he displayed were in bloom or bearing fruit, the plants "never before . . . shown in the United States" drew the knowledgeable and curious alike.[18] Led by exhibit designer Ralph Cornell, who would go on to become a prominent landscape architect, West India Gardens put together a display of its subtropical plants, including ananas (pineapples) and black persimmons from Mexico, feijoas, mangoes, and white sapotes so compelling as to attract the general public.[19] P. D. Barnhart, editor of *The Pacific Garden* and an expert in judging such events, described the avocado portion of its exhibit as

> a revelation to the majority of the residents of this Southland. The fruit has been grown here for years, an isolated tree here and there, some of which are now twenty-five years old, and prolific bearers, but never before have they been exhibited in such quantity and variety, neither [have their] merits been so eloquently and truthfully explained to an inquiring and interested public as was the case at this show by these people.[20]

West India Gardens had grown quickly and now boasted the world's largest avocado nursery, with 50,000 seedlings currently under propagation, and served as one of the regular cooperative stations of the USDA. Fred would soon issue a twenty-page brochure describing his nursery, complete with a photograph of a group of nurserymen in the lathhouse, surrounded by young plants in four-inch pots.[21] Commercial-grade, one-year-old seedling trees ready for budding were photographed in the open orchard. While the Popenoes continued their scouting in Mexico, the *Los Angeles Times* reported on the growing popularity of the avocado, arguably the most valuable plant in the world, and ran an illustrated story featuring their work in the field.[22]

West India Gardens would be remembered as a training ground for promoting the industry—the place where USDA plant explorers were taught, nurserymen began careers, and future horticulturalists honed their skills. As president of the nursery, Fred echoed his son in advertising Mexico as an extension of his domestic enterprise, calling the country "a great experimental garden, in which have originated the choicest varieties of this most valuable fruit" for West India Gardens to tap in producing "budded trees of the finest varieties,—fruits whose development, by the usual processes of plant breeding or selection, would take many years of time and the expenditure of a very large sum of money to secure." In doing so, he forecast successes ranging from solving the problem of world hunger—by using avocados as a meat substitute—to encouraging national prosperity though avocado farming and marketing.[23] The Popenoes felt their efforts in Mexico had been a success but also knew that avocados struggled to adapt to the California climate. A single serious frost could destroy years of work. As it turned out, this much-feared possibility—a factor that had darkened hopes of an avocado industry from the very beginning—would secure the family's horticultural legacy.

While Fred, Wilson, and the staff of West India Gardens were watching and worrying over their fledgling avocado seedlings, the wholesale fruit dealer E. B. Rivers, of Rivers Brothers in Los Angeles, received a basket of the finest avocados he had ever seen. The fruit was shipped from Atlixco by Gabriel Fuentes. Rivers had been in the avocado-shipping business since 1899. Back then, shipments came from Honolulu or Haiti and arrived through San Francisco.

Rivers Brothers obtained avocados from "porters running on the dining cars out of Mexico," who bought them from locals in colorful patterned baskets that added to their allure. The fruit was only served in the most exclusive hotels and clubs. Since several dozen avocados supplied the demand for all of Los Angeles, Rivers never expected to see them grown in California. At six or seven dollars a dozen, more than a day's wages for many laborers, the delicacy was still too expensive to imagine a larger market.[24]

Fuentes made an intelligent investment by sending the sample basket in 1912. Rivers ordered as many avocados as could be provided. He was soon receiving baskets of fifty, packed in excelsior (wood shavings), with cloth covers—first two per week, and then it seemed as if all the trains from Mexico were laden with baskets. Rivers rushed to telegram eastern produce warehouses in Boston, Philadelphia, New York, Chicago, and other major cities. Helped by the Christmas season, he sold all the fruit at a good profit—six dollars a dozen wholesale (more than $175 today). Seeing how well Mexican avocados sold—he had recently handled "Mr. Walker's fruit from Hollywood," at twelve dollars per dozen—Rivers forecast "one of the coming industries of Southern California."[25] The Popenoes agreed. They were already booking orders for their "fine stock of 'novelties,'" the budded seedlings from Mexico, at four dollars a tree.[26]

In addition to avocados, Fred invested in another promising fruit that was just beginning to attract attention in Southern California—the date palm. David Fairchild's efforts to introduce the date in 1903 failed, but now nurserymen were willing to try again with the government's support. Like the avocado, the palm did not grow true to seed. It depended on transplantation from parent plants to be successfully propagated and also took many years to mature. Fred sent his oldest son, Paul, to Algeria, where he secured offshoots of the Deglet Nour variety, but soon after his return, the French government ended such trade with America.[27] The ban threatened to derail plans by Dr. Rebecca Lee Dorsey, a prominent endocrinologist, to launch the largest date ranch in the country. Once again, West India Gardens was well situated to prosper. Dorsey placed orders with Popenoe for more than 4,000 date offshoots, plus an additional 3,000 for a syndicate of Pasadena and Altadena investors. With Algeria and the Deglet Nour variety no longer an option, Fred dispatched Paul, twenty-three, and Wilson, twenty, on a yearlong mission to the Persian Gulf, where offshoots of other varieties could be obtained.[28]

Soon after their departure, the *Los Angeles Times* ran a feature story on Dorsey's endeavor, "the largest single holding of anyone in the country" once the shipment arrived in the Coachella Valley.[29] Fred trusted Paul's fluency in Arabic and Wilson's horticultural experience to see them through, but the year in the Persian Gulf would test the brothers' mettle. The work of collecting nearly 10,000 offshoots, each weighing between fifteen and forty pounds, was a cultural and organizational challenge, and both young men endured months of illness. Paul narrowly escaped death from typhoid, and Wilson suffered from malaria, surviving only due to a daily shot of quinine (for which he must have thanked Hasskarl, Markham, and Spruce).[30]

The Popenoe brothers happened to be setting off on their quest at a moment of increasing tension between federal plant explorers and entomologists. David Fairchild and Charles Marlatt, once the best of friends, were now bitter rivals representing opposing sides of a national debate on plant immigration. Earlier in his career, Marlatt had urged for a laissez-faire attitude toward exchanging plants, but as he climbed the federal bureaucracy and gained power, his position changed.[31] When the Plant Quarantine Act of 1912 was instituted in October, he became head of the Federal Horticultural Board overseeing its implementation. The opening of Ellis Island two decades earlier reignited a perennial debate about immigration, exposing cultural prejudices and jealousies and adding momentum to racist movements like eugenics, of which Paul Popenoe would soon become a noted advocate.[32]

The press capitalized on the relationship between restricting human and plant immigrants, particularly those considered "dangerous and anarchistic." Marlatt saw himself as a hero for defending the United States against "foreign insect enemies."[33] As California nurserymen, the proprietors of West India Gardens were accustomed to state regulations requiring screening for pests and understood the value of such regulations. But as plant explorers, the Popenoes supported the view of Fairchild and eminent horticulturalists like Charles Sprague Sargent of the Arnold Arboretum in Boston, who insisted the world's plants (and the pests that thrived with them) would ultimately spread across the earth, settling in those locations where their needs were met. The federal power to restrict entry of foreign fruits would greatly impact the avocado.

In January 1913, a freeze devastated the fruit orchards of Southern California. For three nights straight, the temperature dropped below twenty-five degrees Fahrenheit. Newspapers throughout the region reported severe losses of the year's fruit crop, particularly valuable citrus. It soon became an event frozen in community memory. Huntington's beloved orchard in Pasadena was so damaged that Hertrich gave up growing avocados.[34] West India Gardens shared in the collective sense of loss, but its proprietors also experienced a personal sense of triumph. Among the blighted trees, seedlings of Atlixco's no. 15 stood tall, unharmed. Wilson's research and Fred's gamble had paid off. Fred had already named this tree El Fuerte (the Strong One, though soon it would be shortened to just Fuerte) as a testament to its buds' vigorous growth compared to other seedlings. The variety had demonstrated its fortitude.[35]

By March, the consensus was that the freeze might have actually benefited the avocado industry.[36] Dan Clower, a recipient of varieties from Atlixco, reported that his thin-skinned Mexican aguacate had borne the trial well. Clower and other "level headed" avocado growers viewed the freeze as a learning experience, realizing the importance of choosing the right variety, as well as forcing trees into dormancy in the fall, rather than winter.[37] Inspired by the success of his hardy variety, Fred began a rigorous campaign to promote the green-skinned Fuerte's smooth flavor, long bearing season, and especially its ability to withstand cold temperatures. His spirits were lifted when John T. Whedon of Yorba Linda accepted forty Fuerte trees from West India Gardens as replacements for frost-damaged trees he had preordered. Whedon was soon planting the first Fuerte orchard in the world on the northern side of Yorba Linda Cove. As he awaited the return of his sons, Fred Popenoe brushed away thoughts of the financial loss the business had suffered from the expensive expedition to Atlixco.[38] He took a stroll around the nursery, examined the young Fuerte trees for pests, and envisioned the success of this vigorous strain, surely California's future variety of choice.

About thirty miles south of West India Gardens, Edwin Giles Hart was walking the property staked out for North Whittier Heights, the new subdivision he managed conveniently located near Whittier and La Habra. For months, his clever newspaper ads had touted the many benefits of buying into a tract with "ideal" conditions for dreamers to venture into fruit growing. Lucky for him, no trees had been planted yet and he could honestly proclaim that "young groves adjoining this property, on land less advantageously located, were not seriously injured by the recent cold spell."[39] He offered not only the rich soil of Whittier but also five-, ten-, twenty-five-, and fifty-acre parcels with complete irrigation systems, calibrated to the needs of fruit orchards (and as an added bonus, "a separate system for supplying domestic water"). Even more exceptional, the Whittier Extension Company, owners of the development, would plant the orchards and care for them as needed.

Anyone could become a grower in North Whittier Heights, but Hart hoped to attract accomplished growers and nurserymen—not enterprises as large as West India Gardens but smaller efforts like

Pollard Brothers of South Pasadena, whose success would inspire the community. Much of the land had been previously cultivated in barley. Now use could be made of the hillsides, undulating terrain ideal for supporting fruit orchards. Hart was busy planning the development's formal opening, scheduled for mid-May. Prospective buyers would enjoy a round-trip ride from Los Angeles; a "real Mexican barbecue" hosted by Jose Romero, celebrated throughout Southern California as a barbecue specialist; and an exhibition of daring equestrian feats staged by a crowd of western cowboys. The celebration would enliven the bleakness of the barley field and inspire future entrepreneurs to dream big.[40]

Hart wasn't the only avocado man taking advantage of inexpensive real estate in the Puente Hills. A year before the freeze, Albert Rideout purchased a tract of about sixty acres in Citrus Heights, above Lemon Street.[41] Despite heavy losses due to the cold weather, he persisted in planting avocado trees on his new property and, when the city refused to assist him, built his own two-mile scenic road traversing the tract. *The Whittier News* described his "series of drives among the hill-tops" as rivaling "the beauty and safety of any mountain roads in this part of the state."[42] A few months after the celebration of North Whittier Heights, Rideout advertised his new development by urging folks to "Get Rightout [sic] and see the Sights."[43]

Rideout offset the costs of his investment by slowly selling off individual lots to prospective buyers. Each property boasted avocado trees and other exotic fruits he had planted, often with the help of his eldest child, Esther. When Esther was six or seven, she and her younger sister would sit on the back porch and peel avocados. The skin was paper thin, and the fruit was just under half an inch thick around the seed. After removing the rich flesh, they planted the seeds in a kind of sandbox to foster germination. By age twelve, Esther Rideout was crawling through the orchard on her hands and knees, planting trees. She learned to bud and graft using her father's unique method. He discovered that rubber bands sealed with Wrigley's chewing gum created as tight a protective seal over a bud as the recommended wax-dipped muslin strips. Esther didn't particularly enjoy gum but dutifully spent many long days chewing it during budding season.[44]

The USDA supplemented the Rideout Ranch with shipments of new fruits to test, and over time, the property evolved into an experimental garden. Rideout's home became a nursery for lots on Rideout Heights and the surrounding region. His development boasted its own water, piped down to individual parcels from a reservoir on the hill.[45] The carefully chosen seedling avocado trees Rideout propagated were one of many heavily advertised benefits of this "frost free" development. Owners with little knowledge of plants could feel confident in his horticultural choices. When potential buyers were skeptical, Rideout had only to mention that his Ganter tree had survived the frost. The celebrity tree was one of his seedlings, planted in 1905 at 622 Magnolia in Whittier and now known as the most valuable tree in America. The hardy Ganter had generated $2,500, through fruits and budwood, in a single season.[46] Two years later, it would gain even greater fame when its owner, H. A. Woodworth, insured it for $30,000 at Lloyd's of London.[47] Rideout received no profits from the productivity of the tree he had launched into the world; he even let its first owner, Ganter, serve as its namesake. For him, it was enough to know people would enjoy the fruit and spread the word. Among his later property deals were an eleven-acre tract sold to a former partner and a seven-room house with five acres of citrus trees to his brother-in-law, H. H. Brokaw.[48]

Popenoe, Hart, and Rideout benefited from the devastating freeze, which not only helped promote new avocado varieties and real estate ventures but also served as the catalyst for expanding government assistance (and regulation) in sustaining California's most valuable fruit industry. Citrus growers lobbied for direct state and federal intervention, passing bills to support further protection of the industry, as well as scientific study. Less than two weeks before the weather emergency, Herbert J. Webber was hired as the director of the Riverside experiment station and leader of the new Graduate School of Tropical Agriculture. Immediately after the disaster, he launched an "investigation" into ways of handling the crisis, incorporating the combined forces of the USDA, the state agricultural school (Berkeley), and the state horticultural commission. One newspaper described it as an effort to "remove freeze fangs," a feat worth millions of dollars to Southern California growers.[49] Webber had dealt with the aftermath of several similar cold-weather events back in Florida and had published his findings.[50] His investigation in California focused on methods of segregating frozen from unfrozen fruit (Floridians gorged on free frozen fruit during the 1894–1895 crises, but contrary to physicians' warnings, none perished), properly treating damaged trees, and educating growers in the benefits of artificial heating and selection of hardy varieties.

Webber was in the midst of executing his study when the University of California launched its first "traveling class in citriculture," a summer school for aspiring horticulturalists. Led by Professor J. Eliot Coit, students took field trips to prominent orchards and nurseries, as well as the government field stations. Knowles Ryerson, a member of Coit's first class in the university's new Division of Citriculture, particularly enjoyed the group's visit to West India Gardens, where he recalled childhood antics with Wilson.[51] As Fred proudly led a tour of the lathhouse and fields, all admired the robust Fuerte seedlings, survivors of the recent tragedy. The freeze had proved to be a worthwhile experiment rather than a setback. Nature demonstrated that some varieties of avocados from Mexico could withstand temperatures lethal to the more sensitive tropical West Indian and Guatemalan varieties. Americans may have once considered avocados a tropical fruit, but this natural disaster would teach them otherwise.

Avocado Fritters

"G.M. Holt of 401 Avenue C. comes forward with a recipe which he calls 'a bachelor's origination' but which sounds so good that it is presented to the women of Miami with Mr. Holt's compliments."

Take one medium-sized avocado, one small onion, one small green pepper and chop up fine. Break in one egg, add salt and pepper, and mix all well together, then stir in one tablespoon flour, one tablespoon Graham pancake flour. Have the lard piping hot, then drop in the mixture, a spoonful at a time, smooth out and fry brown. Celery may be used instead of the onion according to taste.

--*The Miami News*,
November 21, 1914

3 • Birth of an Industry

THE MOMENT COUNTY HORTICULTURAL INSPECTOR A. C. Fleury received the avocado seed, he was overcome with a sense of dread. Pitted and scarred—a hole bored seemingly from the inside out—the seed was devastated. The pest that had achieved this was not only industrious but also capable of destroying an orchard. The avocado weevil penetrated the skin of a healthy fruit, leaving no trace of its entrance, and laid its eggs deep inside the seed. Sometimes a slight softness in the outer shell might indicate a weevil burrow, but there was no way of knowing for sure. The inspector shook his head in despair. A quarantine would have to be considered. The State of California agreed and, during the summer of 1913, issued a temporary quarantine against avocados from Querétaro, Mexico, the origin of the tainted shipment.[1] A yellowish grub, about the width of fingernail, had the power to bring the state's most promising industry to a standstill. The horticultural office should have seen it coming.

Over the last year, Fleury had witnessed a mania among local growers clamoring for new avocado varieties. When an avocado grows from a seed, it never becomes an exact replica of the parent tree, but a good parent typically passes on some stellar qualities. There was no predicting which traits passed through the seed, however, and ambitious growers realized that California's stock of trees was limited. To satisfy their own voracious appetite for seeds to generate healthy rootstalk and crossbreed hybrids, avocado entrepreneurs turned to Mexico.

Fleury and his fellow inspectors had known that large quantities of avocado seeds were destroyed or refused landing because of concerns about injurious insects, including the avocado weevil. It was only a matter of time before some would slither through the cracks. Even with the restrictions passed in the Plant Quarantine Act of 1912, the shipments of avocados overwhelmed inspection stations.

Eight months after Fleury examined the weevil, on March 15, 1914, a federal avocado-seed quarantine went into effect, banning the importation of avocados from Mexico and Central America. Nurserymen took it in stride, assuming the ban would be a short-term problem, easily solved by modern science, a temporary setback until plant scientists discovered a solution. In fact, the quarantine would remain in effect for more than eighty years. Even more surprising, the avocado weevil turned out to be a boon for the developing industry. The fight against this potential menace led to government regulations that furthered efforts to organize, take stock, and strive to create a market standard—the ideal California avocado.[2]

The avocado weevil wasn't the first pest to threaten a California fruit industry. When Fleury was a child, the cottony-cushion scale made international news by compromising citrus. A seemingly harmless pinkish bug, the female scale produced a cottony substance in which to protect her eggs—the more cotton, the more infant scales. Left unmolested, the insects multiplied quickly by feeding off sap from leaves and branches. Trees covered with their soft, white masses failed to thrive and even dropped fruit. Frustrated by decades of battling this persistent pest, the 1886 California Fruit Growers' Convention petitioned for government assistance with the horticultural crisis. The USDA recommended studying citrus trees in Australia, the native home of the scale, but could legally offer no funding.[3]

When the determined growers took their cause to the State Department in 1888, secretary of state Thomas Bayard came up with an ambitious plan. He arranged for USDA entomologist Albert

Koebele to serve as ambassador to the upcoming Melbourne Centennial Exhibition.[4] Koebele visited the new exhibition building and admired the "triumphal arch made up of oranges and orange sprays" in his guise as an official representative.[5] On the sly, he carried out his mission with the help of an ally he met in the Australian groves—the tiny red-coated and black-spotted vedalia ladybug. He quietly arranged to have the insects shipped off to America, and within months of their arrival in California, the cottony-cushion scale had virtually disappeared from the Southland. Decades later, the California Fruit Growers Exchange, known for advertising its highest grade of fruit as Sunkist, looked back on this victory as part of its heritage. When California avocado growers thought about their future, the exchange came to mind as the model for moving forward.

A month after avocados from Mexico were quarantined, Wilson Popenoe returned from his first trip as a plant explorer. On the long voyage to New York, he struggled with the life-changing decision that had been weighing on him for months—should he spend the next four years studying at Cornell University or devote himself to traveling the world in search of plants? Unable to decide, he took the train to Washington, D.C., and sought out David Fairchild, a meeting that led to an offer he could hardly refuse—a substantial salary, a future of government-sponsored adventures across the globe, and the opportunity to contribute to the nation's well-being. After a few months in the USDA Washington office and a quick trip to study mangoes at the Miami experiment station, Wilson prepared for his first voyage as part of a three-man team of plant explorers. In the company of seasoned veterans A. D. Shamel and Dorsett, he would spend the next six months searching for better varieties of navel oranges.

The trip began with an auspicious coincidence. By chance, the plant explorers were scheduled to depart on the steamer *Van Dyck*, in the company of Theodore Roosevelt and his entourage. The former president was en route to rendezvous with Brazilian explorer Colonel Cândido Rondon and had his sights set on exploring the Amazon River, though ultimately chose to map an unexplored tributary, the Rio da Dúvida (River of Doubt), into the depths of the Brazilian jungle. Roosevelt's trip was partially sponsored by the American Museum of Natural History, which charged him with enhancing its collection of wild-animal species. The former president's son Kermit and the famous tropical explorer George K. Cherrie were among those accompanying him on the endeavor.

When the team of adventurers finally arrived, Wilson was surrounded by a crowd of "moving picture operators," incessantly clicking their cameras. Finding his way to the upper deck for a better view, he noticed them lining up again, cameras pointed his way. Roosevelt had appeared at his side, and Wilson found himself playing the part of passenger in a film reel soon to be viewed by tens of thousands. Without missing a beat, he rose to the occasion, acknowledging the crowd with dignity, as he felt a government representative should.[6]

For Wilson, meeting Roosevelt meant more than the obvious thrill of brushing with the most famous man in America.[7] As a teenager, he had visited Riverside to see the celebrated Washington navel orange tree in front of the Mission Inn. The parent tree responsible for launching California's citrus industry was surrounded by an iron fence and marked with a tablet explaining its origin—Bahia, Brazil—and crediting President Roosevelt for taking part in transplanting it to the current location in 1903. The celebrity tree remained in Wilson's imagination as a symbol of the potential of plants to change the world (and spawn horticultural industries worth millions of dollars), leading him to ask the types of questions that would spark his pursuit of the avocado.[8]

During their travels, the trio of plant explorers found little to improve upon California's navel orange but the story of their "thrilling tropic hunt" for "jaca, pitomba, and imbu," among other exotics, warranted a full-page illustrated spread in *The Washington Times*.[9] The Roosevelt-Rondon Scientific Expedition had returned several months earlier, and the relationship between the two Brazilian voyages was not lost on reporters. Roosevelt had also kept an eye out for promising flora. In *Through the Brazilian Wilderness*, a detailed account of his harrowing, near-death experience traversing the River of Doubt, he recommended that the USDA propagate the cajazeira tree. Capybaras gobbled up the fruit, and he considered the sweetly sour flesh delicious. If capable of growing in California or Florida, the cajazeira "would make a valuable addition to our orchards."[10]

The publication of Roosevelt's book in 1914 coincided with the passage of legislation that would transform American agriculture. Six years earlier, as president, he had established a Country Life Commission, led by horticulturalist Liberty Hyde Bailey, to improve the lives of the rural poor. The Smith-Lever Act was one of its legacies. Every land grant college would benefit from a Cooperative Extension Service, allowing university-trained leaders and USDA employees to cooperate in the education of American farmers. Within just a few years, farm advisers with degrees in agriculture were making personal visits to dusty California ranches and offering community presentations on how best to water parched orchards, manage pests, and properly fertilize. Now that the Owens River aqueduct had brought seemingly limitless water to Los Angeles, the future growth of the city and its agricultural bounty seemed guaranteed.[11]

Upon his return to Washington, Wilson drafted a USDA bulletin about the expedition and prepared for his next assignment—propagating mangoes in south Florida. The project required a trip to India, birthplace of the mango. Before departing, he traveled home for a visit.[12] The quarantine had helped galvanize local growers, who dreamed of planning a new organization dedicated to avocados, configured along the lines of the California Association of Nurserymen and the California Fruit Growers Exchange. Monrovia's motto, "smile and boost," underscored the entrepreneurial hopes of local towns aspiring to promote themselves as avocado-producing destinations. Recently, Thomas Shedden, a prominent hotel manager in San Francisco who knew what an avocado was worth, had relocated with the intent of supplying luxury hotels in the Los Angeles region.[13] More than two hundred trees were planted at Shedden's three-and-a-half-acre Florimel Avocado Orchard, nestled in the foothills just north of E. B. Rivers's ranch.

Wilson's visit home was timed to converge with the event of the season—the 1914 California Fruit Growers' Convention in Los Angeles—a gathering of more than 2,000 enthusiastic plantspeople with interests ranging from marketing to improving plant varieties. The group filled the auditorium of the Old Normal School, with individual sessions on tropical fruits scheduled in the nearby Hotel Clark. Keynote speaker J. H. Hale of Fort Valley, Georgia, the "Peach King of the World," famous among peers for accurately predicting the surge in citrus production back in 1890, roused the crowd by proclaiming the industry would bring in an all-time high of $90 million a year by the end of the decade. He then tipped his hat to the California growers for leading the way in packing and shipping fruit, a process much emulated by their peach-growing peers in the East. The spirit of coast-to-coast camaraderie was palpable.[14] And with the opening of the Panama Canal, all could imagine even more efficient collaboration.

Fred took the opportunity to introduce avocados into the discussion during a session on tropical fruits.[15] The future of the industry, he argued, depended on its ability to deliver an avocado with a consistently rich flavor and appearance. Standardization was the key to success. It would take cooperation, self-discipline, and sacrifice, but Fred felt that his cohort of nurserymen friends were sophisticated enough to agree on a limited number of varieties, even if that meant jettisoning those they favored most. In the end, they would all be better off. As propagator of the Fuerte, Fred had every reason to be optimistic. The Fuerte had not only survived the freeze but was growing stronger by the month. Before long, it would begin to bear fruit with potential to become the industry standard. In the meantime, the Popenoes were proud to have introduced new date palms, and Fred pinned all his hopes on their coming to fruition.

The outbreak of war scuttled Wilson's voyage to India. Instead, Fairchild dispatched him to Miami, where he could focus on improving the mango crop at the USDA's Plant Introduction Garden.[16] Wilson was well aware of Miami's important role in the USDA's plant-cultivation efforts. During his trip to Brazil, he heard stories about Walter Swingle's experience in Florida developing the tangelo and helping to establish the USDA's presence on Biscayne Bay. As young men, Swingle and fellow government plant pathologist Herbert J. Webber visited Eustis, Florida, on a mission to save dying orange trees—specifically those belonging to the wife of powerful New York senator Thomas Platt. Working from a makeshift laboratory, soon to be known as the Subtropical Horticulture Research Station, Swingle and Webber studied citrus ailments and ways of helping trees resist them. By 1897, with the support of the state horticultural society, they encouraged oil magnate and railroad entrepreneur Henry Flagler to lease the government an acre of his land for a plant laboratory.[17] Mary Brickell offered an additional six acres to serve as a plant-introduction site. At the station, Webber gained international fame as a plant breeder for his foundational work on what would become known as plant cloning.[18] While Wilson cared about mangoes and citrus, his passion lay with the avocado. He recognized early on that Webber's novel propagation technique could prove the necessary link in creating—and replicating—the model California avocado.

Florida was the birthplace of the U.S. avocado industry, and Wilson worked hard to learn from locals as well as in the laboratory. Over time, he struck up a friendship with the avocado renegade George Cellon. The eccentric pioneer was responsible for introducing the process of budding avocados and developing the Trapp and the Pollock, the first two avocado varieties to be commercially grown. Through these cultivars, he cornered the market on the fruit. Wilson excused his gruff manner and ignored his disparagement of government employees. In return, Wilson gradually gained his trust. He encouraged Cellon to experiment with California varieties of Guatemalan avocados and arranged a deposit on an order of budwood from West India Gardens. Fred was happy to provide the wood and sample fruits. If the government garden hadn't been under quarantine, Wilson would have surprised Fred and the staff at West India Gardens with a sampling of what Florida had to offer.[19]

Wilson's daily routine involved tedious microscope study as well as welcome trips to the mango groves and lunches with visiting scientists. Evenings, he wrote letters home and articles for Liberty Hyde Bailey's *Cyclopedia of American Horticulture*, but he also "tripped the light fantastic," all decked out with his walking stick and the smart new clothes he could afford on his USDA salary. He enjoyed dancing in the Casino at Ocean Beach, cranking out batches of avocado ice cream, and meeting the elite plantsmen and scientists who passed through the USDA facility—including John Kunkel Small, the head curator of the New York Botanical Garden; conservationist Charles Torrey Simpson; and botanist J. Arthur Harris.[20]

As he worked on solving the problems of ailing mango trees, Wilson rightly thought of himself as part of history in the making. In keeping with Miami's rapid growth and the government's mission to support national fruit industries, the station was expanding. Philanthropist Charles Deering had recently agreed to lease the USDA twenty-five acres of his land in the city of Buena Vista, about sixteen miles north of the laboratory. Wilson felt light-headed riding in Deering's Fiat with David Fairchild, skimming past lines of cultivated palms and wild mangrove swamps. Upon arriving at the site, he proudly walked the property in the company of these two accomplished men. The new initiative would mean more funding for agricultural experiments, additional staff, and a brighter future for the avocado.[21]

Spanish Salad, Avacado (Alligator Pear)

Peel and cut in half pears, sprinkle
with salt and sugar twenty minutes
before using, then place in heart of
small crisp lettuce head, pour over
Spanish dressing No. 3.

Spanish Salad Dressing No. 3

Lemon or lime juice. Six tablespoons
to three of olive oil, teaspoon
sugar, one-half teaspoon salt, dash
red pepper, teaspoon onion juice.

--Bertha Haffner-Ginger,
*California Mexican-Spanish
Cook Book,* 1914

4 · **Roots**

ON MAY 14, 1915, WHILE WILSON WAS ENJOYING LIFE in Miami, Fred attended the first meeting of what would become the California Avocado Association. A few weeks earlier, he had received a strange letter. Two men without any connections to the avocado community proposed an association of avocado growers. Their reason was unusual. Victor Killick aspired to write a book about the fruit, a well-informed and popular story that would elevate the avocado to its proper place as a staple of the American diet. His friend had agreed to promote the work, and the future association, as the organization's official lecturer, assuming funds were forthcoming.

If taken aback by the audacity of Killick's plan, Fred was curious. As far as he knew, the letter came from interlopers who could contribute nothing to the serious business of building an avocado industry. Fred and his fellow experts had considered forming such an organization, but no one was willing to take on responsibility for such a risky initiative until the time was right. Success would depend on the cooperation of their tight-knit group. When Fred mentioned the letter to Hart, Taft, and his other associates, he learned nearly all had received an identical summons. No one knew any more than he did.[1]

Five days before the mysterious meeting, a short article appeared in the *Los Angeles Express* titled "Pear Growers to Organize" about a movement to establish an avocado exchange championed by local booster Victor Killick of Glendale. A few days later, Whittier papers covered the California Ahuacate Association's meeting

at the Hotel Alexandria, the most celebrated conference venue in
Los Angeles. More than seventy-five people gathered in Parlor A,
all wondering what would happen next.[2] Killick walked up to
the lectern, said a few words about the value of the industry, and
turned over the meeting to the avocado experts. Any questions
about the founders' ambitions were soon forgotten, as men and
women who had devoted years of their lives to avocados clamored
to be heard.

From the beginning, the group's name was a topic of discussion. As one member pointed out, the USDA had chosen *avocado* as most likely to replace *alligator pear*, and it wouldn't be
easy to battle with the government. Edwin Hart was confident
the association would prevail over the USDA. Dr. Franceschi had
long stood firmly behind *ahuacate* and introduced it to club members as most authentic. Hart appreciated *ahuacate* as a "Castilian"
name long associated with the fruit's origins in Mexico and Central America, whereas *avocado* sounded like "lawyer." (In France
and Spain, the words for lawyer were *avocat* and *abogado*, respec-
tively.) Another member liked the way "ahuacate leaves a pleasant taste in the mouth" and also appreciated that the word never
appeared in conjunction with the dreaded moniker *alligator pear*.
A third agreed, adding that *ahuacate* is "most euphonious" and an
Indigenous name. The cochairman of the meeting, J. J. Crafton,
closed the discussion with a long tribute to the ahuacate's many
virtues—noting that people in the Isthmus of Tehuantepec were
often over one hundred years old, and that some of the "brainiest
men" of Mexico, as well as two of the nation's presidents, lived in
the region where these native fruits reigned supreme. There seemed
no doubt that *ahuacate* best reflected the heritage and promising
future of the fledgling association.[3]

At the conclusion of the meeting, the California Ahuacate
Association elected a three-man "Organization" committee composed of Fred Popenoe, Edwin Hart, and C. B. Messenger, editor of the *California Cultivator*. The new committee took on the

responsibility of naming the board of directors. With the exception of Hart and Professor J. Eliot Coit, the board represented nurserymen from Los Angeles to Santa Barbara. A local reporter covering the event sensed the devotion of the men and women pledged to the fledgling association, even predicting its influence beyond the Southland, when the new organization would issue invitations to the first statewide Avocado Day.[4]

A few days later, Wilson received a letter from his father describing the promising foundation that had been laid for an official avocado organization. The thought of a hack writer like Victor Killick infringing on his territory infuriated Wilson. On his own in Florida, he made plans to strengthen the Popenoe partnership—he would grow what his father sold—and to join in the competition to write the first avocado book. Fairchild was sending him on a quick expedition to Cuba, the birthplace of Florida's varieties, to search for new possibilities. This trip, his adventures in Brazil, and of course experiencing all Miami had to offer gave him an edge over the amateurs in California, particularly that audacious dilettante Killick.[5]

Wilson need not have worried. Killick and his friend never attended another meeting. On the association's ten-year anniversary, Fred would look back and describe how like "a meteor passing through the sky, they came and went."[6] Nevertheless, he recounted the founding story, if only to explain why no member could be honored as founder. A year later, in her regular *Los Angeles Times* column Sugar and Spice, syndicated journalist Alma Whitaker confirmed the "spooky" tale of the "unknown stranger" who launched the organization.[7]

The California Ahuacate Association called a follow-up meeting on May 29 to further its goals, elect officers, and adopt bylaws. Board members met at the Union Oil Building and officially named Edwin Hart president, with William Spinks and Charles Silent as first and second vice presidents. The group encouraged Spinks to publicize its founding with a short history of the organization and dispel some of the myths hindering the avocado's introduction into the American marketplace.[8] Part of the association's mission involved reinventing the fruit's reputation as a tropical fruit.

Since the early nineteenth century, the American press had occasionally mentioned the avocado—describing it as an alluring fruit native to the tropics. An 1831 issue of *The New England Farmer* touted the alligator pears on the Caribbean island of Saint Thomas as valuable and suitable for the table. In the 1850s, readers of *The New York Daily Herald* became acquainted with the "abaca" or "abacaté," a product of the Brazilian Empire resembling a nutty-flavored hard custard and best eaten as a salad with oil and vinegar or a dessert with wine and sugar. The *Monongahela Valley Republican* expected "the Traveler in Cuba" to encounter the aguacate or alligator pear at breakfast; those who had acquired the taste enjoyed the fruit with "expressions of ecstatic pleasure." Armchair travelers also feasted on the fruit, but mostly in their imaginations.[9]

By 1880, those with means and a taste for West Indian avocados could find them in New York City. Thomas J. Murrey, known by fellow gourmands as Terrapin Tom, had worked as a caterer in the Astor House and Rossmore hotels, where he saw the fruit as "beginning to find favor among us."[10] In his *Valuable Cooking Receipts*, Murrey recognized avocados were still new enough to require an introduction. He explained that the main ingredient in his Alligator-Pear Salad tasted like chestnuts and should always be purchased green. When the recipe was reprinted for *Murrey's Salads and Sauces* (1884), he invited readers to visit this native of tropical America at the Everett House Café, where two young trees started from seeds in bottles of water were on display.[11] Later in the 1880s, Maria Parloa, the celebrated founder of Miss Parloa's School of Cookery, provided welcome information about the little-known fruit in *Miss Parloa's Kitchen Companion*. Cooks preparing her Aguacate Salad could purchase "good-sized" (two-pound) aguacates, or alligator pears, for fifteen to twenty cents at a fruit store on Fulton Street.[12]

In 1891, *The American Magazine* was still introducing its readers to "the avocado, or alligator pear" as a foreign import and emphasizing the need to develop a taste for it over time. Author Anna M. Paris compared the fruit to purl, the sustaining alcoholic drink prepared by Dick Swiveller, a character in Dickens's *The Old Curiosity Shop*. Neither could "be tasted in a sip."[13] Despite such efforts to anglicize the fruit, confusion over its name and origins continued to conjure images of exotic, humid climes, not the bright, opportunistic world of Southern California. To move forward, the association would need to show consumers California-grown fruits and educate them in the avocado's nutritional and gastronomic value.

The Boston Cooking-School Magazine, harbinger of food fads to come, profiled the avocado's growing popularity while underscoring the elite status keeping it from reaching a broader audience. Showcased as the seasonal fruit for October 1914–1915, "the Avocado or 'alligator' pear" was "what the terrapin is to the animal kingdom and the truffle to the vegetable . . . in the realm of horticulture."[14] When popular novelist Willa Cather introduced a wickedly indulgent character, Miss Edith Beers, she described her lunching at the Waldorf Astoria, squeezed into a black satin sheath dress and eating "nothing but alligator-pear salad and hothouse grapes."[15] On Broadway, you could expect to pay two dollars for an avocado salad (more than sixty dollars today). Fruit orchardists considered the avocado the most valuable fruit on the American market, despite its limited role as "strictly a salad pear, served with various dressings."[16] But this assessment came from the East Coast, where the avocado had long been known as a tropical delicacy. The California Ahuacate Association knew its success depended on creating a broader market for the fruit, both in terms of culinary uses and public awareness of the avocado's ability to thrive in California soil. In this they received an unanticipated boost from local media.

The freeze happened to coincide with culinary programming newly launched by the *Los Angeles Times* under the direction of Harrison Gray Otis, but most likely encouraged by his son-in-law and soon to be successor, Harry Chandler, both powerful promoters of the city and its enterprises. The two were inspired by the success of the newspaper's cooking contest, introduced nearly a decade earlier. Housewives were encouraged to send in their favorite recipes in specific categories—beginning with soups, then entrées, and so on. Winners were chosen by the number of votes received and monetary prizes awarded to the top recipes. Even better, a selection of recipes from all categories were published in the *Los Angeles Times Cook Book*.[17] When it came out in 1905, the cookbook was further described as "One Thousand Toothsome Cooking and Other Recipes Including Seventy-nine Old-Time California, Spanish and Mexican Dishes." The first recipe, an Alligator Pear Salad, was indicated as "from Mexico," and sent in by Mrs. S. Y. Yglesias. A third cookbook was in production when the *Times* unveiled its ambitious new plan to emphasize the region's growing sophistication: an unprecedented on-site culinary experience presented in a brand-new demonstration kitchen. Bertha Haffner-Ginger, a domestic scientist famed for her cookery, was hired to host an inaugural program.[18] As manager of the new School of Domestic Science, Haffner-Ginger would offer cooking lessons and her valuable recipes to readers of the *Times*. During a free sample class, students eager to learn how to cook "as the Spanish do" filled the school's kitchen on the second floor of the *Times* building.[19]

Haffner-Ginger built her meal around a chicken dish, mesmerizing her audience as she whipped up a dressing and, with a flick of the wrist and a smile, popped it in the oven. No doubt encouraged by her employers to push California's merits, she urged her students to buy from the local city markets and noted that many of the ingredients were "California productions"—the Sylmar Brand of olive oil from the famous San Fernando olive orchards and even the alligator pears that went into the salad were "raised in Pasadena, Whittier and other points in Southern California."[20] She spent time "prowling around" the Los Angeles neighborhood of Sonoratown, among the bakeshops on San Fernando Street, and recommended shopping at Elias & Guzman Spanish Bakery and Eagle Mill, where fresh tortilla dough, corn husks, and chile peppers were sold.[21] When the chicken was piping hot, she lifted the lid to ahs and ohs. Her accompanying salad featured an avocado, curlicues of red cabbage, and green chiles, tossed with a dressing of lemon, olive oil, and vinegar.[22]

During the first months of Haffner-Ginger's tenure with the *Times*, the raging revolutions in Mexico inspired more than a hundred Mexican "soldiers of fortune," to leave Sonoratown and join the fray.[23] Over the next year, poverty and violence became increasingly common, only to increase once the United States entered the war.[24] Having discovered that her Spanish cooking lessons were in demand, Haffner-Ginger compiled her favorite dishes in the *California Mexican-Spanish Cook Book*, America's first with an English-language recipe for tacos. Her version involved folding cooked chiles and chopped beef in a handmade tortilla, sealed with an egg and fried in "deep fat."[25] She reminded readers that what some called Spanish food was actually "Mexican Indian," knowing that if they didn't understand the customs of their Mexican neighbors, many would be familiar with Helen Hunt Jackson's novel *Ramona*, a bestseller that celebrated California's multicultural heritage. Tortillas and other Mexican staples like masa were not native to Spain, but her upper-class clientele gorged on the romance of the Old World and no doubt savored the book's illustrations—conquistadors, Ramona's oven, and the Franciscan missions—along with her "Spanish Salad" featuring avocado.

True to her mission, Haffner-Ginger also included a photograph of Y. Y. Perez making tortillas at the Public Bakery in Sonoratown, proof that "truly the heart of women are the same the world over."[26]

Avocados from Orange Country were highlighted at the Panama-Pacific International Exposition, which ran from February to December 1915. In the months before the inaugural CAA meeting, C. P. Taft did his best to capitalize on that fact. Every ten days, from July to September, he sent at least a dozen Taft avocados to the Orange County exhibit manager, who had mentioned more than once that they attracted the most interest of any fruit display. Consumers paid high prices for avocados, with the best ones selling for as much as a dollar each.[27] After sampling the fruit, the steward of the Hotel Oakland announced he would rather own an orchard than a gold mine. Taft reported his success in the association's first annual report, as his answer to the question, "Will the next (horticultural) craze be over the alligator pear?"[28]

An unanticipated opportunity for avocado promotion arose in early August, when thirty members of the American Pomological Society, the nation's first organization dedicated to establishing fruit varieties, visited the region. Arriving on a special Pacific Electric car, the group was met by the Whittier Chamber of Commerce and "the State school band." Their tour included a visit to the famous Rideout-Ganter-Woodworth avocado tree and to Rideout's ranch, where they admired tropical sapote and papaya trees. After luncheon at the East Whittier clubhouse, Edwin Hart gave a presentation focusing on avocados, which he hoped would soon be known the world over as ahuacates.[29]

Meanwhile, at the University of California, J. Eliot Coit had been experimenting with simpler, less expensive methods of determining the fat content of avocados and when best to pick them. Avocado flesh resembled soft cheese, and Coit discovered that the

Babcock milk tester, commonly used by dairy farmers to measure the butter-fat content in dairy products, could be used for the fruit as well.[30] The *Los Angeles Times* envisioned Coit's discovery as transforming the market. Robust avocados would be advertised as "Fresh Avocados, High Test," and the prices of fruit would range based on fat content, like the cream percentage in butter.

In a speech at the American Association for the Advancement of Science Annual Meeting, Herbert Webber, a citrus man, encouraged planting avocados in orchards, both to reduce dependence on a single product and to introduce a new staple food that he believed could become as common a feature of the American diet as the potato. A newspaper summarized his presentation with the headline "Warns of Citrus Peril, Advises Avocado as Measure of Relief."[31] This shocking pronouncement—coming so unexpectedly from such a devoted citrus expert—helped push the avocado further into the spotlight.

When Wilson Popenoe returned from Florida in the fall of 1915, he discovered Carl Schmidt's notes from the 1911 Mexico expedition amid the West India Gardens nursery records. Now cognizant of their historical value to the new organization and the nation, he began a lengthy transcription project. On the first page of a fresh ledger, he addressed posterity, writing that a copy of the original introductions from Mexico belonged in Washington, D.C., for its "pomological interest." Next, he created a second list of varieties originating in California. A week later, his historical record had evolved into a kind of journal, as he jotted down notes of field trips throughout the Southland in search of nurserymen and their trees.

In Whittier, Wilson met grower Jennie C. Gano and her seven-year-old Ganter trees. The hardworking orchardist had already earned more than $3,000 on the fruit she packed and sold herself to markets and hotels.[32] A few days later, while traveling through San Fernando, he noted that the original seed from the first Dickinson avocado came from a hotel in Guatemala City. According to local legend, a guest named George Williams ate one, brought the seed home, and planted it in 1897. Taft thought this Dickinson variety and the Sharpless the only two with flesh that would not discolor when the fruit was cut. Wilson scrawled down the names and dates of the Walker, Challenge, and Royal—all varieties that came from the Murrieta Place as young plants, and then reminded himself to write Murrieta (over Fairchild's signature) for data on his introductions. These records would soon become the basis for a new method of thinking about avocados—as seeds native to specific geographical locations, with qualities based on climate, soil, and water level, and each demonstrating individual flavors, textures, and hardiness. Over the next year, his work would become vital to the new association's mission.[33]

As Wilson obsessively traveled and researched, local newspapers began to report on the California Ahuacate Association's preparation for its first semiannual meeting. The avocado men had learned from the citrus industry's battle against pests, freezing temperatures, and unregulated marketing practices. When speaking to reporters, they made a point of emphasizing the conservative nature of their enterprise, its solid foundation, and support from the USDA and university experts. The CAA growers had the time, money, and willpower to experience failure. In fact, they accepted it as part of their experimental work. Everyone knew the story of William Hertrich, who gave up growing avocados for Huntington after the 1913 freeze. When he went to remove the damaged trees, new shoots were sprouting from the stumps. The next summer brought further growth. Now he was a grower again with steadfast admiration for the hardy avocado and an example for all those who doubted the fruit's resilience.[34]

Area newspapers and horticultural publications gave the upcoming meeting considerable publicity. The *Los Angeles Times* called the event "epochal," not to mention proof that the "exotic product" had already taken root in California. Some trees were more than twenty years old, and thousands had been budded by the state's most experienced growers, like Taft, who had been in the business for sixteen years.[35] During the weeks leading up to the event, however, the papers also publicized confusion over what to call the product. Was it ahuacate or avocado? And why not alligator pear? The organization's leaders seemed to agree about almost everything except their own name. When Edwin Hart learned that a government bulletin had included the term *ahuacate*, he leaped at the opportunity to reinforce his favorite appellation. Charles D. Adams, a charter member of the CAA, saw Hart's endorsement in the *California Cultivator* and responded with an essay of his own. Adams described the citrus industry's unsuccessful effort to change *grapefruit* to *pomelo* and urged CAA members to accept the term *avocado* or risk being forever plagued by *alligator pear*. Even Hart would ultimately back down when confronted with that dreaded possibility.[36]

As the big day grew near, such dissention among the ranks was replaced by anticipation: the world's first avocado association was about to convene for its inaugural annual meeting.

Avocado on Toast

Remove the flesh with a spoon and
mash with a fork. Spread thickly on
a small square of hot toast. Add
a little salt and pepper. This is
one of the nicest ways of serving
avocado.

--California Avocado Association
Annual Report, 1915

5 · The Fuerte's Rise

ON OCTOBER 23, 1915, EDWIN HART STRODE UP THE
marble steps of the Hotel Alexandria, just down the street from
his real estate office, now the headquarters of the California Avocado Association. He had reason to feel confident as he entered
the hotel's Palm Court, its stained glass skylight casting a warm
glow. In addition to serving as president of the association, Hart
was publicly announcing the founding of Hart & Barber Avocado
Company, the merger of his nurseries with those of T. U. Barber,
Fred Popenoe's former manager. The new venture had the advantage of Hart's downtown location in the Union Oil Building,
his nurseries in North Whittier Heights, and Barber's orchards
in Hollywood. The partners already considered themselves pur-
veyors of the "largest most perfectly grown and selected stock of
budded trees in California," in thirty varieties. The glamorous hotel setting reflected Hart's hopes to jump-start the nascent industry. He smiled broadly as he surveyed the ballroom, where rows
of healthy seedlings were displayed. Chandeliers glittered above.
The Alexandria's manager had rolled out the red carpet. Visitors
mingled among the trees, some five deep, craning their necks for
a better view of the specimens. Growers proudly exhibited their
thin-skinned varieties, two rare seedless examples among them.
Some of the nursery trees, budded seven months ago, were already
five feet tall.[1]

Among the seventy-four charter members of the CAA, Margaret
(Mrs. J. L.) Stewart stood out in the crowd. Hart knew her as the
owner of an advantageous parcel of land in San Fernando. A society

lady, she shocked her social set by planting an avocado orchard adjacent to her small lemon grove. Margaret made no little plans. She aspired to become a commercial grower and assumed her fellow members did the same.[2] It was said she even passed up a trip to Europe in favor of tending the young avocado trees. While her husband was abroad, Margaret bribed her chauffeur to shade her one-foot seedlings with shingles during a particularly hot summer. She planted more than ten acres and lost hundreds of trees and at least $1,000 to drought but remained undaunted. Hart hoped her perseverance would inspire others to invest in avocado land. As president of the CAA, he considered it his responsibility to keep tabs on planted acreage, not to mention boost the economy by fostering potential real estate transactions.

When he stepped up to the podium, Hart looked out over an audience of more than three hundred. He was pleased to recognize USDA staff, scientists from Riverside, and Berkeley professors among the crowd. If the industry were to move forward, these minds would lead the way. After a warm welcome, Hart opened the meeting with a simple principle: the association dedicated to the culture, production, and marketing of the avocado was determined to stifle any overhyping of the infant industry, an issue of particular sensitivity given the fabulous profits. It was up to the association, he argued, to protect the public against that "class of boomers who made the raising of eucalyptus and spineless cactus a craze." Devoted to moving the avocado from "fad" to legitimate industry, Hart outlined a range of promotional plans—from semiannual exhibition meetings in which experts could demonstrate their experimental varieties to the distribution of 10,000 folders of recipes with directions for fruit selection.[3]

A lineup of speakers chosen for their expertise and ability to advance the CAA's agenda followed. Professor Ira J. Condit of Berkeley focused on hastening the standardization process by keeping a scorecard for each variety. Growers would rank key traits such as size, form, stem, and skin to create a personal profile of each tree, and these statistics would be compiled to determine the varieties best suited to the industry.[4] Professor Myer Jaffa, head of the division of nutrition at Berkeley, promoted the avocado's health appeal. As far as fat content, the olive was its only competitor but lagged behind in terms of nutrients and required extensive processing. Along with the avocado's healthy fat, the fruit's indescribable combination of texture and flavor, summed up as "succulency," identified it as both delicious and the superfood of its day.[5] Any doubters were invited to his exhibit of avocado oils, avocado flour, candied avocado seeds, and other edibles—just a taste of the wonders in store for avocado lovers.

A *Los Angeles Times* reporter covering the meeting remarked that at a dollar a fruit, the market was "confined to the banker, retired capitalist and the millionaire."[6] The avocado's reputation as a luxury food would be hard to shake. Nearly twenty-five years earlier, Santa Barbara's *Daily Independent* had noted that since its debut at Delmonico's, the fruit was considered a delicacy.[7] Celebrated New York chef Charles Ranhofer included sliced avocados seasoned with salt, pepper, and vinegar and garnished with lemon as a side dish in his famous cookbook, *The Epicurean*.[8] Little had changed since then, and the endorsement of renowned citrus grower Egbert Norman Reasoner, who called avocados "'the most valuable fruit in America,'" did not suggest that the fruit would become affordable over the next few decades.[9] Well aware of its image problem, association leaders focused on the first steps toward bringing avocados to the average American's kitchen table: standardizing the product and educating the public in the versatility of this "everyday food."

At midday, the crowd enjoyed a spectacular array of avocado delicacies, courtesy of the hotel. Three years earlier, Charles C. Frey, head chef of the Hotel Alexandria, had recognized the value of growing his own fruit and purchased forty acres in Baldwin Park, near Covina.[10] The hotel's banquet tables displayed the fruits of his labors. There were "sliced avocados, dainty avocado sandwiches, avocado cocktails, and mixed avocado salads with beautiful decorations."[11] Along with the food samples, participants were encouraged to take free recipe folders, replete with dishes like avocado toast and Cuban salad, easily assembled by placing three stuffed olives in the cavity with a sprinkling of lemon or lime juice. For dessert, a choice between avocado ice cream or avocado and chopped dates whipped together with sweetened cream—delicious! Hart reminded everyone that additional recipe booklets were available at the CAA office, where he also hoped to sell some prime avocado land.[12]

An interested group gathered around a box of thin-skinned, well-traveled avocados. The battered crate had been shipped to Chicago and back to test different methods of packing the fruit. Those wrapped in paper were blackened and bruised, but contrary to popular expectation, the fruit loosely covered in excelsior fared well. A few avocados withstood the trip without any visible damage. The association made a point of explaining that, with the exception of a single large, thick-skinned Sharpless reserved exclusively for the event, all the varieties were of the thin-skinned type typical of the season.[13] Growers noted such details, and marketers heaved a sigh of relief at the success of excelsior as packing material.

When the meeting resumed that afternoon, A. D. Shamel brought the audience's attention back to the importance of accurate recordkeeping, as outlined by Condit and modeled after methods used by the Riverside experiment station for citrus breeding.[14] This invaluable set of records would benefit from a concurrent project led by Fred Popenoe.

Popenoe had taken on the herculean challenge of developing a list of documented avocado varieties. From several hundred, he identified eighty-six, divided by geographic origin into three types (West Indian, Guatemalan, and Mexican) and further differentiated by "California" or "Foreign" origin. Fred asked his fellow nurserymen to contribute to the growing body of research in hopes of soon standardizing the fruit. Everyone knew he was keen on advancing his own pet varieties—the Puebla and the Fuerte—and given their promise, West India Gardens had reason to be confident.[15]

A highlight of the day was Webber's demonstration of loyalty to the cause. At the Riverside Citrus Experiment Station, he daily encountered possibilities for developing the industry. Imagine annual seedling exhibitions, with medals awarded, an incentive dating back to early America, when the Massachusetts Horticultural Society used this method to improve fruit breeding and the English successfully enlarged the gooseberry from three-eighths of an inch to the diameter of an average hen's egg. Just think how much more progress could be made in the modern age! The Citrus Experiment Station would contribute its ever-increasing knowledge of fertilization, applying its successful efforts in using winter cover crops like bitter clover and purple vetch to enrich the soil with nitrogen and organic matter. At this very moment, a tract of nearly five hundred acres was being outfitted with laboratories, hothouses, barns, and an irrigation system in preparation for next year, when the station would begin planting its first experimental avocado orchard.[16] After his rousing speech, Webber was elected an honorary member of the association. The most famous representative of citrus was now an avocado man.

Before the end of the meeting, the association resolved to petition the secretary of agriculture and the USDA to send a plant explorer to Central America in search of more hardy, frost-resistant varieties. Members left full of enthusiasm for the work ahead. Together, the association offered the fellowship and progressive thinking necessary to envision a California avocado industry. And it was even easier to imagine their chosen explorer, Wilson Popenoe, returning from the Guatemalan wilderness with saddlebags full of green gold.

After Wilson's experience in Florida, rejoining the fraternity of avocado enthusiasts was like returning to his childhood home. He felt comfortable and appreciated but harbored a sense of superiority that he struggled to keep hidden. Continuing his research, he gathered more information on Santa Barbara varieties and began revising Condit's scorecard methodology, a task that reflected Wilson's increasing expertise. He consulted Harris Perley Gould of the Bureau of Plant Industry, and the two further refined the scorecard. In mid-December, when Wilson returned to Washington, D.C., he ran a new version by G. N. Collins, who thought it "satisfactory for practical purposes," which was Wilson's intent.

Since the October meeting, association officers had thought carefully about choosing members for its Committee on Registration and Classification of Varieties. Certainly, those selected should not be involved in the commercial avocado industry, a limitation that significantly reduced the field. All were relieved when Webber accepted the chairmanship and Condit signed on. Having a representative from Riverside and one from Berkeley provided regional representation and lessened any sense of favoritism among the close-knit Southland growers. William Hertrich, Huntington's personal nurseryman, was welcomed as another nonpartisan committee member. An amateur enthusiast, H. M. Haldeman, kept himself busy managing the Boynton Company, manufacturer of pumps, and Charles Adams, known for his experience with the California Fruit Growers Exchange, rounded out the group. The five men were responsible for registering the most desirable fruits as certified CAA varieties, judging nursery stock and trees at the association's annual meetings, and awarding certificates to growers of CAA-endorsed avocados. Over the next year and a half, the committee would determine the fate of individual growers and commercial nurseries.[17]

Two days before the CAA's spring gathering, the Committee on Registration and Classification of Varieties held a meeting at the Hotel Clark. Their agenda summarized the progress achieved over the winter. The group adopted a temporary scorecard shaped by Wilson's work, determined that upcoming CAA exhibitions should focus on varieties producing superior fruit (not just the largest number displayed), and agreed that a fine should be levied on members using the barbarism *alligator pear*. Members were enlisted to help with the project by ranking the committee's list of California varieties. The compiled results, among other factors, would determine the final list. Finally, the committee resolved to emphasize the importance of standardizing the market by annually awarding gold, silver, and bronze medals to the growers with the most notable new varieties. Looking ahead, they envisioned an official variety orchard at the Citrus Experiment Station. Growers hoping to introduce additions to the list would be asked to furnish five good trees on budded and approved stock for testing at the station.

The forthcoming list was foremost on the minds of the members with a serious stake in the outcome. Edwin Hart and T. U. Barber took the opportunity to get ahead of the competition by advertising their "fifteen-acre avocado orchard on frost-protected slopes of North Whittier Heights," which also served as a plug for the real estate business. Fred Popenoe thought it brazen of Hart to suggest his list as authoritative, but since both the Fuerte and the Puebla were on it, he couldn't complain. In fact, he was planning his own brochure—a pamphlet exclusively pushing the Fuerte as the exemplar. Hart's endorsement couldn't do any harm.

In the meantime, on behalf of the California Avocado Association, plant explorer Wilson Popenoe planned another trip abroad. He hoped to discover more productive, better-tasting avocado varieties capable of thriving in the state's semitropical climate. His USDA colleagues, the veterans Cook and Collins, gave him advice on how to prepare and what to expect. During the months leading up to his voyage, he made many visits to the Library of Congress, where he found John Lloyd Stevens's classic *Incidents of Travel in Yucatan*, William T. Brigham's *Guatemala: The Land of the Quetzal*, and Anne Cary and Alfred Percival Maudslay's monumental *A Glimpse at Guatemala*. Reading these romantic accounts, filled with descriptions of brightly colored flora and fauna, conjured visions of stumbling upon the wild avocado emersed in its native landscape. The primeval avocado—the origin of the species—had the potential to unlock countless botanical mysteries, not to mention add his name to the history books. Knowing it might not exist made the hunt that much more alluring.

At last, in September 1916, the twenty-five-year-old avocado expert set off on the *Sixaola* of the Great White Fleet, bound for Puerto Barrios, a port on the Caribbean coast of Guatemala.[18]

Thomas Shedden was fed up. Once again, the CAA had promised to do away with the crippling misnomer *alligator pear*, but nothing had changed. Alligator pears appeared in the newspapers, on hotel menus, and even in conversation with fellow avocado men (despite the threat of a fine). To consumers, all avocados were alligator pears. Shedden knew the marketing power of a name and wouldn't rest until the alligator pear was extinct.

Back in 1905, botanist G. N. Collins had also taken a stand against the alligator pear. His definitive government bulletin attempted to discourage the "misleading designation" while it was still little known. He envisioned puzzled consumers equating the fruit with common pears and "annoying complications in statistical classifications" in places where both fruits were grown. His research revealed more than forty-three names for the avocado—a "curious and undignified jumble" including *midshipman's butter*, *custard apple*, *butter pear*, and *vegetable marrow*. It had all started in ancient Mesoamerica.[19]

The Aztecs knew the avocado as *ahuacahuitl*. They understood the shape of the fruit as representing its ability to pass on strength and virility.[20] In the modern version of Nahuatl, the Aztec language during the Spanish conquest, *ahuacatl* was the word for avocado and testicle. When conquistador Pedro Cieza de Léon came upon the ahuacahuitl in the early sixteenth century, he called it *aguacate*.[21] This was the beginning of a long series of variations derived from the Aztec word. One of these came from Henry Hawks, an English merchant, whose *aluacatas*, encountered on his travels through Mexico in 1572, were the first mention of the fruit in an English publication.[22] More than a hundred years would pass before the word *avocado* appeared in print as part of a 1696 catalog of Jamaican plants written by Sir Hans Sloane, who also called it the alligator pear. Later British adaptations included *avocato*, *avigato*, and *avocado*, but *alligator pear* was easiest for Americans to pronounce and remember.[23] And now, thanks to elite hotels on both coasts, alligator pears were everywhere. At a time when members were too preoccupied with the list of varieties to think of much else, Shedden vowed to wage war on the alligator pear.

Curiosity in the industry and its challenging task attracted more than 1,000 to the May meeting at the Normal Hill Center in Los Angeles.[24] Shedden stepped up to the podium armed with bullet points. The fruit was cursed by a name suggesting something beastly "crawling and sprawling" on the ground. Among hotel guests, *alligator* gave rise to unpleasant thoughts, and hotel staff called the fruit *gators*, leading to all sorts of problems—like the time one new employee delivered a box of gators to a guest assuming they were shoes. Shedden held the floor for much too long, encouraging fellow "avocranks" to join him in engaging in defending the fruit they loved.[25]

At the conclusion of his speech, Shedden read a paper sent by Victor Hirtzler, chef at the famed Hotel St. Francis in San Francisco, his friend and ally in the effort to unseat the alligator pear. Chef Hirtzler had served the avocado at every course, both raw and cooked, from cocktail to ice cream, always calling it by its proper name. He tempted palates with one of his culinary masterpieces, Avocado en Surprise. To prepare this delicacy, the chef

scooped out half of an avocado, mixed it into a paste with mayonnaise, and returned it to the shell. Then about a tablespoon of
flesh was spooned out and combined with a cooked egg yolk dyed
brown with a few drops of soy sauce. Finally, the depression was
filled with the brownish mass, creating a mock seed in the half
shell. Accomplished gourmands might test their skill on even more
elaborate dishes, like the dessert Avocado Queen Liliuokalani
(named after the Hawaiian queen), a recipe that challenged the
cook to remove the seed of an avocado, reconstruct the fruit, fill
the cavity with anisette, and mount it on a ring of genoise sponge
surrounded by whipped cream and strawberry sauce topped with
crushed nougat.[26] Shedden felt that he and Hirtzler had done their
best to honor the versatile avocado and its distinguished history.
His hopes were confirmed when the association elected him as its
third president.

On October 25, 1917, the day before the fifth annual meeting,
the CAA issued "Circular on Varieties," the committee's "Avocado
Varieties Recommended for Planting in California," also known
as "Circular No. 1."[27] The chosen few were the Fuerte, Sharpless, Dickinson, Lyon, Taft, Puebla, and Blakeman. West India
Gardens claimed two varieties on the list—the hardy Fuerte and
its cousin the Puebla. Each avocado was graded based on color,
shape, weight, size of seed, and oil content, the quality considered
its nutrition content. The Fuerte measured a whopping 30 percent
oil, the Lyon a mere 16 percent. Other factors such as bearing
habits were implicit in the committee's decision.

Representing the board of directors, T. U. Barber praised the
committee and emphasized the necessity of its actions. Although
he and Hart had covered all their bases by planting a range of
varieties, Barber commiserated with the crowd who, "with plantings already started . . . felt somewhat disappointed because all
selections were not recommended."[28] The CAA vowed to maintain
a committee on varieties and to adjust the list of recommendations based on evolving knowledge. All were reminded that the list

would never become final. The board of directors felt a momentous step had been made. The avocado industry was ready to move forward by establishing a marketing plan similar to that of the citrus exchange with its Sunkist label. In response to any disappointments, planters were encouraged to begin "top-working" and nurserymen to discontinue varieties in little demand.[29] Topworking was an age-old horticulturalists' technique to trick Mother Nature, a way to grow something new from something old. The nurseryman cut mature trees down to stumps, sliced a few notches just behind the bark, carefully slipped in sticks of budwood from a new scion, bound or girdled the graft with cloth, and waited for the budwood to bond with the soft cambium beneath. In a few months, if all went well, the old tree, reborn, produced a completely different kind of avocado.

Wilson returned from Guatemala in December 1917, arriving in Washington just before Christmas. Adjusting to life at the Bureau of Plant Industry was always challenging after a long trip. With no directives from above and World War I raging, he felt increasingly isolated. David Fairchild had promised to keep an eye out for any opportunities and kindly asked him to lunch at the Cosmos Club. The club gathered together men who shared Wilson's interests—scientists and geographers mingled with plant explorers and professors. Wilson's brother Paul had been elected a member shortly after publishing his book on dates, and Wilson hoped he, too, would receive this honor. On a few occasions, he ran into Sylvanus Morley, an archaeologist for the Carnegie Institution of Washington he had met while traveling through Guatemala City. Morley revealed himself as a spy for the U.S. Navy. His work digging for artifacts in foreign countries served as the perfect cover. Intrigued by the thought of mixing travel and espionage, Wilson listened carefully as Morley confided that Charles

A. Sheldon, chief of naval operations, had asked him to compile a list of potential recruits. With Fairchild's blessing, Wilson proudly signed on. As a legitimate plant explorer, he would hunt for promising new avocado varieties while keeping an eye out for German submarines probing the coast of Mexico.[30]

By February, the necessary steps had been taken to secure funding for an exploratory trip to Mexico, courtesy of the University of California's College of Agriculture. Herbert Webber, A. D. Shamel, and the staff at Riverside experiment station were eager to host a welcome-home dinner.[31] Before the event, Wilson spent a few days with his family in Altadena. As usual, his father had news of his latest investment, sure to yield a fortune. His twenty-six-acre loquat orchard in Vista had taken off, and he expected to ship as much as 30,000 pounds of the exotic fruit. Wilson applauded his efforts, while also cautioning him not to overextend himself. Brushing off any doubts, Fred launched into his latest plan—planting several acres of avocados in Fallbrook, an up-and-coming avocado district.[32]

Wilson was recovering from his final typhoid vaccine while corresponding with Charles Sheldon regarding necessary preparations. The plant explorer hoped to establish friendly relations with scientific men in Mexico City and travel to Veracruz for a visit with botanist Carl Purpus, known for contributing thousands of Mexican plant samples to the UC Berkeley herbarium. In official naval documents of the Office of Naval Intelligence, Wilson was known as No. 219.[33]

It was only a matter of weeks before the plant explorer set off on his secret mission, which included a side trip to a place he had long yearned to visit—"the mecca of California avocado growers," Atlixco, Mexico, birthplace of the Fuerte. Traveling in wartime was difficult, but he managed to find a berth aboard the SS *Break-water*, a banana boat traveling from New Orleans to Veracruz. During the rough passage, he suffered in his cabin, "sucking lemons, nibbling on soda biscuits, and counting the hours."[34] Since

receiving the mysterious letter from Riordan with the ancient pictograph, he had imagined a place much like his memories of Costa
Rica, not tropical but vibrant like the hardy native fruit his father
had named Fuerte.

Traveling by train, just as the sun rose over the hills across the
valley of Puebla, Wilson caught a glimpse of the Great Pyramid
of Cholula and the snow-covered volcano Popocatepetl before de-
scending through the Tentzo hills to the village. He expected to
find a mountain valley crowded with pines and a quaint settlement nestled among roses and fruit trees, but instead encountered
"a series of low, rolling hills, as brown as barren as those of Southern California in September." A moment later the view opened
up, and he felt transported to the fertile San Joaquin Valley. Only
the volcano seemed out of place. A new landscape unfolded before
him—groves and gardens, fruits and flowers . . . and avocados—
the gardens of Atlixco, home of the parent Fuerte![35]

The journey was not without its risks. Atlixco was frequently
occupied by the Zapatistas or in danger of their raids. The volatil-
ity kept many avocado enthusiasts from visiting. Wilson himself
had canceled a much-anticipated trip to meet Carl Purpus at his
home, writing that he feared traveling to Zacualpan. Trains passing through the region were commonly the target of rifle-wielding
youth who robbed passengers of everything except their under-
wear. Although Wilson avoided this experience, he nevertheless
prepared by wearing his best undergarments on Mexican trains.[36]

Not all of the trip was so harrowing. During a week in Mexico
City, he visited the Dirección de Estudios Biológicos, the country's premiere botanical library, and toured the museum with its
director, Professor Alfonso L. Herrera. With Herrera's assistance,
he obtained access to the herbarium and to rare works on Mexican
botany, horticulture, and agriculture, as well as to the collections

of the Museo de Historia Natural, under the professor's charge. Botanist and professor Maximino Martínez accompanied them to the Museo Commercial, where Wilson admired a display of Mexican flora ranging from fiber- and oil-producing plants to sources of rubber and Mexican hardwood.[37]

Finally, he had a chance to delve into "the musty tomes" at the Museo Nacional de Arqueología. After nearly eight years of wondering, this was his opportunity to learn more about the origins of the Aztec pictograph. On the shelves of the main library, he discovered a book with renditions of a series of pictographs, said to have been taken from Emperor Montezuma's "tribute rolls" discovered during the conquest. The names of the towns offering tributes were represented, as were the desired items—cacao beans, rabbit skins, and other valuable commodities. The town of Ahuacatlán's pictograph was a tree with three branches, from which little ellipsoidal fruits issued to indicate ahuacates. Teeth in the tree trunk signified "place where." When puzzled together, Ahuacatlán was "place where the ahuacate abounds." Now more than ever Wilson felt a kinship with Mexico and Atlixco, for him the sister city of Altadena, where avocados flourished.[38]

In his search for the ahuacatl, Wilson found guacamole among the pages of philologist Rémi Siméon's Nahuatl dictionary.[39] The dish Siméon called a "ragout," made by mashing avocado pulp, lemon juice, and chopped onion, was known as ahuacamulli, a combination of *ahuacate* and *mulli*, the word for sauce or soft food. Delighted by the discovery, Wilson recorded yet another example of how ancient civilizations shaped modern cuisine.[40]

Many hours of research and collaborative work contributed to Wilson's respect for this familiar yet foreign land. A letter of introduction from his friend botanist William E. Safford introduced him to Zelia Nuttall, the prominent California-born archaeologist known for her studies of Indigenous culture. Her expertise had been demonstrated years ago, after she identified a valuable Indigenous manuscript, painted on animal skin, and used her connections to secure its publication.[41] The rare Codex Nuttall shed new light on the culture of Mesoamerica. Shortly after sending his letter, Wilson received an invitation to visit Nuttall at her home, Casa Alvarado, in Coyoacán, just outside Mexico City. Already charmed by her insight into the horticultural history of the Aztec nation, he sat spellbound as she described her long and storied archaeological career, much of which was sponsored by the philanthropist Phoebe Hearst and the University of California. Nuttall described the Aztecs' original system of plant nomenclature, a precursor of the Linnaean classification system, and questioned him about his exploration of the ancient Aztec picture writings depicting avocados. When he showed her the pictograph, she explained that two ancient towns were named after the avocado, Ahuacatlán (in the state of Nayarit) and Ahuacatlán (now Aguacatán in northern Guatemala).[42] In the spacious sala of Casa Alvarado, itself a veritable museum of Mexican antiquities, the two sipped tea and lost themselves in their mutual admiration of the ancients.[43]

Wilson found in these collections of national treasures a culture he admired and a horticultural tradition to emulate in the orchards of Southern California. During one of his research forays, he came across an essay by a Señor Carlos Gris, who as early as 1896 predicted that local avocados could become a considerable source of income to Mexican exporters. Wilson wasn't convinced but applauded the concept, writing in his journal, "Congratulations, Señor Gris. If the avocado weevil had not put in an appearance, you would probably have won out!"[44] Looking forward, Wilson predicted that Atlixco would become known for its relationship to the California avocado industry in the same way that Bahia, Brazil, was identified with the state's citrus industry.[45] Both were backdrops to an American success story and would share the honor of nurturing a mother tree that changed the world.

Early one morning, with Carl Schmidt's notes and diagrams in hand, Wilson set off to search for a property belonging to Matildi Dion. He learned the tree was now owned by Dion's cousin, Alejandro Le Blanc, a Mexican of French ancestry, and grew in his garden at 2 Calle Manuel Buen Rastro. Le Blanc's son answered the door and kindly showed Wilson around the grounds. The Fuerte parent tree filled one corner, close to a high wall across from the nearby house, an area of clean, level, uncultivated ground. Healthy and vigorous, it was not considered large, measuring about thirty feet tall, and most likely had lived between thirty and thirty-five years. Alejandro knew the tree's value and gave it extra attention. When his reservoir irrigated the garden, the exceptional tree soaked up extra water from a special drain below the ground a few feet from its trunk.[46]

The Le Blanc family recognized the unusually rich flavor of the Fuerte and appreciated the high yield of flesh resulting from the small seed. The fruit ripened over a longer season than its peers, yielding about six hundred avocados each year, all of which stayed in the family. Lesser trees on the property provided produce for the marketplace. Alejandro's son pointed out the small branch bearing Carl Schmidt's copper band, labeled only "15." As the tree grew, the band was carefully loosened. Wilson took photographs of Le Blanc proudly standing in front of the parent Fuerte and enjoyed a dish of peaches offered by his son. Before he left, the Le Blancs encouraged him to select a few avocados for himself. Fruits were ready to pick when the bright-green skin showed a yellowish tinge.

In a letter to his father sent on New Year's Eve, Wilson mentioned having taken many photographs of the Fuerte and reading a frightening story in that morning's paper. A man named Rodiles, the owner of a prominent hacienda only a few miles away was "caught by the Zaps, held for ransom, and when he didn't pay it was pretty generally slashed and mauled about." Recently, Wilson had reluctantly turned down an invitation to Rodiles's aguacate plantation, fearing the unsettled conditions in the countryside.[47] He hoped Rodiles would recover from his ordeal and that, one day, he might meet this industrious grower and tour his famous orchard, the first of its kind.

On January 1, 1919, Wilson ushered in the new year by cutting open an avocado picked from the tree that spawned California's most famous variety. Now fully ripe, it tided him over until dinner. Looking back, he would remember the pilgrimage to Atlixco as one of the red-letter days of his career.[48]

Among Guatemalans of European blood
the pulp of the avocado is very
commonly added to meat soups at the
time of serving. It is the custom of
many hotels to place a ripe avocado
in front of each guest, who opens the
fruit, removes the pulp, and places
it in his soup. The flavor imparted
is exceedingly pleasant. This mode of
serving the avocado seems worthy of
adoption in the United States.

--Wilson Popenoe,
The Avocado in Guatemala, 1919

6 · Mission Avocado

WHEN WILSON RETURNED FROM HIS MISSION, HE SET-
tled down to work at the Bureau of Plant Industry in Washington. Sitting at a desk all day was a challenge after his peripatetic
existence in Central America. Time passed slowly as he compiled
his observations and the detailed survey of Mexican avocados for
Webber.[1] The reports were part of a full day's work that also included regular communications with the Office of Naval Intelligence. Although unable to discover any Germans sneaking into
coastal ports, he had mapped out key transportation routes and
their geographical features.

In the spring of 1919, Wilson was charged with representing the
USDA in the effort to convince Florida growers to make "small,
experimental plantings" of the hardy Guatemalan avocados he
had sent to the states. His assignment—to identify the sections
of Florida best suited to growing the fruit—included stops in Fort
Myers, West Palm Beach, and Punta Gorda.[2] He contacted local
newspapers in advance of his arrival to invite potential growers
to meetings. Those willing to experiment with growing the trees
would receive them courtesy of the government and could expect
a USDA representative to follow up with a visit to record the tree's
growth.[3]

While in Florida, Wilson received a letter from Fred with a
special enclosure, a letter from Alejandro Le Blanc, the eighteen-
year-old son of Señor Le Blanc. Wilson began a correspondence
with the young man and encouraged his father to do so as well,
"because you may want to keep track of the crops produced by

the parent Fuerte."[4] During the months that followed, Wilson increasingly counseled his father. Always seeking the next opportunity, Fred now dreamed of making Vista the family "horticultural headquarters."[5] The loquat grove continued to do well, and he liked the idea of being closer to the family date ranch. As usual, his father had too "many other irons in the fire."[6] However, when the topic came up that spring, Wilson supported the venture, provided they could get rid of West India Gardens. By midsummer, his scheme further along, Fred considered selling off a section of the family property to pay off the mortgage on another parcel and some of what was owed on the Vista land.[7]

Back in Washington that fall, Wilson attended a lunch with Otón "Jim" Jiménez, a young Costa Rican botanist, at the home of Mary Agnes Chase of the National Herbarium.[8] Chase was an exceptional botanical artist and prominent agrostologist, who used her expertise on grasses to understand the natural world. Speaking in Spanish, Wilson and Jim were soon engaged in fascinating conversation and parted hoping their paths would cross again.

Wilson was enjoying his time in the limelight as a plant explorer and a patriot when a controversy shook his sense of well-being. The eminent anthropologist Franz Boas published a letter in *The Nation* condemning the United States government for encouraging scientists to serve as spies. Although Boas did not name names, both Wilson and his friend Sylvanus Morley were among those suspected. Boas had been denounced by a majority of American Anthropological Association members and his membership in the National Research Council rescinded, but the conflict hung in the air, causing Wilson to consider his personal ethics and strengthening his resolve to do his patriotic duty.[9]

On the home front, Wilson found himself with additional responsibilities. In his rush to experiment with new California fruits, Fred once again faced financial ruin. He had underestimated the cost of his investments. The dates were slow growing, and principal investor Rebecca Dorsey had been exposed as a fraud.[10] Her trial cast a pall over the project. Loquats might serve to temporarily alleviate his immediate financial problems, but Fred needed a long-term solution. On Wilson's advice, he retained a three-acre parcel in the eastern part of the nursery, where the fertile soil supported two parent Fuerte trees, a Puebla, a *Feijoa sellowiana*, and several Queensland nut and Hachiya persimmon trees.[11] Although disappointed by his loss, Fred soon moved on. The newly elected president of the Vista Water Company, he busied himself with plans for bringing more water to the region, perhaps even by damming the San Luis Rey River.[12]

West India Gardens, once known for its "widespread fame throughout the country," was sold by the end of the year.[13] The prominent commercial nurseryman R. M. Teague, who primarily dealt in citrus, purchased the nursery and now owned a respected line of budded avocados.

Paul Popenoe responded to Fred's change in lifestyle by moving to the Coachella Valley, where he and his wife, Betty, managed the family investments in avocados, grapes, and cotton. They built a cabin designed by the architect Rudolph Schindler, a protégé of Frank Lloyd Wright.[14] It was there that Paul began writing about the human race, developing a warped version of his intellectual passions—eugenics, sociology, and horticulture—and leading the Human Betterment Foundation, an organization that encouraged racism and advocated for forced sterilization. After the Second World War, Paul wisely changed his focus to satisfy readers of the *Ladies' Home Journal*, where he became an editor and penned the magazine's most popular column ever, Can This Marriage Be Saved?[15]

Knowing that Paul and Betty were managing things in California helped Wilson focus on meeting his book deadline. When Liberty Hyde Bailey commissioned him to write *Manual of Tropical and Subtropical Fruits*, the first comprehensive study of its kind, he couldn't refuse but also felt that his reputation was on the line. Research in Mexico had whetted his appetite for history.

He decided to begin with "early voyagers": Gonzalo Fernández de Oviedo's 1526 account of the tree in Colombia, Pedro Cieza de Léon's memories of seeing avocados eaten by Spaniards in the Isthmus of Panama, and a report by Francisco Cervantes de Salazar, who described a fruit sold in Mexico City markets in 1554 as an aguacate. Wilson was fascinated to come across Garcilaso de la Vega's 1605 mention of *palta* as a name given by the Incas, in honor of the Palta province. But the discovery that sent chills down his spine was Bernabé Cobo's story. A priest whose travels took him to the Yucatán and Peru, Padre Cobo appeared to be the first European to mention the Guatemalan avocado. Aided by nothing but his own senses, Cobo developed a classification system in 1653 that the CAA, backed by science and technology, was hard-pressed to improve upon hundreds of years later.[16]

Wilson's manual began with a nearly eighty-page chapter on the avocado and grew to more than four hundred pages, the last completed shortly before his next assignment. Early in 1920, Wilson set off for a grand tour of major avocado-producing countries. The journey would begin in Guatemala and take him to Costa Rica, Panama, Colombia, Ecuador, and Peru and Chile (where the fruit is still called *palta*). Although the Bureau of Plant Industry funded his travels, Wilson had also made arrangements to engage in more freelance spying for the Office of Naval Intelligence.

Finally equipped with a vetted list of the eight recommended varieties, the CAA had taken the first step toward developing a standard of quality essential to building a brand. L. B. Scott, a leader in the selection process, suggested a partnership with the California Nurserymen's Bud Selection Association, a group that distributed budwood from the state's leading standard fruit varieties to commercial nursery firms. The committee also provided scion budwood to growers for topworking. Now the CAA could not only standardize its own budwood but also receive assistance with the recordkeeping so crucial to launching an industry.[17]

The association acted on Scott's advice immediately. CAA secretary Agnes McNally, the former office manager for West India Gardens, accepted a position as head of the prestigious "bud selection committee."[18] McNally placed an advertisement in the annual report emphasizing the importance of the department as the catalyst for improved packing, shipping, and marketing. As an incentive, the CAA published a list of nurserymen using selected, high-quality buds.[19] McNally was responsible for tabulating the performance records crucial to determining the very best. Customers could make their selections with confidence.

Adjusting to the new system was a challenge to growers like Albert Rideout, who had invested so much in a single variety. Rideout began to worry about damage to the Lyon's reputation. Even though it made the list, his favorite tree—short, stalwart, and fruitful—was increasingly described in less-than-glowing terms by fellow members of the association. It had been called a filler tree, bushy, and undependable. Eager to push it to the top, he hoped to spread news of the Lyon's courage, an attribute that revealed itself over time, when the tree emerged from a frost without a droop or suddenly bore dozens of fruits on a single limb. To prove his loyalty to the association, despite its poor judgment, Rideout offered a prize of five avocado trees to the person who enrolled the most new members.[20]

As another way of attracting members, the CAA planned a special luncheon designed to demonstrate the food value of the avocado as the centerpiece of its October 1920 meeting. Over twice the number of anticipated attendees arrived. Agnes rushed off to request the third hotel dining room. The bill of fare certainly impressed, but would the 1,200 ripe fruits feed more than four hundred people?

The banquet began with an avocado cocktail and an avocado salad accompanied by sliced tomato and cottage cheese. A plate lunch followed: an avocado scallop, mashed potatoes, and carrots. An attractive buffet featured sliced avocados accompanied by thin bread, crackers, salt, lemon, and French dressing. For dessert, all were offered avocado ice cream, as well as cake and coffee. To the relief of the association, the 403 guests went home well fed and surely convinced of the avocado's future as an American staple.[21] The successful event marked a turning point for the establishment of a cooperative. If a few members felt maligned by not making the roster of recommended varieties, the majority rallied behind the organization. More than the fear of failure, older members dreaded losing the sense of camaraderie that made the CAA such a valuable part of their lives.[22]

When the association's yearbook was published, members read Wilson's "Letter from Ecuador," an update on his travels over the last eighteen months. While exploring in Costa Rica, he and Otón Jiménez discovered a long-sought-after "wild avocado" on the slopes of the volcano Irazú. Dark green and the size of a baseball, it was encased by such a thick shell that a stone or mallet was necessary to crack it open. Virtually all the qualities Americans desired in an avocado were lacking—the skin was too hard, the seed too large, and the flesh almost inedible. The locals rarely ate the anise-flavored fruit. If not appropriate for eating, however, this venerable ancestor might provide the hardy budwood California growers so desperately needed to survive cold temperatures. A rancid-tasting avocado just might bolster the industry.[23]

Wilson didn't mention that his search for avocados included another mission—the mapping and surveillance of key travel routes for the Office of Naval Intelligence. In December 1919, he had begun writing "reconnaissance" reports on his trips from Cobán to San Cristóbal in Alta Verapaz, Guatemala. He kept up this type of work throughout his journey, traveling "by water, by rail and by cart road" to Livingston Port and on to Puerto Barrios, Guatemala; reporting on conditions at the Port of Champerico; and by the summer, reaching Puntarenas and

San José, Costa Rica. Throughout his travels he sent packages of documents to Fred F. Rogers, commander of the U.S. Navy, via diplomatic pouch. When he finally received his first response at the end of August, the apologetic commander attested to the value of his work and encouraged him to continue. In his formal reply, Wilson added a personal note. While taking pictures in the small town of Catacocha, in southern Ecuador, he was arrested and accused of being a Peruvian spy. The chief of police eyed his binoculars, aneroid barometer, and compass with suspicion, but Wilson finally managed to talk his way out of captivity. Near the end of his travels, he complained of the tedium involved in "reconnaissance." The commander's assurance that his work was of high value to both the navy and the army appeased him, but he was ready for this mission to end.[24]

Wilson was traveling back from Central America on October 22, 1921, when the CAA formally announced its decision to sign a marketing agreement with American Fruit Growers Inc. The festivities had begun two days before at the California Flower Show and Horticultural Exhibition in Exposition Park. More than four hundred attended the banquet at the Ambassador Hotel. One reporter surmised that each guest consumed about a pound of avocado, "in its various delicious forms." These included the now-standard cocktail with Thousand Island dressing, avocado salad on lettuce, plates of unadorned avocado slices, the requisite avocado ice cream, and as a special treat, layer cake with avocados between the layers and as a topper. Dining in the company of the California Association of Nurserymen and the director of the state department of agriculture, the avocado men and women felt they had finally arrived.[25]

All was well in the Southland until a bitter wind blew through on Thursday, January 19, 1922. Avocado growers throughout the region woke up to find some trees frozen past recognition and others barely scarred. Old-timers who experienced the frost of 1913 could see some progress—varieties like the Fuerte that had survived then were much more prominent in orchards now. Recalling the devastation of his orchard at the Huntington estate, William Hertrich made a project of surveying the damage throughout the region.[26]

Morale was already low, and now the year's crop would be light. Many active CAA members had refused to accept the marketing agreement, seeing it as flawed. When it came time to sign on the dotted line, devoted avocado men grew doubtful, and the spirit of bonhomie that had always pervaded the meetings began to fade.

At this challenging moment, Wilson Popenoe lifted spirits with news of a new avocado region in the Chota Valley of northern Ecuador. Coming upon this fruit in the remote Andes was a highlight of his career, and securing its budwood proved the most difficult task he had yet undertaken. The enterprise would not have been possible without the help of José Félix Tomayo, an Ecuadorean educated in Connecticut, who introduced him to local guide Jorge M. Benítez. Cutting the wood in the sweltering heat, carrying it by mule more than a hundred miles to the railroad, connecting to a New York–bound steamer, and packing the wood to endure travel through the tropics was a grueling process that faced steep odds. Indeed, most of the wood was dead on arrival. Luckily, two of the most promising varieties were among the five survivors currently being introduced in Washington. Despite the hardships of traveling to the Chota Valley, Wilson recommended the government sponsor a follow-up trip to examine all the trees in the surrounding region.[27]

Not every avocado grower was pleased by the introduction of new varieties. Many longtime members of the CAA, including Albert Rideout, were already having trouble persuading fellow members to support favored varieties. The last thing they needed was more competition. Rideout was suffering greatly from the slow descent of his Lyon. To add insult to injury, in an article for the *Los Angeles Times*, Ernest Braunton cited Hertrich's recommendation that only Fuerte and Puebla varieties should be planted. Braunton characterized the Lyon as "generally considered a poor tree," successful only in "restricted zones or favorable local spots."[28] The CAA agreed and even added other criticisms about its size and dependability. His patience worn thin, Rideout vented his anger in a professionally printed brochure featuring his wife picking a Lyon on the cover and his own sketch of a lion as a concluding illustration. Flipping through the pages, Rideout was pleased with his work except for one omission. Beneath the Lyon sketch he wrote, in his best cursive, "My nursery trees were not injured at all during the recent freeze."[29]

Rideout attended the November meeting—even exhibiting the Lyon, along with an exceptional collection of little-known varieties—but ultimately, he let his membership lapse.[30] He knew that his revenge could only come through besting the Fuerte, and he would, even if that meant discovering a variety more productive than his beloved Lyon. Now on his own, he redoubled his efforts, promoting the Lyon while also experimenting with new methods of breeding. A. B. Stout's presentation on the topic had captured his imagination. Productive filler trees might actually surpass their more popular peers as the link to increased productivity. The Lyon just might have the last word.

The *Los Angeles Times* called it "the sensation of the year in Southern California horticulture circles."[31] Botanist A. B. Stout, director of laboratories at the New York Botanical Garden, had unlocked the secret of avocado reproduction. A subtle biological process, lost on the growers and plant explorers, was not only revealed but also promised to revolutionize avocado-tree husbandry. The avocado's tiny flowers held the answer. By understanding how pollination occurred, and when, growers might boost production and encourage promising new cultivars. Enlightened avocado enthusiasts could look forward to tinkering with Mother Nature.

The CAA launched Stout's project in 1922, after publishing a paper by a graduate student from India, B. S. Nirody, who had chosen "Investigations in Avocado Breeding" as his master's thesis at Massachusetts Agricultural College and traveled to Florida to carry it out.[32] Nirody's pioneering work inspired the association to arrange for Stout to spend a year in California, performing similar research on breeding. Pomona College sponsored his project in exchange for part-time teaching.

In "Clocking the Avocado," Stout revealed that avocado trees are hermaphrodites of two types—A trees and B trees—with flowers that open as male or female. Their unisexual flowers open and close on a single tree synchronously, each variety sticking to the same schedule, like clockwork.[33] On May 5, 1923, Stout witnessed the action at Thomas Shedden's ranch near Monrovia. Luckily it was sunny, without fog the night before, perfect weather for photography. Having already identified compatible trees, he set up his camera and wrote the date on chart I, his hourly record of the flowers' behavior throughout the day. At midmorning, he recorded the opening of flowers on group A trees, noting they were female and receptive to pollen. After an hour or so, the flowers closed and, in the afternoon, predictably opened again as male. The periods of opening for the flowers of group B trees were reversed, and both trees changed cycles at the same key moment, between one and two o'clock. The fieldwork confirmed Nirody's thesis and Stout's hopes—Shedden and his fellow growers could use his charts and data to match trees with compatible flowering cycles. Although trees depended on this system to discourage self-pollination, Shedden realized that proper interplanting could increase fruit production, thus leading to "the ideal avocado, from the standpoint of self-fruitfulness."[34]

The *Times* agreed that Stout's "practical research work, properly followed up by the growers themselves, bids fair to open a new era in avocado culture."[35] Already, lists of compatible trees—those As and Bs with complementary schedules and desirable qualities— were circulating to encourage interplanting. Pairing Fuerte with Dickinson was judged a good bet for reciprocal cross-pollination. Looking ahead, ambitious growers and scientists planned their own experiments with artificial pollination and companionable varieties. For some, the limitless possibilities of scientific breeding would become an obsession.

Honeymoon Salad

Place crescent-shaped slices of
avocado on plates that have been
covered with a mixture of shredded
lettuce, grapefruit cubes and chopped
red and green peppers. Cover with a
lemon French dressing mixed with a
small amount of chili sauce. Garnish
with walnut halves and ripe olives.[1]

--Chef A. C. Wyman,
Los Angeles Times,
October 2, 1923

7 · Calavo

BACK IN WASHINGTON, WILSON WAS FILLING IN FOR DA-
vid Fairchild, whenever necessary, and adjusting to the life of
a bureaucrat. He liked to think his role in procuring new avocado varieties would help launch a California industry, and the
Times interview was certainly a step in that direction. With the
passage of the Capper-Volstead Act, farmers gained the power to
form their own cooperatives. Wilson thought the time was ripe
to launch a successful marketing venture to promote the avocado,
assuming association members had learned something from the
last attempt.[2]

In the summer of 1923, Wilson met Dorothy K. Hughes, an
accomplished British archaeologist who had recently joined the
Bureau of Plant Industry as a botanist and plant illustrator. The
two struck up a whirlwind romance and soon planned to wed. On
November 17, Fred received a Western Union telegram describing
the marriage as taking place "at sunrise under trees in Rockcreek
Park." The Fairchilds hosted a reception at their Chevy Chase residence. After a short honeymoon to Miami, the newlyweds moved
into a house on Biltmore Street in Washington, and Wilson resumed his job at the USDA. His carefree days as a plant explorer
were over. At first, working as an administrator and likely successor to Fairchild seemed an admirable position for a married man,
but soon he felt a growing sense of wanderlust. Luckily, he had
married a woman with an equal yearning for new discoveries and
foreign adventures. Less than two years passed before he, Dorothy,
and their young son, Peter, settled down in Tela, Honduras, the

site Wilson had chosen for the Lancetilla Agricultural Experiment Station, on behalf of his new employer, United Fruit Company.[3]

When George B. Hodgkin accepted the position of secretary for the California Avocado Association, it was with high hopes for a new career in the marketing business. His colleagues at the California Fruit Growers Exchange advised the association to take charge of selling its own fruit. The Exchange had developed over decades of trial and error (mostly the latter), before organizers realized that a profitable organization needed to be formed "of growers and for the interests of growers," preferably in small groups organized by regions, with a manager as the only salaried officer. Hodgkin believed the same was needed for the CAA and the avocado.[4]

The time was right. During the summer of 1923, consumers were more interested in avocados than ever before. At least 100,000 visitors had pushed through the turnstile of the avocado exhibit at the Valencia Orange Show. If still a curiosity, the avocado nevertheless attracted crowds who seemed to recognize its potential. Even more promising, the association anticipated a bumper crop— between 200,000 and 600,000 pounds of fruit. This good news came with a price, however, and the CAA's coffers were empty. To handle the surplus, the association scraped up money to hire a marketer by taking on loans from members. In July 1923, thirty-year-old George Hodgkin was hired at a salary of three hundred dollars per month. It was only a part-time job, but the challenge of leading a promising endeavor fed his sense of ambition—perhaps he had stumbled upon the chance of a lifetime?[5]

Hodgkin worked out of a temporary office at 2160 East Seventh Street in Los Angeles within the American Fruit Growers packinghouse. On his first day, he planned trips to all the avocado-bearing acres in Southern California in order to get a reliable estimate of the crop and to explain the marketing contract to shippers. Hard-working and goal oriented, Hodgkin felt guided by providence as the region was divided into twelve districts and meetings were scheduled to elect representatives from each who would form a marketing board.[6]

The American Fruit Growers had been handling many of the CAA's packing needs, but as the industry grew, the need for a separate organization just for avocados became apparent. On January 21, 1924, Hodgkin formally announced the opening of the California Avocado Growers Exchange. Under the new arrangement, the American Fruit Growers would no longer take part in handling avocados, and in May, all ties were severed with the association.[7]

Hodgkin prided himself on making smart moves quickly. When an excess of fruit overwhelmed the existing packing facilities, leaving avocados to rot and causing the market to plummet, he wasted no time relocating operations closer to the wholesale terminal market. His efforts paid off. A grand total of 93,638 pounds of avocados were sold in just seven months. Hodgkin also opened a retail store, a "not for profit" venture intended as a form of educational outreach. A staff member ran the operation, distributing leaflets, handing out samples, and taking notes on consumer opinions and preferences to develop new ideas for advertising. In his next annual report, Hodgkin documented marked progress. Although the store had been turned over to private ownership after six months, more than 20,000 customers bought fruit, and hundreds of thousands had visited. All profited from spending time with avocados.

Advertising was clearly a worthwhile investment. At a cost of more than $1,000, the exchange printed 5,000 recipe booklets for chefs, 20,000 leaflets for retailers and public exhibits, 100,000 recipe bags, and 1,000 display signs for distributing to dealers. Progress had also been made in grading fruit—segregating it first by variety and then by quality (culling the scarred from the irregular)—and in packing materials, choosing the coarse wood excelsior over any form of paper. A special ventilated crate called a lug was chosen as the standard packaging for two dozen medium-to-large fruits. Hodgkin saw these achievements as the product of teamwork, the only means of sustaining a cooperative supported by a group as eccentric as the CAA. Over the last year, he had learned that being a "kook" or "nut" about avocados served the community well. All in all, the members of the CAA were in it for the fruit and recognized that any personal gain depended on group solidarity. This spirit of a cooperative helped Hodgkin weather the market's ups and downs.[8]

The tenth anniversary of the association gave old-timers like Fred Popenoe a chance to reminisce and literally take stock of the trees that were now orchards feeding a new industry. To the surprise of his audience, rather than extolling the virtues of his Fuerte, Fred claimed the increase in avocado real estate prices as the true standard of the CAA's success. Recently, Carlsbad, the site of the Fourth Annual Field Day, had treated the CAA and all comers to a free avocado luncheon, featuring a special lecture by Dr. Philip Lovell speaking on "Avocados and Health." A few years earlier, an acre in Carlsbad went for five or six hundred dollars. Now you were lucky to pick up one for $2,000. The craze for avocado land had caused prices to skyrocket—such was the power of the association![9]

Advertising also came unexpectedly in the form of self-described health nut Clarke Irvine, a former newspaperman from Culver City determined to share his recipe for improving well-being and achieving mental freedom. In June, Irvine walked 133 miles, from Los Angeles to San Diego, eating nothing but avocados during the six-day journey. The fruit was his "ideal 'single menu.'" It also served as a natural laxative, a soothing tonic to the nervous system.[10] Irvine continued his avocado-only diet another two weeks, with plans of presenting the results of his experiment to the University of California, Berkeley.[11] His stunt supplied free advertising for the CAA at a time when the health angle was resonating with consumers.

One of the many Americans persuaded by the media to invest in avocados was a postman from Milwaukee named Rudolph Hass. A former door-to-door salesman of men's furnishings and Maytag washers, in 1925 Hass had taken a more stable job with the Pasadena post office to support his wife and children. While doing his rounds, he wondered what else could be done to improve their lot. An artist's rendering of an avocado tree with leaves like dollar bills came to mind. Why not look into things further? The newspapers were full of ads for avocado properties at La Habra Heights, where an ordinary family man like him might make quite a bit of money in a neighborhood "ranch" perfect for kids, or so the ads said.

As Hass contemplated his venture, Morris Saperstein watched his dreams come true. Like so many, Saperstein was lured to California by the region's growing reputation for healthful living. On his way across the country, he acquired a medical degree and reinvented himself as Philip M. Lovell, ND (doctor of naturopathy), a name he thought would resonate with the local elite. In 1923, he hung up his shingle. One of his first clients was Harry Chandler, publisher of the *Los Angeles Times*. Chandler, a transplant from the East Coast, hoped the California climate might cure his lung ailment. Lovell impressed Chandler, and when longtime author of the *Times'* popular Care of the Body column, Harry Ellington Brook, passed away, Chandler appointed Lovell his successor. Around this time, Lovell joined the CAA, and in August, Care of the Body consisted of a full-page endorsement of the avocado.[12]

CAA members lucky enough to own radios and tune into the *Los Angeles Times*–owned station, KHJ, at just the right moment had already heard Dr. Lovell's inspired words. In an authoritative voice, he proclaimed the avocado "a food concentrate much more sustainable than meat." The avocado yielded greater value "pound for pound, or dollar for dollar than any other fruit known." In his article for the *Times*, Lovell outlined more benefits, geared toward marketing the avocado to conscientious mothers and an increasing number of Americans seeking solutions to serious health problems. Lovell, always a bit excessive when it came to promotion, added "More" to the CAA's existing motto, "Eat Avocados." As he explained, this magical fruit played a central role in the body's clearinghouse by discharging the toxic materials responsible for a litany of illnesses.[13]

The type of detailed analysis presented at CAA conferences by scientists like M. E. Jaffa, if priceless for nutritionists, scientists, and horticulturalists, had no place in the lives of average consumers, but Lovell's message reached an audience eager to act on recommendations for good health and longevity. The reputation of California as a place for healthful living, bolstered by real estate advertisements, slowly began to raise the profile of the avocado as a sound investment. The CAA's support helped Lovell transform himself into a health guru. In later years, his enthusiasm for sunbathing and exercise even influenced the world of modern architecture when he commissioned two iconic homes—Rudolph Schindler's Lovell Beach House in Newport Beach and Richard Neutra's Lovell Health House in Los Angeles, complete with avocado trees.[14]

Along with Lovell and other high-profile influencers, the association counted on an increasing number of middle-class dreamers like Hass to sell the California avocado. Banking on the fruit's reputation as an incentive, members called a special meeting of nurserymen and real estate agents interested in selling avocado land. "Fruit as thick as huckleberries" was predicted for 1927, between 2 and 4 million pounds.[15] To prepare for this deluge, the association recommended extending its advertising committee in the East before distributing the heavy shipments became a problem. Property agents were asked to pledge a dollar for every acre of avocado real estate they sold and nurserymen five cents for every tree. The fund would launch an advertising campaign necessary to successfully ship the anticipated bounty. Among those contributing were former West India Gardens employee Carter Barrett, Edwin G. Hart, Armstrong Nurseries, Rancho Leucadia, and Cascade Ranch.[16]

Eager to rebrand itself, the California Avocado Growers Exchange had turned the exercise into a publicity opportunity by conducting a nationwide naming contest. After two years and more than 3,000 entries, on January 8, 1926, the exchange announced their selection: Calavo. Sixteen prizewinners, several from outside California, had independently happened upon the clever combination of *California* and *avocado*. Knowles Ryerson laughed when he learned of the contest results. He recalled hearing the trademarked name before. His wife, Emma, had come up with Calavo instantly but never entered the contest. One of the successful entries came from Don Francisco, the advertising manager for Sunkist. All winners received a box of avocados, each stamped "Calavo" in yellow.[17] The new name reinforced the avocado's indelible tie to California.

On March 7, *Los Angeles Times* reporter W. C. Tesche introduced the official brand with a full-page story in the *Farm and Orchard Magazine* section, calling the avocado "California's Butter Fruit." It was a high-profile endorsement, and proof of the fledgling cooperative's success was predicted in the form of a 2,000 percent increase in acreage, resulting in 13 million avocados by 1930. Marketing director George Hodgkin personally endorsed the product by substituting butter fruit for cow's butter on his toast every morning for six months.[18]

At that year's annual CAA meeting, Fred Popenoe looked back

on the last decade with pride for the group's achievements. Foremost in his mind was respect for the men and women who had "prevented any stampede or boom or wildcatting in connection with the industry." More typically, particularly in the Southland, such endeavors were "made the vehicle of unscrupulous promoters, as a get-rich-quick business." In this respect, the association could not only boast a clear conscience but also claim the best avocados in the world. Continuing in an almost religious tone, Fred admitted to not always agreeing with Rideout, "especially where he makes the Lyon jump out of its cage and eat up the Fuerte," but admiring his work ethic and selfless devotion to improving the avocado. All judgments aside, Rideout had "a thousand hybrid trees, and among them may be the tree to bear the perfect fruit we are looking for."[19] He continued to make strides with the Lyon, one of the eight varieties recommended for the Calavo stamp of approval by the CAA, soon to be shipped off to eastern markets.[20] As it turned out, Rideout's greatest contribution to the industry came not through a variety of avocado but through his willingness to guide a novice grower.

Rudolph Hass saw promise in the rich, well-drained alluvial soil of La Habra Heights, so he took out a loan to purchase two acres. He had faith in this "frost free land" and in the man who sold him three hundred sprouted avocado seeds of Guatemalan stock, Albert Rideout.[21] Optimistic about the future, Hass planted his orchard using the standard method: in tar paper tubes measuring two by two by eight feet set across the property on a twelve-by-twelve pattern.[22] Most were of Rideout's preferred Lyon variety, but he also included an assortment of others. Once the seeds became seedlings, Hass consulted G. R. Calkins of Montebello, a known expert, for help grafting the trees to Fuertes. One stubborn baby tree refused to accept the graft, even after multiple attempts. It seemed best not to waste any more time or money on a dud. But if the expert grafter thought he should see how the tree grew, well then, he would let it alone.

From that recalcitrant seedling would spring a new variety, destined to revolutionize the industry.

A week before Christmas 1926, George Hodgkin arranged for the growers exchange to ship a carload of Calavos to Chicago. The record-breaking shipment—2,184 boxes—was nearly four times larger than any previous attempt and valued at $12,000. Avocado growers proclaimed it "the first effort at national distribution on a large scale." Hodgkin himself met the carload in Chicago, a smart means of garnering further publicity for the exchange. Avocados were distributed throughout the Windy City before continuing on to New York, as well as points east and south. It was a tacit challenge to the Florida industry on its own turf. The Californians were here to stay.[23]

Calavo Sailboat Salad

It is one of the easiest salads in
the world to prepare. Cut one of
the large Calavos into quarters.
You now have a Calavo boat. To make
it a sailboat just insert a square
cracker, point downward, into the
prow of the boat. Fill the boat with
a cargo of your favorite fruit--the
little oranges are particularly
good looking sliced, using a cheese
cracker sail. Or serve with just a
simple dressing.

--"Requested Recipes by Marian
Manners, Director, Home Services
Bureau," *Los Angeles Times*, 1932

8 · Envisioning an Empire

GEORGE HODGKIN, MARKETING DIRECTOR OF CALAVO Growers, pushed open the door of the Calavo packing plant and paused to survey the scene. The whir of machinery and the woody smell of excelsior almost overwhelmed him with a warm feeling of prosperity. These days, so much was done before avocados even arrived at the plant. Each individual fruit was laboratory tested, guaranteeing a level of quality unknown in the early stages of the California Avocado Growers Exchange. Now the state required a minimum 8 percent oil content to meet the standard. Once certified, Calavos were carefully picked with clippers (leaving the end of the stem in place) or long poles and dropped into canvas catch sacks. Trucks transported the fruit to the Vernon packinghouse in Los Angeles' Central Manufacturing District on the very day it was picked.[1]

Workers dressed in sanitary uniforms (with "Calavo" stenciled on the back in bright-yellow letters) carefully placed each avocado on a conveyer belt. The fruit went through a blower—a machine with revolving brushes and a fan that blew away all the dirt. From there, the shiny clean fruits rolled down to the sizing belt, where they were divided by weight and hand sorted for quality. Inferior fruits were removed. Those that remained traveled along to the stamper, to be certified "Calavo" in yellow ink directly on the peel. The mechanized parts—the bins, chutes, and dumps—were well padded with excelsior and cotton, a vital precaution to prevent bruising and ensure a first-class product. Workers packed avocados in standard boxes, labeled with the variety and number. Those destined for the East were loaded on flats in one layer to facilitate precooling at forty to forty-five degrees Fahrenheit for forty-eight hours before shipping. The plant's two state-of-the-art electric refrigerators could cool up to 3,000 flats each. The process was a model of efficiency and attention to detail. Fifteen employees working at regular speed could pack an entire carload of Calavos every day.[2]

The industry also received a helping hand from local real estate agents. The Encinitas district of San Diego had recently become a desirable avocado region, with 300,000 pounds of "green gold" the previous year. Along with this success came soaring land values, and Edwin G. Hart capitalized on the boom with compelling ads selling La Habra Heights that appealed to savvy buyers. The newspaper's real estate section paired Hart's ads for "proved" avocado land with Dr. Frank McCoy's endorsement. The "internationally known health expert" added the avocado to the tenth edition of his bestseller *The Fast Way to Health*, further augmenting Calavo Growers' efforts to demonstrate the multifaceted benefits of their aristocratic fruit.[3]

Hodgkin and his cohort realized that many of the problems plaguing the avocado men in the past—the preponderance of varieties, the high price, and the ignorance of the purchaser—could be solved through marketing. Language describing the new product was scientific and sometimes accompanied by images of growers testing fruit for maturity in their own laboratories. Here the Calavo plant itself offered an opportunity for national advertising. Advertisements featured the Calavo operation and described how a decade of scientific research and experimentation had resulted in a powerful "new" food. Establishing the Calavo brand also settled the long-running controversy over the fruit's name. It was now best known nationwide as the avocado.

In May 1929, when Whittier's big avocado show opened with a radio address from Governor Young, CAA members felt the weight of their achievement.[4] Among the prizewinners for best fruit at the show was R. G. Hass, of La Habra Heights, who won first prize for his plate of the Fuerte variety.[5] In the wake of this grand endorsement, newspapers throughout the country reported on the Calavo, and the Cooperative Extension Service sponsored a series of radio talks on station KFI. An up-and-coming advertiser named Leigh Crosby, a representative of the famous Chicago advertising firm Lord & Thomas, spoke on "Advertising Calavos" in July and "Advertising Avocados" in August.[6]

Still, the avocado faced headwinds. *Los Angeles Times* columnist Alma Whitaker estimated that only one in 10,000 United States citizens had ever even heard of an avocado, much less tasted one. Nevertheless, she acknowledged the growing prestige of the fruit in her column, Sugar and Spice. A jaunty drawing of couples conversing during a ballroom dance illustrated her story. If mocking the CAA's elite image, Whitaker knew her audience. She went on to cover the highlights of a meeting attended by seven hundred growers. Paul W. Armstrong of the Orange Growers' Association advised the crowd on how to sell a crop of unprecedented dimensions. The three main marketing points—the avocado's appeal to appetite, health, and style—were crucial to attracting customers. Whitaker understood what the CAA was up against.[7]

Public interest in the roots of the avocado industry did not grow spontaneously. Calavo Growers of California predicted an enormous increase in production over the next year and saw no option but to put all they had into expanding their customer base. Hodgkin and the CAA gathered their forces, focusing less on expensive ads in periodicals and more on personal contacts, store displays, and new ways of encouraging avocado consumption. During the winter of 1930, when naysayers scoffed at the possibility of marketing such a pricey delicacy, the avocado men and women were hard at work, building their membership and creatively preparing for the upcoming "emergency."[8] In addition to promotion, the CAA fought the claims of hucksters who promised absurd returns for avocado orchards, thus further adding to their problems by overstimulating production.

During the robust 1930–1931 growing season, Hodgkin had been momentarily concerned by a fierce December storm, the worst since 1923, fearing the loss of a significant amount of the crop. This time the damage hadn't been devasting, in part because overproduction was an issue, but he wanted to be prepared for the next bout of bad weather. For nearly a decade, the university had been experimenting with using culled avocados, unfit for retail sale, in the manufacture of consumer items. The experimental oils and candied pits displayed at early avocado meetings were the result of these labors.

Other investments in culinary delights appeared to have potential. By this time, the *Los Angeles Times* counted twenty-seven creameries producing avocado ice cream, hands down the most successful use of damaged fruit to date, though a treat admittedly best suited to the local climate. Calavo's experiments with bread had also produced some promising results. Six bakeries were using avocado-based shortening in baked goods, including doughnuts, cupcakes, and pastries. Experiments in extruding avocado oil and creating avocado-seed-based products were ongoing.[9]

The monumentality of the cooperative avocado-marketing achievement wasn't fully recognized until the spring of 1931. Over the last year, production had risen a phenomenal 800 percent, but Calavo had kept pace with the abundance of fruit—packing 1,394 boxes in August and an estimated 30,000 the following March. Despite the Great Depression, membership in the California Avocado Association more than doubled: from 480 in October 1929 to 1,140 a year later. Based on this show of strength, banks increased the CAA's borrowing power by $50,000—an extraordinary indication of faith in this time of national fiscal hardship. Reporter Bruce Buttles summed up the cooperative's success against all odds: "The Fruit Was Sold: Avocado 'Co-op' Did the 'Impossible.'"[10]

The industry's potential and its current plight were not lost on the powerful influencer Harry Chandler, now publisher of the *Los Angeles Times*. He hired Ethel Vance Morse to serve as the director of the *Times'* new Home Services Bureau, a kind of think tank designed to attract an influx of female readership and to spread the word about California-grown products. Under the pseudonym Marian Manners (inspired by Chandler's wife, Marian, who was also Harrison Otis's daughter), Morse taught classes in the new *Times* building, traveled to other venues throughout the city for cooking demonstrations, and published her own "tested" recipes in the *Times*. Marian Manners frequently included avocados in her recipes, always branded as Calavos, emphasizing that only this California brand garnered her stamp of approval. Her cookbook, *Mexican Dishes; Dishes of the Dons*, which would be published in 1933 by Richfield Oil Co., included a recipe for tacos requiring one avocado and movie star "Ramon Novarro's own" guacamole recipe consisting of two avocados, half a can of green chiles, and a pound of grapes. Pomegranate seeds were a highly recommended, if obscure, grape substitute. Novarro, known widely to moviegoers as the Latin Lover, was born in Mexico but had been recast as a Hollywood heartthrob of Spanish descent. The year *Mexican Dishes* was published, he starred in *The Barbarian*, also known as *A Night in Cairo*, risking death for love alongside Myrna Loy.

Seizing these successful marketing ventures, and with a nod to Marian Manners, Calavo Growers expanded its by-products department.[11] In addition to Calavo Crushed Fruit Flavoring, the secret behind Calavo Ice Cream, Calavo Bread Shortening had proved a successful ingredient for baked goods. A "delicious tidbit" marketed as Avocado Dutch Toast could be purchased in markets from San Diego to Seattle. Even more exciting, the official bakers of Melba Toast had signed on to produce Calavo Melba Toast—a triumphal partnership for the company and the American diet. Avocado oil, although not yet profitable for cooking, found its place in high-end cosmetics. These marketing achievements represented a significant step forward for Calavo Growers, which benefited from free advertising while squeezing income out of piles of damaged avocados.

Calavo and association members may not have been aware of an elite fashion fad inspired by their favorite fruit. "Avocado green" appeared as a color choice for high-end women's dresses in 1928 and by the mid-1930s as an option for fashionable coats, handbags, and shoes in the best department stores. Livingston Brothers of San Francisco advertised "flat crepe frocks" in avocado green, sponsored by Chanel, for prices as high as $98.50 ($1,900 in 2024 dollars). Those shopping for a bargain might move on to Louis Gassner Inc., where an "untrimmed Chanel version" of an avocado-green fox-trimmed coat with "all the chic in the world" sold for the equivalent of $700.[12] At Henry Morgan & Company, in Montreal, a matching dress shoe, priced at $290, could be purchased "in that romantic spring color—avocado green" and accented with brown suede and gold kid piping. For the first time, the avocado's aura was abstracted to represent the exotic, precious, and fashionable, a status that likely evolved from its long association with elite hotels.[13]

While avocado enthusiasts searched for trendy products, Knowles Ryerson and Robert Hodgson collaborated on efforts to shift avocado studies from Northern California to the Southland. In 1928, University of California regents had agreed to move the entire division of subtropical horticulture to Los Angeles and located a ten-acre parcel for an experimental orchard. When the CAA visited the "pioneer college" at the University of California, Los

Angeles (UCLA), for a field day in October 1929, the citrus trees had been planted, and as Hodgson explained to fellow members, planning for avocado plantings and experiments was well underway. Hodgson, a professor in the division of subtropical horticulture, moved to Los Angeles from Berkeley in 1932, shortly before the first classes in agriculture were taught at UCLA.[14] Under his direction, the university would team up with the CAA to create a variety collection (supplied primarily with cultivars discovered by Wilson Popenoe), and the orchard would grow to become one of the most esteemed in the world for teaching and research of subtropical fruits.[15]

During the spring, Calavo launched an initiative to register promising seedlings. The project, pushed by J. Eliot Coit, gave members an opportunity to study young trees and perhaps even stumble upon the next superstar. Sixteen had been registered between December and May, and the CAA provided descriptions of those most likely to succeed. Local farm bureau variety committees were encouraged to observe, test, and propagate the selected trees.

A variety called the Hass bore the smallest fruit, weighing only seven ounces, less than a third the size of the robust Fairfax, and its flavor rating was a mere "good minus." Nevertheless, Rudolph Hass was thrilled. Secretly, he had long felt the Hass had great potential—his kids loved the fruit beyond any other and the neighbors agreed. This lucky break would give the public a chance to weigh in on his what the CAA officially dubbed a tree with "meritorious" fruit.[16]

A year later, Hass received a permit from the Board of City Directors to sell avocados from his porch at 786 Lincoln Avenue. The fruit was so popular that within just a few months, he had been robbed three times.[17] Hass knew he had a good thing going but lacked the knowledge to manage his windfall. Experienced nurserymen like Rideout and Calkins had guided him this far. Now he needed someone to handle growing, promoting, and distributing. As his circle widened, he worried about retaining control over his discovery.

While Hass mulled over the prospects of his namesake, George Hodgkin focused on expanding distribution and increasing consumer demand. Since 1929, he had benefited from the advice of Leigh Crosby, a shrewd adman and small-scale grower. While working back east on a project for Sunkist, Crosby had adopted one of the strategies *The Delineator* used to raise its profile. The famous fashion magazine, owned by the creator of Butterick patterns, informed its content through a network of 1,000 "housewives," from "all walks of life and in all income groups and in all areas in the country." The editor sent these correspondents questions about homemaking issues, and their combined responses comprised "a sort of laboratory on home-making."[18]

Having read *Selling Mrs. Consumer*, nationally famous home economist Christine Frederick's groundbreaking book on advertising, Crosby understood the power of the female purse in the average American family. Frederick herself was already known as "the distinguished authority on household efficiency," and her endorsement of avocados was worth its weight in green gold.[19] In the late twenties, she had traced the growth of interest in the fruit, noting that the increasing demand for luxury foods—particularly tropical and imported delicacies—led to its popularization. Among the trends Frederick identified as characterizing current American dietary habits were the focus on health (particularly "slenderizing"), greater diversity in food choices, less consumption of starches, and an increase in fresh fruits and vegetables. American housewives were not only more likely to try new foods than their foreign counterparts but also to react positively to "snob appeal."[20] The avocado's reputation as a "smart" entrée, touted by elite hotels and copied at home by their clientele, was slowly trickling down to the middle class.[21] By directly targeting the housewife, Calavo could spread the word about avocados as fast as newspapers were printed.

In 1932, Crosby convinced *The Delineator* to send out a questionnaire to the women that would pinpoint regional differences, reveal knowledge about key facts (like the ability of a typical buyer to determine ripeness), and identify prejudices to clarify the focus of a future ad campaign. Following Frederick's lead, he boiled down the typical housewife's dilemma to the five questions she confronted every day: What will I serve for dinner? Will my family like it? How do I prepare it? Is it too expensive? Is it nutritious?[22]

The results of Crosby's survey were revealing. In the Southwest, a quarter of respondents served avocados once a week or even more often. Elsewhere, however, avocado households dropped to a mere 13 percent. Now that California avocados were shipped to all regions, how could Calavo give first-time buyers the confidence to try one? Calavo paid for Crosby's services and turned over the results of the survey to the industry "for the good of all," a clever way of spreading the word through newspapers.[23]

While Calavo expanded its operation and mulled over strategies to expand the avocado's footprint, a new problem cropped up. Back in 1902, when the Republic of Cuba was established, nobody felt threatened by duty-free avocados from the tropics. Times had changed by 1929, when representatives Ruth Bryan Owen, a Florida Democrat, and Philip Swing, a California Republican, joined forces to push for an avocado tariff.[24] California boasted 10,000 acres of avocados, proof of a growing industry, and they argued for a level playing field. Despite this effort, inexpensive avocados from Cuba had continued to stream into Florida. And now President Franklin Roosevelt's new Reciprocal Trade Agreements Act of 1934 merely restricted Cuban avocado imports to June, July, and August, prime time for California growers. George Hodgkin wrote to Wilson Popenoe, lamenting this development. His frustration involved more than the numbers of imports; Cuban avocados, free of Calavo's rigid quality standards, threatened to undermine the fruit's carefully managed reputation. The Cubans' alligator pears benefited from his marketing campaign while sullying the pristine image of the California fruit. Hodgkin vowed to continue efforts to limit Cuban competition.[25]

Powerless to bend Roosevelt to their position, Calavo Growers capitalized on his popularity and promoted their brand by sending him Calavos for his fifty-third birthday dinner on January 30, 1935. The scheme was carefully orchestrated. On a stormy night, the boxed fruit was shipped "special delivery" to the capital aboard the new American Airlines transcontinental service. Washington, D.C.–based Calavo Growers representative Sandy McPhail, trained in the Los Angeles office, met the plane and transported the gift to the White House. The menu for the intimate private dinner appeared in newspapers throughout the country. In addition to turkey with chestnut stuffing and all the trimmings, the president and his guests feasted on avocado-and-grapefruit salad. Two weeks later, Calavo Growers received thank-you letters from both Franklin and Eleanor Roosevelt—giving Hodgkin and his staff another opportunity to contact the press.[26] The marketing department hoped to attract American women who might strive for a little White House panache in their own homes.

The atmosphere of the CAA's twentieth-anniversary spring meeting was electric, as predictions of reaching $1 million in sales were among the many good tidings circulating among members. That weekend, Christine Frederick advised her readers to "take advantage of the avocado in May," citing its reasonable price, nutritional benefits, and perhaps most persuasive, ability to add a dash of elegance to the middle-class hostess's repertoire.[27] For growers, the primary focus shifted from limiting production to joining together in a united front to broaden markets outside the state. Two million potential dealers and wholesalers were waiting, and Frederick's vote of confidence suggested consumers were, too.[28]

More good news for Calavo came in July, when the cooperative struck a deal to market 80 percent of the Florida avocado crop. Increasingly, Florida growers were choosing to sell their fruit through Calavo's eastern distributors. During the summer and early fall, the eastern offices helped boost national demand and retain the "better-price business" secured over the last year. Stable prices boded well for the California offices, which would increase shipping of Calavos to the East in late fall. To supplement the Florida market, Calavo branched out into "sideline" items, particularly limes and dates, a decision that played a key role in building awareness of its brand.[29] Best of all, Calavo had "supplied the whole of the United States with Christmas avocados."[30]

Rudolph Hass found himself in a quandary. His dream of growing robust avocados had materialized, but unforeseen expenses cut into an already slim budget. Through the grapevine, he learned that a woman named Jennie Gano had boldly registered a patent for an avocado at the U.S. Patent Office. The very idea that one could patent a fruit seemed preposterous, but recent legislation allowed for the patenting of certain plants. Gano had taken advantage of an opportunity that just might solve Hass's predicament.

To apply for a patent, one need only prove the uniqueness of the "invention." Hass had no doubt that he could meet the standard. Practically impervious to high winds, Hass trees stood tall, shipped well, bore a consistently heavy crop, and produced a rich, buttery fruit of an excellent, nutty flavor. Marketers would instantly perceive the value of an avocado that matured during the summer months, when prices were at their highest. Securing the patent would end up costing hundreds, but Hass believed in his invention, both as a means of feeding his family and contributing to local agriculture. He submitted the application on April 17, 1935.[31]

Less than four months later, on August 27, Rudolph Hass became the official holder of U.S. Plant Patent 139, otherwise known as the Hass avocado. In an interview with the *Santa Ana Register*, he snuck in a bit of advertising by inviting anyone with interest in the new patented fruit to visit his grove on Saturday and Sunday afternoons.[32] He also advertised his product in the want ads under "Miscellaneous," noting its 22.41 percent oil content among other fine qualities, at a price of "$2.50 in quantities."[33] On weekends, he proudly introduced the Hass to more than a few friends, neighbors, and out-of-town guests, all of whom admired the handsome fruit, but sales were never enough to make a dent in his bountiful crop. It would be past maturity soon, and something needed to be done quickly.

Hass offered Rideout's brother-in-law, H. H. Brokaw, a deal—75 percent of the profits if he would grow, promote, and distribute the patented avocado. The nurseryman hesitated. Green avocados were hard enough to sell. When the Hass matured, it turned black, a color suggesting spoilage. Brokaw would have to work hard to convince the public of its many virtues—its copious production and unusually long growing season.[34] On the other hand, the timing couldn't be more perfect. In 1935, seven times more avocados had been sold than in the previous year, and the forecast was equally bright for the future. Brokaw accepted the commission. In 1936, he planted 150 Hass trees. Within two years, he would add another 1,050 to the orchard.

As Hass and Brokaw worked to slowly expand their plantings, Calavo Growers' strategic advertising campaign for 1936 capitalized on its last successful year, with national newspaper stories aimed at appropriate regional markets across the country.[35] All of a sudden, it seemed, the possibility of lowering the price to fit the budget of a middle-class housewife had become a reality. Calavo Growers used the feedback from Crosby's survey to develop ads targeted at different regions. Calavos were delivered in refrigerated train cars to supermarkets throughout the tri-city area of Davenport, Iowa, and Rock Island and Moline, Illinois.

In Detroit, Calavos sold for ten to fifteen cents, and that discount down from seventy-five cents also came with new benefits—the former salad fruit had proved itself extraordinarily versatile and now could star as a main course or memorable dessert. One example, Chipped Beef Croustades, was a filling meal of an equal amount of Calavo and beef, topped with a generous helping of gravy and served in a crisp bread shell.[36] In Pittsburgh, Calavos were advertised as a means of keeping up with the Joneses.[37]

In less than seven years, Calavo Growers had grown from its single warehouse in downtown Los Angeles into a national brand name, with offices across the country. The organization owned a subsidiary—Calavo Subtropic Fruit Company—responsible for "two division, ten district, and thirty-one sales and distributing offices" located at strategic locations throughout the United States. Calavo employed a staff of more than ninety in its sales and advertising department alone. The mastermind behind this network, and its growing success, was George Hodgkin. During the earliest days of the industry, back when he oversaw a single warehouse, Hodgkin had used every trick of the trade to build the customer base and keep one step ahead of disaster. Now he had established a recognizable brand name, garnered public trust in his product, and successfully produced returns for the growers year after year. Nevertheless, Hodgkin recognized the fragility of a product that depended on the whims of nature. During the winter of 1937, the crisis he had foreseen hit hard: not one devastating January freeze but two. More than 45 percent of the crop was damaged. The crisis seemed insurmountable. He had no choice but to announce the truth—the weather events were "without question the greatest catastrophe that has ever hit our industry."[38]

Calavo directors went into triage mode. They lowered salaries and cut down on excess operating expenses, but the priority was getting salvageable fruit off the trees as quickly as possible. Working seven days a week and taking on extra shifts, employees began the massive harvesting job. Hodgkin anticipated that maintaining the Calavo standard would be a problem, so he persuaded Dr. F. F. Halma of the UCLA Division of Subtropical Horticulture to create a method of grading the fruit to an acceptable standard of quality. Segregating the fruit in this way would by necessity result in significant loss, but Hodgkin recognized that a marked drop in avocado quality could destroy the Calavo brand, which was built on prestige and consistency.[39]

Growers came by the hundreds to drop off their crops. Dealing with the chaotic mess of accepting, sorting, and grading piles of fruit was a marketer's nightmare. Having foreseen such contingencies, however, Hodgkin kept a level head. The previous year, he had set in motion a plan to have major California supermarkets carry avocados in the first two weeks of January as part of a local "agricultural push." Despite the freeze (and thanks to the carefully designed standardized packing crate), the chain stores kept their promise. Safeway actually sold 16,669 flats, filling ten full refrigerated carloads. Eastern and midwestern markets also rallied to the cause by following through on their commitment to accept avocados in January and February. When Calavo asked the Pacific coast Safeways to repeat the push, another sixteen carloads were sold. Leftovers—a half million pounds of culled avocados—were reduced to avocado oil.[40]

Even with chain stores' assistance, Hodgkin doubted Calavo could have survived without two additional initiatives he had worked to develop over the years—the massive outreach campaign to educate the public (particularly so-called Mrs. Consumer) and income from sidelines to offset the eight-month California avocado-growing season. In the past, advertising campaigns centered around benefits like nutrition, but this year, the emphasis focused squarely on quality, particularly the fact that an avocado didn't need to look perfect to taste great. The USDA pitched in with a nationwide broadcast of *Housekeepers' Chat*, urging consumers not to be wary of the avocado's varying shapes and colors—and explaining that the fruit was ripe when it yielded to gentle hand pressure.[41] In addition, Calavo benefited from a lineup of specialty tropical fruits sold during California's offseason; along with Florida avocados, there were limes, dates, figs, and occasionally South American grapes and Hawaiian pineapples. All the products fit into Calavo Growers' marketing scheme, which made their distribution simpler and much less costly. Against all odds, Calavo could report to the CAA an income of $100,000 in sideline crops.[42] The hard winter had been a test of the industry's mettle, and Calavo Growers of California had proved resilient.

Aguacates (Avocados)

Peel as many fruit as you wish,
allowing one-half to person. Remove
the seed and fill hollow with
pimiento cream cheese to which some
finely chopped nuts have been added.
Place in hot oven five minutes before
serving. Serve as a vegetable.

--"Recipes Given for National
Dishes on Mexican Menus,"
Los Angeles Times,
April 22, 1936

9 · Mother Tree

DURING THE AUTUMN OF 1936, ARCHIBALD SHAMEL and his wife set off on an automobile trip to visit the Fuerte parent tree, a dream the two had long shared. Their journey was enhanced by having read William H. Prescott's *History of the Conquest of Mexico* years earlier and, more recently, popular titles like Joseph Henry Jackson's *Mexican Interlude*. Archibald looked forward to practicing his Spanish with their local guide, Ernesto Santa Ana.[1] The Shamels admired the fine automobile roads leading travelers through magnificent mountain passes with dramatic scenic vistas bordered by ornamental plantings of willow, eucalyptus, and Mexican cedar trees. From the Puebla Valley, they enjoyed a distant view of snow-covered Pico de Orizaba, towering over 18,400 feet, and corn and bean fields, apple and pear orchards, and wildflowers of every shape and color.[2]

Upon reaching Atlixco, the Shamels found their way to 3 Poniente 24 and drove through a gateway into the Le Blanc garden.[3] Here at last was the parent Fuerte tree, in the corner by the wall, near the entrance to the house kitchen. Señora Delfina Smith Le Blanc warmly welcomed them and apologized for her husband's absence while expertly answering their questions. First recognized as significant in 1908, the tree boasted a circumference of more than four feet and stood forty-five feet tall. Le Blanc explained its lack of foliage as the result of a water shortage; the town irrigation system had been broken for three years. Shamel wondered if the soap from their washtubs might be at the root of the problem. Boron or salts in the water may not have drained properly.[4]

For many years, avocado enthusiasts had visited the tree, taken photographs, and benefited from Señor Le Blanc's hospitality. Despite his diligent stewardship, Le Blanc had never received "a peso" for his vital contribution to the California avocado industry. Shamel aimed to change that. His efforts bore fruit. At the May CAA meeting, President Carter Barrett moved to acknowledge the California industry's collective gratitude to Mexico, and specifically to Le Blanc, for his devotion to the world's most famous avocado parent tree. Dr. Hurley of La Mesa proposed that the association commemorate the tree with a bronze tablet and present its caretaker with a gold medal. Wilson Popenoe composed the bilingual text for the tablet, to be mounted on a stone base. The next step was to contact the Mexican consul in Los Angeles. If all went as hoped, the Mexican department of agriculture and the USDA would participate in the ceremonies.[5]

The plan quickly gained widespread support. Soon those making the pilgrimage to Atlixco included friends of the industry and growers.[6] By October, the trip known as the "Mexico event" was described as an "international good-will tour and pilgrimage" intended to further the beneficial relationship between the two countries. California represented the largest avocado industry in the world—with more than 10,000 acres of trees, 75 to 80 percent of which were Fuerte avocados.[7] The CAA created the "Le Blanc Fund" to offset costs for the memorial, medals, and commemorative programming and also welcomed support from new members, who would receive the organization's yearbook along with all the rewards of joining the association.

Around this time, another book captivated the attention of CAA members. In what *The New York Times* called "smooth, colorful, and vigorous" prose, *The House in Antigua: A Restoration* by the popular writer Louis Adamic provided a glimpse into the heart and mind of Wilson Popenoe.[8] In 1930, the Popenoe family had moved from Tela to Guatemala City, where Wilson continued his work as an agronomist, just an hour's drive in the family Ford from Antigua. Drawn back to a place he loved, Wilson introduced his wife, Dorothy, to the ancient city, and the two soon purchased a ruin at its outskirts known as Casa del Capuchino, after a stately capuchin cypress tree on the property. This was no ordinary old house in need of repairs but the carcass of a once-eminent structure built in 1634, laid bare by the earthquake of 1773, and long left untended. Dorothy, having recently completed a study of similar ancient ruins, was highly qualified to restore the house to its original condition. Wilson's old friend Jorge Benítez supervised the laborers and craftsmen necessary to realize her vision.[9]

Two years into the restoration, Dorothy died tragically at age thirty-three. An expert botanist, she had consumed an ackee, a fruit known to be deadly if eaten raw.[10] *The House in Antigua* was a tribute to her memory, invoking the presence of the past Adamic absorbed, as well as her highly sensitive restoration. The book expressed Wilson's desire to focus on her achievement rather than his own.

The Popenoes' restoration would entertain a stream of guests, the Fairchilds among them. Strangers (who obtained a card of admittance by writing to Wilson) were also welcome. Louisa Jane Church of California visited twice and was so taken with the house that she had its plans copied. After marrying Curtis Peck, she built a replica of Casa Popenoe at 1100 South Grand Avenue in Pasadena, about five miles from the former West India Gardens, on land Wilson knew as once occupied by beer magnate Adolphus Busch's famous public garden.[11]

By January, the pilgrimage to the parent tree had evolved into a seventeen-day tour of Mexico highlighted by an "international goodwill" ceremony on Easter Sunday at the Le Blanc garden. Calavo and the CAA, cosponsors of the event, were subsidized by donations to the "Voluntary Fund for the Le Blanc Commemoration." Contributors included Wilson Popenoe, George B. Hodgkin, and Rudolph G. Hass, among more than forty others.[12]

While the association collaborated on fundraising, Alejandro Le Blanc was suffering from his own financial problems and a heartrending secret. The property nourishing the Fuerte, owned by his mother, Doña Mathilde Dion Dumont, had been liquidated to support the family. When he heard of the pilgrimage, Le Blanc was overcome by a crushing sense of shame. His days as caretaker of the tree were numbered and its future uncertain. After a long struggle with this seemingly unsolvable predicament, he realized that the tree could be memorialized in a document. Slowly and painstakingly, he created a plan of the garden showing the location of the tree and indicating the details of its surroundings. Then he wrote a letter to the CAA describing his desire that the plan become part of the association's archive and expressing his very deepest gratitude to the association for honoring him, his city, and his country by spreading the Fuerte's fruit around the world, in "the genuine Spirit of Cooperation." Three weeks before the celebration, he asked Albert Grego to translate the document into English for the CAA.[13]

The day of their departure, the travelers assembled at the Los Angeles train station destined for El Paso. From Texas, they made further connections to reach Mexico City, where cars were hired for the remainder of the tour. The projected itinerary included motoring through the Querétaro and La Cañada valleys and the southern tropical regions of Oaxaca, Mitla, and Monte Albán. Stops would be made in Cuernavaca and Taxco, as well as the "ultra-fashionable" city of Tehuacán. Mexico City, with its famous floating gardens, was on everyone's agenda as a must-see.[14] A few days before the celebration, Wilson Popenoe flew in from Guatemala.

On Easter morning, a cavalcade of ten automobiles reached Atlixco, where a surging crowd brought them to a stop beneath the city's "Welcome Arch." The guests were greeted by locals and Mexican music as they pushed their way out of the cars and found themselves at the entrance to the city, encircled by eager photographers. Mayor Gabriel Cuevas's welcoming speech was followed by Judge Frank Halm's gracious reply, all of which was translated by Señor Servin (a representative of the Mexican National Railways who traveled with the American party). A foot-long silver master key to the city, presented to the judge by the mayor, would travel back to California as a token of goodwill.[15]

Soon all were marching into town, led by a band and urged on by schoolchildren in festive outfits, a mass of humanity moving toward the city hall, the Palacio Municipal. Arches of red, white, blue, and green bunting hung across the street at forty-foot intervals, creating a mile-long ceremonial pathway to city hall and then on to the celebrated destination. At the palacio, the names of the American guests were called and each stepped up to receive an inscribed commemorative parchment.[16]

For the next hour, the Americans greeted their Mexican hosts and vice versa, and a lucky few managed to get lunch at the California Cafe. In the midst of the chaotic fest, a whistle was blown. At the signal, participants rushed to their cars and drove to the Le Blanc home, guarded by a military platoon. Halm, Webber, and their party were ushered into the courtyard, to reserved seats in front of the honored tree. The CAA's monument stood before them, circled by the flags and colors of the two countries. When the judge called the meeting to order, silence fell.

Many speeches followed. Shamel spoke for the USDA, Wilson Popenoe added the perspective of a plant explorer, and Consul-General James B. Stewart, of the American embassy, spoke of America's gratitude to Mexico. Representing Mexico were a host of public officials, including Dr. Jose Parres, secretary of agriculture; Ernesto Hidalgo, secretary to the minister of foreign affairs; and General Gomez, chief of the army in Puebla. Powerful local politicians like Puebla governor Maximino Camacho, whose brother would soon become president of Mexico, had their own reasons for showing up for this small-town celebration of international diplomacy and Mexican pride. Just a month earlier, Mexico had nationalized its oil production, a move the American government had reluctantly tolerated. Fresh off that victory, Mexican leaders were eager to boost support for the country's natural resources, particularly in rural areas where they feared uprisings by struggling farmers.

After the speeches, another hush fell on the audience. Standing on either side of the monument, Judge Halm and Governor Camacho each lifted the flag of his country, unveiling a bronze tablet, inscribed:

He aquí el árbol
cuyos vástagos han desempeñado un papel de
importancia primordial en la formación de
una nueva industria en California, E.U.A.
esta placa ha sido colocada como
testimonio de gratitud y aprecio por la
California Avocado Association
1938

This tree
has, through its progeny, played a major
role in the development of a new industry
in California, U.S.A.
In testimony of our gratitude and
appreciation, this tablet is placed here by the
California Avocado Association
1938

The cheers of the crowd were almost as loud as the Mexican national anthem.

Throughout a twelve- (or maybe fifteen-) course feast following the ceremony, toasts of pulque, tequila, wine, and beer were enjoyed in the shade of tropical trees. The sun was low in the sky when guests were ushered to cars for the hundred-mile trip back to Mexico City. As the procession pulled away, a scream rang out and the crowd surged, forcing the lead driver to a stop. Onlookers made way for a frantic woman holding a painting. She passed it through the car window, warning Judge Halm that the paint was still wet. He had just enough time to thank Marcia García Leon for her portrait of the Mother Fuerte before the car moved on.[17]

Reporter Jorge Labra traveled from Mérida, more than six hundred miles east, to cover the story for his paper, *Diario de Yucatán*. When he first heard of the assignment—a ceremony drawing high-ranking Mexican officials—he found it newsworthy, but once he learned that the honoree was an aguacate tree, he had to laugh. How would the Mexican contingent manage to keep a straight face? By the time Labra arrived at the city, his opinion had begun to change. The festivities were more of a cultural celebration than he expected. And the Mexicans put on a good show. A city considered cheerful but dirty and known to harbor frightening swarms of flies had cleaned itself up. For the Californians, this was a long-anticipated occasion, a moment of brotherhood and gratitude. But the very idea of gathering around a tree and showering it with praise seemed ludicrous—should they pretend to be serious or smile?[18]

Labra watched as the tree, "silent and solemn, . . . received the homage, listening attentively to the speeches and feeling a shudder of satisfaction run through its rough trunk when Governor Ávila Comacho unveiled the Plaque in its honor." The tree seemed as perplexed as the crowd, until the senior official of the secretary of foreign affairs stepped up and saved the day. The ceremony did more than honor this single tree, he proclaimed, it gave thanks to all the earth gives us—land, trees, and animals, who ask only for our "solicitous care." This was a good message for everyone to hear, but Labra wasn't quite satisfied with it as his article's conclusion because, after all, the Americans had done quite a bit of work to make this tree valuable. He reminded his readers that California farmers care for their trees in ways that make them profitable. Mexicans, he opined, would benefit from being a little more attentive and developing a more "active conscience that takes care of its own wellbeing." His column was picked up by *La Opinión*, the Spanish-language newspaper in Los Angeles.[19]

Although the ceremony marked the culmination of a pilgrimage, it was only the beginning of Archibald Shamel's adventures in Mexico. Months earlier, as the principal physiologist of the Division of Fruit and Vegetable Crops and Diseases for the USDA, he had planned a six-week study of Mexican avocados, focused on identifying summer-bearing varieties for introduction to the United States. From his decades of plant exploration, Shamel knew that success depended on access to regional avocado-growing districts and surrounded himself with local experts accordingly: Dr. Juan A. Gonzalez, director of rural economics at the Mexican department of agriculture; Señor Alejandro Le Blanc, award-winning Fuerte grower; and Ernesto Santillana. All agreed that the Atlixco region stood apart as the only region supplying avocados throughout the year, usually at altitudes of above 6,000 feet, in well-drained soils mixed with volcanic loam.[20]

Shamel hadn't intended to analyze the Mexico avocado market, but his insider's view of California's progress opened his eyes to the country's emerging industry. He looked more closely at the methods of harvesting and marketing practiced throughout the area. The Tochimilco district was home to 5,000 trees at all stages of growth, and avocados were central to the region's economy. Most cultivated avocado trees resided in huertas like Le Blanc's, but at the Rodiles hacienda, about four miles from Atlixco, he saw more than 3,500 trees cultivated in twenty-five-foot-by-twenty-five-foot rows. No wonder Wilson was disappointed not to have visited twenty years earlier. Here, in contrast to the typical casual maintenance—annual plowing perhaps or stirring of the soil—the "clean cultivation" reminded Shamel of Southern California orchards.[21]

At harvest time, pickers maneuvered long poles with baskets or hooks fixed to the ends. No one seemed to care much about bruising, and there was no such thing as a proper packing crate. The fruit was carried away in baskets, nets, bags, sacks, whatever could be found, and if sorting took place, it was limited to size and color as part of the market-stall display. Traveling by train, truck, muleback, or person (growers were known to carry as much as two hundred pounds of fruit on their backs), the avocados were sold in village and city public markets. The small "corriente" (common) avocados were essential to the national diet. Still, larger, more expensive fruit was always in demand. By the end of the survey, Shamel had exchanged information with his Mexican colleagues on subjects ranging from new varieties and bud propagation to rootstocks and marketing. He returned to America with budwood from eight promising trees, all proved to bear in the spring and summer, and a new perspective on how both countries might mutually benefit from future collaboration.[22] He also brought with him a very special piece of wood—a limb from the Mother Fuerte.

Writing about his findings for the CAA yearbook gave Shamel a chance to mention an "interesting study" he couldn't fit into the itinerary. Rumor had it that indigenous avocados were thriving in a forested mountain valley, extending over thirty miles, near Uruapan, in the neighboring state of Michoacán. He made a mental note to visit the region during the next bearing season.

Early that summer, the Mexican press and California newspapers reported the suicide of Alejandro Le Blanc, attributing it to poverty.[23] Occurring just weeks after their successful expedition, the tragic act left Shamel shocked and guilt ridden. He felt strongly that something needed to be done to honor his friend's noble aspirations on behalf of Mexico and the avocado industry. A month after Le Blanc's death, Shamel attended the Avocado Institute in La Habra. At the end of the program, he presented the avocado departments of the Los Angeles County and Orange County Farm Bureaus and Agricultural Extension Service with the limb he had secured from the Mother Fuerte. At the next CAA meeting, the association was offered a gavel made from the celebrated Fuerte's wood. In this symbolic way, repurposed in the form of gavels calling meetings into session, the tree branch would remind Californians of their debt to Mexico and Le Blanc.[24]

Stuffed Avocado Ideale

2 (6 1/2 oz.) cans crabmeat or 2 cups fresh
  cooked crabmeat
1 cup celery (cut into small, matchlike
  sticks)
1/4 cup salad oil
Salt & pepper
2 avocados (cut in half lengthwise)
2 Tbs lemon juice
1 Tsp finely chopped chives
4 anchovies
1/4 cup Russian dressing

Separate crabmeat into large pieces.
Marinate crabmeat and celery separately
for 15 minutes in seasoned salad oil. Scoop
out balls from avocado, being careful not
to break shell. Scrape out remaining pulp,
mix with chives, and reserve. Sprinkle
a few drops lemon juice over balls and
pulp mixture to prevent darkening. Place
crabmeat in centers of empty shells;
surround with avocado balls. Group celery
sticks at each end of avocados and place
one anchovy ring on top of each serving.
Serve on crisp lettuce, in a bowl of
cracked ice, with Russian dressing mixed
with remaining avocado pulp and chives.
Yield: 4 portions.

Note: Be sure to use avocados that are
neither too green nor too ripe.

--Recipe by Chef Yter Jardin, from
Grace Turner, "Streamline Your
Dinner Parties," *The Birmingham
News*, November 19, 1939

10 · **Wild Avocado**

WHEN THE NEW YORK WORLD'S FAIR OPENED ITS GATES on April 30, 1939, visitors eagerly stepped from Flushing Meadows Park into "the world of tomorrow." President Roosevelt inaugurated the celebration with the hope that new products, initiatives, and ideas would steer American consumers in the right direction as the country emerged from the Depression. The USDA-approved Food Focal exhibit, by modernist designer Richard Wright, featured an avocado replica studded with five jewels representing the essential components of a healthy diet.[1] Here was the opportunity to launch the avocado onto the world stage, and what better spokespeople than the king and queen of England. At the fair, the royal guests lunched on "typical" American fare that included New England Sea Food Cocktail followed by Jellied Gumbo Louisiana and Breast of Capon Middle Western Style, with corn fritters and lima beans on the side. An avocado-and-grapefruit salad complemented the meal. In the wake of the royal visit, the Florida state exhibit began selling the popular salad from its venue.[2]

Visitors interested in regional foods could buy a copy of the *New York World's Fair Cook Book*, by the film producer and food influencer Crosby Gaige.[3] California was represented by an avocado-and-tomato salad, the Southwest with a ranchman's soup requiring five types of meat and a slice of avocado for each plate, and Texas with half an avocado filled with caviar. For those unable to attend the festivities, newspapers ran celebratory recipes, such as Stuffed Avocado Ideale, which gained its superlative from spiking the avocado and crab with the tang of anchovy. The country was ready to believe in itself again, and the avocado, once a luxury of elite hotels, was now billed as a nutritional powerhouse within the budget of Mr. and Mrs. Consumer.

Among the many visitors introduced to avocados at the fair was teenager Pierre Franey, newly arrived from France. Nearly forty years later, Franey would dish out relatively simple recipes to *New York Times* readers of his column, the 60-Minute Gourmet. His Salade Niçoise included avocado, and Avocados with Crab Louis borrowed its dressing from the St. Francis Hotel's cookbook.[4] For Franey and thousands of others, the fair displayed an optimistic vision of a future guided by science and technology. For the avocado, it was an international debut as the epitome of nutrition, rubber-stamped by the USDA.

As the Great Depression waned and Americans faced the threat of war, Southern Californians were distracted by two construction projects that tested the limits of modern technology—the massive Colorado River Aqueduct and the Arroyo Seco Parkway, the state's first freeway. For avocado growers, this seemingly bottomless source of water would ensure nourishment for orchards, allowing for the expansion necessary to develop an industry, and the increase in vehicular routes would not only supercharge the state's agricultural industries but also transport the population crucial to regional development.

Despite these auspicious projects, CAA members worried about the future of the industry. All the excitement over the aqueduct seemed ironic in the face of problems caused by excess water. Beginning back in 1936 and 1937, heavy rains had caused some avocado trees to suffer. At first, it had seemed like an inevitable result of too much water. Stunted leaves wilted and turned brown, branches died back, and fruit dropped early. A few trees even died. Whispers of decline, apoplexy, and asphyxiation creeping through orchards over the last few years were uttered by some, while others just shook their heads. But as spring came, and years passed, the symptoms continued, soon in epidemic proportions.

Professor William T. Horne, an international expert on avocado pathology at the Citrus Experiment Station in Riverside, had long anticipated this type of epidemic. Over the course of his thirty-year career, he had studied a wide range of pestilence and disease: sun blotch, tipburn, crick-side, and many more, but root rot posed the most serious threat to the industry.[5] Fungus was both friend and foe—essential to life and yet easily turned. It could nourish a tree with essential nutrients or bring one down by suffocating its roots. Horne spent endless hours hunched over his microscope, hypothesizing that a fungal pathogen capable of swimming through the water might be at the root of the avocado growers' troubles.[6]

His supposition was confirmed in 1939, when graduate student A. Vincent Wager of South Africa, a fellow at the experiment station, determined the culprit was *Phytophthora cinnamomi*, the deadly fungus busily killing America's revered chestnut trees. Avocado growers were instructed to pay special attention to soil—its composition, water tolerance, and depth—and even advised to survey their entire property by hand with a shovel or other tool before, during, and after irrigation to determine the optimal soil conditions throughout the orchard. Not all trees were affected, which meant that hardier strains could be grafted.[7]

For Wilson Popenoe, the disease attacking avocados gave further credence to his ongoing obsession with the wild avocado. Beginning in 1941, president of the United Fruit Company Samuel Zemurray had charged him with finding a location for a new agricultural school. Perhaps this institution could become a leader in the international quest for a new variety, one that was hardy, buttery, and resistant to disease.[8]

H. H. Brokaw remained optimistic about his Hass, as it increasingly rose among the ranks of its fellow varieties. He knew that the black, pebbly-skinned fruit was a tough sell. Even though Calavo

had pulled out all the stops to get its green-skinned Fuerte recognized as the ideal, the Hass's superior attributes could not be
denied. It predominately bore in the spring and summer, and for
a longer amount of time than the fall-winter Fuerte; it was a more
trustworthy producer, too, held its own against high winds, and
possessed the necessary tough skin for shipping.

Rudolph Hass had allowed Roger Magdahl, a California Avocado Society (CAS) member based in La Cruz, to propagate his
patented Hass in Chile—both an act of "Good Neighborliness"
and a calculated move to help supercharge development of the
Hass by testing it in a different climate.[9] The gambit paid off. In
1945, as the society looked to the future, the Hass was on the
rise.[10] The flaws of the Fuerte had become more apparent with the
passing of time. Its diminished strength opened an opportunity
for Hass and Brokaw.

While Hass continued to expand his orchard in La Habra
Heights, Henri Gilly was planning an orchard of budded Fuerte
trees at his famous cattle ranch, Hacienda Xahuentla. He sent an
employee to meet CAS member Carl Crawford and secure budwood at a local avocado nursery in Santa Ana, California. Since
then, Crawford had visited Xahuentla many times, helping Gilly
select seed for rootstocks and teaching his nursery manager how to
care for more than 1,000 budded Fuerte trees. The orchard would
soon expand to become a thirty-five-acre testing ground for new
Rodiles varieties.[11]

The discoveries at Rodiles's were especially meaningful since
the tragic death of the Fuerte mother tree. Wilson Popenoe had
examined the tree in the fall of 1942 and given it only months to
live, but it hung on for three more years.[12] Carter Barrett proposed
a second pilgrimage, this time to honor the dead Mother Fuerte
on the tenth anniversary of the society's first celebration. The "gesture of good neighborliness" would involve not only speeches and
a plaque but also a selection of the "best Fuerte progeny raised in
California," the grandchildren of the mother tree.

Before the event, Carl Crawford secured permission to saw off the trunk, counting sixty-one rings. He did his best to preserve what was left—setting the trunk on its stump and propping it up with wooden supports. Over the next three years, the anniversary pilgrimage would grow to become "a big business," involving a train, a travel agency, and a cost of more than $800,000, despite endless pro bono hours put in by society members.[13]

During the spring of 1946, Harlan B. Griswold, Carter Barrett, and Carl Crawford traveled to Antigua to honor Guatemala's contribution to the California avocado industry with a plaque in the park adjacent Wilson's home, Casa Popenoe. The commemoration was the first of many expressions of the society's gratitude (the organization had changed its name in 1941, swapping Association for Society to suggest its many cultural activities) and led to thoughts of other ways of sharing the wealth—through new introductions, perhaps, bestowed upon countries around the world. On the way home, the three stopped off at Henri Gilly's ranch to see the budded Fuerte orchard Carl Crawford couldn't stop talking about.[14]

Just a few months after this visit, Crawford accompanied H. B. Griswold to the new Escuela Agrícola Panamericana Zamorano outside Tegucigalpa, Honduras, the agricultural school funded by the United Fruit Company, where the two presented school director Wilson Popenoe with the CAS's emblem of honor. For him, it was an opportunity to renew ties with the society and continue his search for the elusive wild avocado, now with the additional incentive of discovering a potentially tree-saving rootstalk. Griswold had his own interests in mind as the owner of the Griswold Ranch in La Habra Heights. The explorers bonded on a hike through a nearby cloud forest, dense with vines, moss, orchids, begonia-like flowers, and ferns, a primeval forest harboring wild avocados. Testing with an auger revealed an unbelievable three feet of soil saturated enough to squeeze water from. Wild Guatemalan avocados produced very small fruit—seeds less than an inch in diameter surrounded by a mere eighth of an inch of flesh—but, importantly, they showed no sign of decline in the saturated soil. Over time, the rootstalk must have evolved to manage excess moisture. Down in the valley, budded year-old trees with West Indian rootstalks, planted in clay soil, already showed signs of root rot. On their hike out, Wilson gathered seeds for testing in California. Before returning home, Griswold and Crawford took his advice and went out of their way to stop at Pico de Orizaba in search of the primitive fruits once thought to be the origin of the species. The experience left them eager for more.[15]

Griswold acted quickly, appointing a Foreign Exploration Committee to continue the hunt for rootstalks resistant to the deadly fungus. Wilson was delighted to volunteer. While others concerned themselves with details related to the *Phytophthora cinnamomi* outbreak in California, he would dig deeper in search of "wild forms and species" that could one day lead to the creation of a cultivar resilient enough to reach markets across the globe. Recalling his hubris at discovering the "first" wild avocado on a climb up the volcano Irazú in Costa Rica, he blushed at his youthful enthusiasm. Later a similar tree was discovered on the Caribbean coast of Honduras, but Wilson still saw promise in its ability to withstand moisture, a requirement of a resistant rootstock. Now there was the wild avocado of Tecpán, discovered at 9,300 feet (a record elevation for the fruit in Central America); a similar discovery in the cloud forests near Tegucigalpa, Honduras; and another relative at 7,500 feet, above Acultzingo in Veracruz, Mexico. Avocados had been cultivated in Mexico and Central America for more than 1,000 years, so every expedition brought with it the possibility of coming upon a tree in its truly indigenous state.[16] In the company of Griswold, Barrett, and the Escuela's botanist Dr. Louis O. Williams, he not only predicted a successful exploration but also felt a familiar restlessness to begin the quest immediately. Before heading to more distant locations, the explorers would visit a unique collection of native trees in the land of the Mother Fuerte.

A seasoned explorer at age fifty-five, Wilson was a little embarrassed not to have experienced the Rodiles orchard, established near Atlixco around 1917. Almost thirty years ago, he'd declined a chance to meet Adolfo Rodiles at Hacienda San Diego and tour the avocado plantation in its infant state. Looking back, he couldn't help but speculate on how a collaboration with Rodiles, at the time when the Fuerte was just coming into its own, would have transformed avocado production in both countries.

Driving though the familiar landscape of valleys and mountains, with Popocatepetl as a natural compass, Popenoe expected to be surprised by a cultivated orchard on the edge of town. The reality was beyond expectation. Row after row of mature trees in all shapes and sizes revealed to his practiced eye a living family tree going back several generations. From a distance, there appeared to be little order to the collection, but as the group ventured into the grove, the trees organized themselves into three terraced spaces, each with its own central irrigation canal, and in distinct stages of growth. Those most recently planted seemed less hardy, but the oldest trees, in the central section, were Fuerte-like in appearance . . . and flourishing.[17] Rodiles had spent more than two decades carefully crossbreeding the progeny of the best Mexican and Guatemalan avocados in local markets. The Rodiles ranch was by Wilson's estimation, "probably the most valuable avocado orchard in the Americas."[18]

For Wilson, Rodiles's collection of varieties (which he dared to consider a potential "hybrid race") suggested that California might gain even better avocados at a time when his prized Fuerte seemed vulnerable. Among all the youngsters boasting the best qualities of the Fuerte, there were sure to be those with a longer growing season or the potential to thrive in regions unsuited to the prevailing variety. He charged an employee with preparing budwood for the Escuela. President Griswold went home with twelve varieties destined for the College of Agriculture in Los Angeles.[19] In a few years, perhaps as little as twenty months, a tiny tree might lead the way forward.

Carter Barrett, chairman of the tenth-anniversary pilgrimage, had planned the event for more than two years when the first public announcements went out in December 1947. The Hillman Travel Service Inc. of Santa Ana, hired to manage promotion and logistics, ran a succession of photographs and newspaper stories. First the publicity group gathered around a map of Mexico. The following month, a color movie at the women's club was described as a preview to the pilgrimage, with Mexican officials as honored guests and children from the Los Niestos School singing and dancing to songs of "old Mexico."[20] More than three hundred participants attended a kickoff party in February.

As the date approached, a prominent *Los Angeles Times* advertisement called attention to "a few reservations now available to the public."[21] Governor Earl Warren formally endorsed the goodwill mission, writing a letter of introduction to President Miguel Alemán Valdés and passing on his remarks to CAS president H. B. Griswold, now considered his "emissary" to the Mexican president.[22] A few weeks later, Beckie Hillman was pictured passing a $26,000 check to a Southern Pacific Railroad agent, the down payment for exclusive rights to a train for the "'Friendship Tour'" to Mexico.[23] The train claimed to be the first traveling from California since before World War II and to contain more drawing rooms and compartments than any previous "special." On the day of departure, April 7, 127 travelers boarded. The most important passengers were fifteen Fuerte trees, contributed from Armstrong Nurseries of Ontario and nurserymen from Fallbrook, Vista, and La Habra.[24]

In Mexico City, the human visitors enjoyed a sightseeing tour and accommodations in the Hotel La Reforma. Their official mission began with a reception at Los Pinos (President Alemán's home) and the planting of the first commemorative Fuerte seedling on the grounds. All admired the bronze commemorative plaque. Later, Alemán would write to Governor Warren expressing his gratitude for an avocado tree "that, over time, will be a permanent symbol of the friendship that links our two peoples."[25]

After a second ceremony and planting at the nearby national botanic gardens at Chapultepec park, the tour moved on, stopping for a few hours in Veracruz, where dancers performed at the station, and continuing to Fortín de las Flores, a "tropical paradise" of glittering waterfalls, fruit plantations, and gardenias. Although moved by the beauty of the landscape, Carter Barrett was equally intrigued by a typical Indigenous village—Coscomatepec—a place seemingly untouched by modern improvements, where old avocado trees called to mind the fruit's ancient heritage.[26]

Traveling on a road at 8,000 feet, with a view like that from an airplane window, the pilgrims traversed the tropical valley from Maltrata to Acatzingo before arriving in Puebla, a city of almost 100,000. Barrett was among the select group invited to Henri Gilly's Hacienda Xahuentla, where the rancher's white Charolais cattle impressed him as much as the avocados. Guests also visited Trinidad, an Indigenous village notable for the large avocados growing in nearly every courtyard. Although Barrett would never let on, the final ceremony at Atlixco depressed him. The city had rolled out the red carpet once again and set up a permanent concrete base for the plaque in the plaza's park, but the young Fuerte tree almost seemed to be in mourning. Barrett consoled himself with thoughts of the additional trees to be distributed to Carl Schmidt and members of the Mexican government. For some reason, these seemed less associated with the death of their relative.[27]

The remaining days of the trip were filled with new sites, tastes, and experiences—so many that by the end Barrett yearned for home. For him, a highlight of the return trip was a border stop.

Before leaving Mexico, all passengers disembarked from the train to walk through troughs of chemically treated sawdust, while soldiers sprayed the floors of the cars. In Barrett's opinion, this method of controlling foot-and-mouth disease had proved effective, and the whole process was more streamlined than American customs. He left Mexico with a new perspective of "our sister republic" and a sense of relief in having completed his pilgrimage.[28]

Less than six months after the gala anniversary celebration, the Foreign Exploration Committee was back at work, organizing yet another CAA trek. Since its fieldwork at the Rodiles orchard the year before, the committee had been planning a summer expedition in the hope of finding trees bearing ripe fruit before Fuerte season. Word spread quickly, and by August 1948, the trip had evolved into "the largest gathering of professional avocado enthusiasts, bound on a serious mission, which Mexico has ever seen."[29] The seasoned explorers, Wilson Popenoe and Louis O. Williams from Honduras and J. Eliot Coit, Knowles Ryerson, and Carl Crawford from California—were eager to meet three members of the Texas Avocado Society, the CAS's sister organization, founded that spring, with its headquarters as the USDA Citrus Rootstock Laboratory of the Texas Agricultural Experiment Station at Weslaco. Dr. Rafael H. Cintron served as the chairman of the society's variety committee and William C. Cooper, a USDA employee, as secretary/treasurer. J. R. Padgett, of Rio Farms Inc., the owner of three hundred recently planted seedling avocado trees, was one of ninety-six members.[30] Little did they know, this was the first of twenty society-sponsored trips to Mexico over the next eight years.[31]

Carl Schmidt met members of the expedition at the Mexico City airport. Shortly after arriving in the city, they visited the young

Fuerte in the park. A moment of silence ensued while they stood before the tree reading the memorial plaque.[32]

Este árbol de aguacate
de la variedad "Fuerte" de California
permanecerá al través de los tiempos
como un símbolo de gratitud hacia Atlixco,
donde esta incomparable calidad fue originada.
Este hijo viene al pais de su padre,
lleno de orgullo para perdurar su clase
como su padre lo hizo por muchos años.
Sembrado por la California Avocado Society;
en abril 18, del 1948.

This Fuerte avocado tree from California
stands as a symbol of gratitude to Atlixco where
this peerless variety originated.
The son returns to the home of his father
to perpetuate his kind.
Planted by the California Avocado Society
April 18, 1948.

The tree looked well enough, though without new growth. Its trunk was encircled by a concrete rim, leaving just an inch of soil visible. Perhaps this unusual planting method had stunted the young seedling? Fortuitously, Salvador Sánchez Colín, Mexico's young director general of agriculture, was a member of the party. An avocado aficionado, he had been working in collaboration with the Rockefeller Foundation's Mexican Agricultural Program, which began in 1943. When asked to look into the issue, Sánchez Colín promised to rectify the situation.[33]

After three days of scouring the Rodiles grove for "Fuerte-like hybrids," the team of explorers agreed on eighteen trees as likely candidates. Budwood from these was cut, numbered, and tagged with copper labels identifying their location in the orchard. Having completed their work in Atlixco, the expedition split into two groups. The three Texans, all of whom were fluent in Spanish, translated for Coit on a tour of Veracruz, in search of hardy Mexican seedlings that could be grafted to West Indian stock. They set their hopes on creating West Indian–Mexican hybrids capable of surviving the harsh temperatures and salty soil of the Rio Grande Valley. Although this region had yielded few successes, the Hoblitzelle Ranch planted eight acres of avocado trees within 750 acres carved out of the sand hills near Mercedes, Texas.[34] Ranch-O-Hills, the hobby of theater magnate and philanthropist Karl Hoblitzelle, depended on an intricate irrigation system and the knowledge of agriculturalists from Texas A&M University, as well as its ranch manager, Dr. Cintron, an expert in tropical fruits from Puerto Rico. California had stumbled upon its record-breaking Fuerte. Texas's big avocado might be just around the corner.[35]

The more experienced group, obsessed with the ongoing search for new varieties, wasted no time in continuing their travels. Sánchez Colín served as their guide through the state of Michoacán. At Zitácuaro, they met Jesus H. Contreras, a horticulturalist who mentioned that he had brought seeds to the region from the Rodiles orchard years earlier. Over time, the avocado experts had become increasingly discerning. Budwood was secured from only one tree, a Guatemalan-Mexican hybrid at Nabor Contreras's garden in the nearby village of Curungueo.[36]

All in all, forty selections from the Rodiles orchard, collected during the 1948 trips, were sent to be planted in California, Texas, and Honduras. Budwood from the best of these went to Florida, South America, and Johannesburg, South Africa. Wilson was determined to spread the wealth to locations around the world where Fuerte relations could thrive. Trees budded in Honduras had yielded mature fruit in just twenty months. Two were already worthy of names—Aztec and Toltec—and among the Mexican names waiting in the wings was Mixtec, a choice ultimately dropped because it sounded to some like *mistake*.[37]

Henri Gilly's Xahuentla orchard and Rodiles's orchard had impressed the CAS visitors with their diversity and hardy growth, and for the first time, Californians began to wonder about the potential for competition from Mexico. Back in 1928, the CAA acknowledged "an awakened interest in the fruit" after the Mexican department of agriculture published "El Aguacate," a "very creditable" bulletin heavily based on the association's yearbooks.[38] The general directorate of agriculture collected production and harvesting statistics beginning in 1927, when it reported 27,303 tons of creole (criollo) avocados.[39] Now the country was producing over 30,000 tons more than the previous decade and hoping to develop weevil-resistant varieties with greater commercial appeal.[40]

Despite government support, Wilson and Carl agreed that the Mexican industry faced many hurdles. The unpredictable, wide-ranging quality and varieties of avocados in Mexican markets would not attract an American market, especially one accustomed to a standard package of high-grade Calavos. And even if quality and standardization improved, importers were blocked by the quarantine, and if that were ever lifted, the seven-and-a-half-cent-per-pound import duty significantly impacted profits. For now, the California industry seemed safe.[41] But there were more intangible dangers to consider.

Back in the spring of 1948, Griswold located a diseased tree on his land, had it removed, and sent a root sample to the Citrus Experiment Station. Plant pathologist George Zentmyer planted the wild avocados of Aquila and Acatzingo in a triangle, one foot on each side, alongside a "check tree," a variety known to flourish in the region. In less than a year, both the Acatzingo and the "check tree" were dead. The Aquila lived on, proving its resistance to root rot. Of all the specimens collected over the last decade, the Aquila seemed to have the most potential. Whether or not it would serve as a rootstalk was another matter. Wilson had failed to establish the Aquila in Honduras, though he did see success with varieties that offered little potential in California.[42]

In 1951, CAS president Elwood Trask set out with Griswold on yet another trip to Mexico in search of wild avocados and brought along Zentmyer to identify cases of root rot. Although no new wild avocados were discovered, at the local markets they were introduced to round, black fruits, about an inch in diameter, only large enough for a taste of savory avocado, and eaten with the skin. These grew wild everywhere—from forests to cultivated land—a finger food free to all. On the return trip they made the required stop at the shrine of the Fuerte parent tree, reduced to a mournful stump. Out of thirty trees in the area tested for root rot, Zentmyer found only one case of infection.[43]

Before leaving Mexico, the group spent a weekend at Gilly's Hacienda Xahuentla. Now boasting sixty acres, his crop was primarily Fuerte and the promising new variety Griswold was banking on, the Hass. Both were selling at good prices in Mexico City. On the drive and flight home, they speculated on how scientific studies, improvements in technology, and international collaboration could eventually lead to a breakthrough: the ideal, invincible avocado.[44]

Part II

The Hass Mother Tree

(born 1926, La Habra Heights, California)

Hass mother tree, La Habra Heights, California. California
Avocado Society Yearbook, 1945. *(From the collection of the
Lenhardt Library of the Chicago Botanic Garden)*

California Sunshine Cup

You want just the perfect Christmas dinner starter, and here is one of the best.

1 large avocado
2 8-ounce cans grapefruit sections
1 cup seeded red grapes, sliced
1/2 cup sherry
Dash Angostura bitters

Cut avocado into cubes or balls. Cut grapefruit into bite-sized sections; seed and slice grapes. Combine all fruits with wine and bitters and serve in stemmed cocktail glasses.

Makes 6 servings.

--Helen Bauer and Roberta Logerman,
The Avocado Cookbook, 1967[1]

11 · **Believers**

RUDOLPH HASS RETIRED IN THE SUMMER OF 1952 AF-
ter a thirty-year career with the Pasadena post office. He died three
months later. His loved ones laid him to rest at Mountain View
Cemetery in Altadena, a short walk from Fred Popenoe's grave
and across Calaveras Street from the original home of West India
Gardens. The brief obituary in the *Los Angeles Times* heralded his
loyalty as a civil servant but made no mention of his namesake
avocado, whose patent expired that same year.[2] The Hass variety
had yet to rise above the crowded field of favored avocado varieties
growing in Southern California. For that to happen, Hass needed
a champion.

William Henry Brokaw, known as Hank to his friends, was a
new member of the California Avocado Society when he walked
into the Maie Ellis Elementary School in Fallbrook for the group's
1958 meeting. He carried a special pedigree: twenty-five years earlier, his uncle Harold Hazzard Brokaw had the foresight to strike
a deal with Rudolph Hass to propagate and sell his patented avocado commercially. Hank grew up working alongside his father
and Uncle Harold in the family's Whittier nursery. Whether it
was nostalgia, ambition, or simply a hunch about a great-tasting
black avocado, Hank had been drawn into the family business,
and he was eager to learn as he moved among the impressive
crowd of ranchers, University of California scientists, marketing
experts, and produce-industry executives. He heard university
researchers report on an irrigation-and-fertilizer study involving
Hass avocado trees planted at the Citrus Experiment Station; tests

of the leaves showed that zinc, copper, and boron levels declined on trees that received a nitrogen treatment.[3] Hank made a mental note. Back at his new avocado nursery in Oxnard, he had rows of young Hass trees waiting in pots for ready customers.

On his way home, Hank passed acres of young avocado orchards. Many of them were Fuertes. The dominant variety had a reputation for bearing erratically but still accounted for nearly seven in every ten avocados sold in California. Calavo would pack more than 37 million pounds of the green-skinned favorite that season. Most American housewives, the industry's target customers, had never heard of the fruit, let alone knew what to do with it. When Barbara Faber of Garretson, South Dakota, first got her hands on one in the early 1950s, she tried to cook it like a potato. The heat turned the pulp into a bitter, mushy paste. Years later, her son Ben would grow up to be one of the University of California's leading avocado experts, but in the mid-twentieth century, the fruit was still an anomaly in much of the country.[4] Those familiar with the diversity of avocados in Mexico knew that black-skinned avocados could be delicious, but in much of the United States in the 1950s, American shoppers typically thought the good ones were green.

In the decades-long race for the ideal California variety, the black-skinned Hass trailed far behind, a distant second with just 11 percent of Calavo's harvest.[5] A report from the University of California had recently decreed that if its alternate-bearing habit could be controlled, the Fuerte would remain unrivaled as the preferred California variety. Even with its flaws, the report said, "it will doubtless be many years before the Fuerte supremacy is seriously challenged."[6] But up and down Southern California, the Hass was on the rise. Growers were topworking old trees, more than 50,000 in the past two seasons alone, grafting most of them with Hass budwood.[7]

Back in 1922, Uncle Harold's Whittier nursery was the first in California solely dedicated to growing avocados.[8] His brother-in-law, Albert Rideout, inspired him to plant Lyons, but he also sold Prince, Fuerte, Dickinson, and other varieties.[9] When Rudolph Hass turned to Uncle Harold to propagate and promote his prize avocado, he negotiated with the local cooperative and got the Hass to market.[10] Even when people disparaged an avocado that turned black when it ripened, Uncle Harold never lost faith in its potential.[11] Now, a generation later, others were beginning to see it, too.

Hank grew up around Hass avocados, eating the fruit fresh from mature trees and working his first job at his family's avocado nursery. He served in the U.S. Navy, came back to attend community college, then studied medicine at Harvard, but the avocados drew him back. When he decided to start his own nursery in Oxnard, he chose the Hass. As avocados go, the Hass was hard to beat: the trees were productive summer bearers, the seeds weren't too big, and the fruit shipped well, peeled easily, and tasted great. As California's avocado acreage grew in the 1950s, the CAS urged growers to commit to a trio of "commercial varieties"—Fuerte, Hass, and Rincon—but not everyone listened. A veritable alphabet soup of avocados, from Anaheim to Zutano, grew all over the state. Calavo still packed (somewhat grudgingly) the "cats and dogs," an eclectic list of more than 150 cultivars.[12] Calavo answered to the growers and wouldn't turn them away, but handling many varieties required more sorting, more labor, and more costs. As the industry grew, so did pressure to streamline.

The cats and dogs had history. They included varieties from Atlixco as well as cultivars developed by California's avocado pioneers. Calavo picked more than 17,000 pounds of Pueblas (a Carl Schmidt selection) in the 1956–1957 season, enough to fill 426 forty-pound field boxes. Albert Rideout's favorite, the Lyon, filled 740 field boxes that season, and Jennie Gano's namesake variety, the first avocado to receive a patent, contributed five hundred pounds to Calavo's harvest. In Santa Barbara County, where more than four hundred farmers grew 1,500 acres of avocados in a narrow strip from the Santa Ynez Mountains to the Pacific, three in every ten trees were MacArthurs, a thin-skinned, dark-green avocado that, like the Fuerte, ripened in the fall and winter. Others in the county grew Anaheim, Dickinson, Edranol, Nabal, and Ryan. Zutano trees bore well down south in Riverside County, where people seemed to tolerate the fruit's watery flavor, and in Los Angeles County, a population boom was threatening farmland, but growers still tended 2,400 acres of orchards in foothills from Whittier to Monrovia. Society president George Bowker, a Santa Paula rancher and Calavo board member, tried to clamp down on the diversity. Prices had plummeted, and everyone was pointing fingers. Bowker begged growers to think of the consumer, who expected—and would pay for—uniform, top-quality fruit.[13]

Beneath the chaos, Hank began hearing a consistent message. Despite the Fuerte's dominance, and even as consumers seemed lukewarm about an avocado that blackened when ripe, the farm advisers' reports were filled with accolades for his uncle's favorite variety. The University of California employed farm advisers in every county in California. Funded in part by the USDA and housed in county agriculture offices, the advisers were a result of the 1914 Smith-Lever Act's push for an agricultural extension service.[14] Public servants in work boots, they served as on-call horticulturalists who helped farmers implement the university's research in California's orchards. Their annual updates to the avocado society—some lyrical, some technical, some seasoned with regional bias or a folksy aside—also reported on trends in each county: how many acres of avocados, what challenges the growers faced, what innovations made trees more productive, what varieties showed promise.[15] The "Hass is outstanding in fruit quality and has a good record of production," the Riverside County farm adviser said. In Los Angeles County, word was that "the Hass variety has proved to be a very consistent producer suited to all warm, frost-free areas."[16] Farther up the coast, farm adviser George E. Goodall noted many of the lesser-known old-school varieties around Santa Barbara were being topworked to Hass, which he expected would dominate the county in a few years. Overall, in the past year Calavo's Hass haul more than doubled, from 73,366 field boxes in 1957 to 150,307 boxes in 1958. Hank knew some of that variation could be chalked up to the tree's unpredictable bearing cycle, but it was still an impressive number. With each field box weighing forty pounds, that was more than 6 million pounds of Hass avocados ripening from green to purplish black on American kitchen counters. And if the farm advisers had it right, many more were on the way.

Some farmers worried about oversupplying the market, but a new state-backed marketing association, the California Avocado Advisory Board, promised to help find new customers and keep prices from dropping dramatically. Championed by a group in Fallbrook and voted in by growers, the board formed in 1961 to take advantage of two Depression-era laws that permitted farmers, ranchers, and in some cases, distributors to pool resources to promote their commodities, fund research, and set quality standards.[17] The new avocado board charged mandatory assessments, and while some argued against it ("another step towards socialism," one farmer grumbled), Florida avocado growers had already made a similar move.[18] Faced with fluctuating productions and increased competition from their peers in California, Florida growers and handlers voted in a federal marketing agreement in 1954.[19] California's growers followed a model already set by California dairy, apple, fig, grapefruit, lettuce, pear, and raisin farmers.[20] The marketing board gave the avocado industry a new voice in California. Unlike the CAS, a volunteer association that had international members, or the packinghouses that competed for the farmers' fruit, the new board unified the state's growers around a shared economic goal: selling as many avocados as possible and keeping profits high.

Ellen McGiffert knew that when she married Hank, she was also marrying avocados. The couple met in the glee club at the University of Chicago, where Hank was studying anthropology after graduating from Harvard. Ellen, an undergrad, was the daughter of progressive Christian pastors, and her father led the prestigious Chicago Theological Seminary. Ellen grew up with parents who prized social justice, and she appreciated that Hank had spent the summer working with Indigenous tribes in South Dakota. She saw he wanted to make a difference in people's lives.[21] In a ceremony officiated by her father, a Congregational minister, Ellen and Hank married in May 1954 in the First Unitarian Church of Chicago, then decamped to Los Angeles, where Hank got his teaching credential at UCLA.

When Hank landed his first job as a math teacher in Ojai, he also planted hundreds of avocado seeds in coffee cans in their backyard and built a little greenhouse to shelter the seedlings during cool nights. As Hank's seedlings and ambitions grew, the couple borrowed $10,000 from Ellen's parents and bought an acre in Oxnard on a former riverbed with nutrient-rich soil. Their home was a forty-foot metal Quonset hut on the property. Hank transferred his avocado seedlings from the coffee cans to larger tar paper pots and bought bundles of wooden stakes at a closeout sale at Abbott & Mason Nursery in Camarillo.[22] Once the seedlings sprouted and were vigorous enough to withstand a bit of a shock, he collected budwood and grafted the seedlings one by one. His father, Robert Brokaw, drove up from his home in Whittier to help out. A few didn't make it, but Hank learned from his mistakes. Soon scores of baby trees were thriving on the Brokaws' Oxnard acre.

The Nursery Stock section of the *Ventura County Star* classifieds only included one ad on March 23, 1957. It read: "Avocado Trees. Hass, Fuerte. W.H. Brokaw Nursery." The Brokaws were open for business. A year later, the same year he joined the avocado society, he sprung for a half-page display ad in the society's 1958 yearbook: "W.H. Brokaw Avocado Nursery. PREMIUM 1-year budded and grafted trees in king-size pots," followed by Hank and Ellen's home address and phone number. The book was mailed to more than 950 society members in nineteen states (including Michigan, Montana, and New Jersey) and twenty countries from Morocco to Mozambique, Australia, Israel, Lebanon, and Peru. There were sixty-seven international members, including nineteen from Mexico, the most of any country outside the United States.[23] Advertisements weren't the only way the Brokaws marketed their trees. To sell their avocados in the early years, Ellen put a grafted tree in the back seat of their DeSoto sedan, nestled her firstborn baby, Debbie, in a basket on the front seat, and went cold-calling at Ventura County farms. Farmers who saw the tree began to place orders, and the nursery expanded fast. Hank soon moved the nursery from the Oxnard acre and rented a larger parcel in nearby Ventura.

Between 1941 and 1961, the California Avocado Society members invested $32,000 in research at the University of California, Riverside, on a range of avocado-related matters including breeding; fertilizer, insecticide, and soil studies; and experiments using parasites, beetles, and other natural enemies of mites and greenhouse thrips.[24] They learned how Hass trees responded to thirteen kinds of insecticides and Southern California's various climate zones and soils.[25] A team of scientists at UC Riverside and UCLA released two types of beetles into the orchards to see if they would devour harmful pests, while others used calipers and machinist gauges to measure the diameter of Fuerte and Hass avocados to fractions as small as one one-thousandth of an inch, eager to learn how heat and irrigation affected the volume of pulp in maturing fruit.[26]

Hank joined an avocado world that had grown considerably in the half century since his uncle first opened his nursery. Reports came in from growers and society members as far away as Israel, Australia, and Chile; researchers were analyzing orchards in Jamaica, Mexico, and Puerto Rico; and university scientists were receiving shipments of seeds from Brazil, Costa Rica, Argentina, Colombia, and Peru, hoping to find promising varieties to breed with California cultivars. The avocado society sponsored a field trip to experimental macadamia and carob groves at UCLA, forming useful ties with those who grew and studied subtropical fruit. Alongside the farm advisers and dozens of field and laboratory researchers, the University of California had two full-time professors dedicated to the avocado, Berthold "Bob" Bergh and George Zentmyer, one to breed new varieties and the other to study pests and diseases. To top it off, the regents of the university system invested in a 220-acre farm in Orange County, where the avocado scholars could plant orchards, breed new cultivars, and conduct experiments on fertilizers, water management, pesticides, and more.

By the 1950s, farmland in Southern California was disappearing fast. In Orange County, dozens of new tract houses replaced orange groves, Disneyland opened in 1955, freeways carved through the countryside, and the local water district, eyeing the postwar population boom (and anticipating increasing land values to come), was suing its neighbors for a greater share of the region's groundwater. Urban development around the UCLA campus in Westwood had been encroaching on avocado research since the late 1940s. Even the Citrus Experiment Station in Riverside was competing for space. The CAS formed a small committee to tackle the challenge and in December 1954 struck a deal with the regents of the University of California to buy a sizable tract of land from the Irvine Company for $465,000.[27] The Irvines turned the Saddleback and Santa Ana Valleys into sheep pastures, then dry farms tended by sharecroppers who grew lima beans, row crops, and later, citrus as far as the eye could see.

Christened the South Coast Field Station at Tustin, the site soon saw improvements including roads, fencing, pipelines, and gravity-flow and pressure irrigation systems. A laboratory, greenhouses, a garage, and a small residence followed.[28] The Irvines, who helped fund some of the work at the field station, continued to part with farmland at a rapid clip: the federal government had recently grabbed 4,700 acres for the El Toro Marine Corps Air Station, plus more for a blimp station nearby.[29] The university regents had their eye on another prize: 1,510 acres of the open land for a new, state-of-the-art public research university that would bear the Irvine family name. The open land wasn't all the university wanted. The Irvines had water. After a severe drought in 1912, James H. Irvine, whose immigrant father started buying up the area in 1864, spent more than $3 million drilling 1,200 wells in the valley, powered with electricity from the Southern California Edison Company. While these pumped the groundwater up to the surface, the family formed a water company to capture rainfall and find ways to pool, block, and redirect mountain streams for agricultural use. All told, the family erected eight dams, laid 2,500 miles of pipe, and built the Santiago Canyon Reservoir, also known as Irvine Lake. Water from the reservoir was pumped through pipes to irrigate the university's new research station, which lacked its own well to do the job.[30]

The university's new station did not capture much media attention, but the sprawling University of California, Irvine, campus became a national story. By 1963, William L. Pereira, the charismatic planner hired to design the university and surrounding neighborhoods, was on the cover of *Time* magazine, and more than 15,000 people showed up to watch President Lyndon B. Johnson dedicate the land the following year.[31] The local newspaper reprinted the dedication speeches, and a congressman quoted the Bible and marveled at the modern buildings, jet planes, and freeways amid the farmland, all shining examples of the "wondrous world of tomorrow."[32] Amid all the fanfare, the press paid little attention to the young avocado trees taking root.

The California Avocado Society members wanted land dedicated exclusively to avocado studies, and the regents agreed to make avocados a priority. The 1956 California Avocado Society yearbook reported on twenty-two separate avocado-related studies underway. Avocado breeding, also known as Project 1131, aimed to breed the ideal avocados for Southern California climate zones, a goal that dovetailed with the CAS's ever-expanding marketing ambitions.[33]

Obsessed as the California growers were with varietals, some feared the industry was growing too slowly. Wilson Popenoe's dream that the avocado would one day rival the orange in importance to California hadn't been realized. Popenoe, writing to the CAS board in 1959 while traveling through Europe hunting down avocado trees, called his dream "the exuberance of youth," adding, "I hope I can be forgiven for that."[34]

Growth was not what kept Hank—and just about every other grower in California—lying awake at night. That dubious honor went to the looming threat of avocado diseases. "Our number one problem is still our old nemesis, root rot," society president George Bowker announced. He hoped Zentmyer could solve it.[35] If Hank wondered at first what this "almost boyish looking" professor could teach a roomful of farmers, he quickly saw that the young plant pathologist was up to the task.[36] The University of California was taking root rot seriously, undertaking an almost mind-boggling range of experiments to identify, treat, and study its ways. Zentmyer seemed willing to go anywhere, meet anyone, and try anything that might lead to a cure.

In a two-year study that concluded in 1959, Zentmyer and colleagues gathered 2,425 avocado seeds from ten varieties and immersed them in hot water, eager to see what temperature would kill the fungus without harming the seed's ability to germinate.

After soaking the seeds and then planting them in fields and greenhouses, they reported to the avocado society members that 120-degree-Fahrenheit water for thirty minutes would do the trick.[37] Zentmyer studied fungicides and soil fumigants, injecting some into soil, spraying some under tarps, adding others to water, and watching what happened. Funded by grants from CAS, he ventured through Central America, the Caribbean islands, and South America, looking for promising examples of wild avocados that might be resistant to *Phytophthora cinnamomi*. He consulted Wilson Popenoe (by then director emeritus of the Escuela Agrícola Panamericana in Honduras), and the more he learned about the fungus, the more he was certain that Popenoe was right: if wild varieties resistant to the fungus could be grown in California, they could potentially serve as rootstocks for Hass and other varieties favored by California farmers. The fruit of the wild avocado wasn't his focus; its roots, however, could save the industry.[38]

Hank was impressed by the rich abundance of avocado trees Zentmyer encountered on his travels: anise-scented trees in the hills above the Lancetilla Valley in Honduras; native avocados growing at 9,000 feet in the mountains of Guatemala; trees with small fruit in Veracruz, Mexico; budwood samples shared by Henri Gilly.[39] On one of Zentmyer's journeys, in the company of Professor Efraim Hernandez and botany students from the Escuela Nacional de Agricultura in Chapingo, he collected 1,400 seeds and budwood from eight trees, some of which would show promising resistance to root rot in field tests back in Irvine. In a market in Acayucan, Mexico, he discovered an array of unusual avocados, some tube shaped, some with grainy white flesh, others just two inches long. In Chiapas, he noted avocados that were "huge, weighing 2 pounds or more." He collected budwood from a tree at a remote village twenty miles from the town of Jesús Carranza, accessed "by dugout canoe down the Rio Jaltapec and a hike by trail and, with the aid of machetes, through the dense forest." Zentmyer was especially thrilled by discoveries of wild

avocado trees growing amid oaks, pines, and native shrubs in the
mountains near Montemorelos, which he found with the help of
E. E. Calles, a scientist from the Mexican agricultural secretary's
office, and José Ramirez of the USDA. He surmised that the fruit,
known locally as "aguacatillo," less than an inch and a half in
length and "with very little flesh," was likely an ancestor of the
common avocado.

While the plethora of avocado varieties in Latin America presented exciting opportunities, back in the United States, avocado
diversity was causing costly headaches. In the early 1960s, Florida growers, who were cultivating a range of green-skinned West
Indian and Guatemalan varieties, sought to import their harvest
into California. The two states, however, had different maturity
standards that governed when avocados could go to market. In
California, where most farmers grew oil-rich varieties like the
Hass, the state department of agriculture set a minimum thresh-
old of 8 percent oil, while Florida growers, whose fruits were less
oily, followed a federal rule based on fruit size and weight. The
dispute went all the way to Supreme Court. The Floridians alleged
that the Californians were disrupting interstate trade, and in a
season filled with landmark civil rights cases, the nation's highest
court heard two avocado cases that hinged on two ripeness laws,
one state and one federal. In a 5–4 decision penned by William J.
Brennan Jr., the court ruled in 1963 that a district court in California had jurisdiction to decide.[40] The Californians lost the case.

In 1968, Hank took a seat on the CAS's board. It was a heady
time for the industry and a fractious one. Despite the efforts of
the new marketing board, as acreage and production grew, consumer demand (and price) didn't always follow. Hank watched the
old systems begin to fracture. Calavo was doing its best to market avocados to Americans, even sending enough "flash-frozen"

avocados to serve 5,000 people at President Lyndon Johnson's inaugural luncheon in January 1965, but growers were looking for better prices.[41] Some turned their backs on Calavo, hoping to join smaller avocado cooperatives like Hank's uncle Harold's in Whittier or sell their fruit through new for-profit packinghouses including Green Goddess, King Salad Avocado, Henry Avocado, Foster Avocado, and Del Rey Avocado Co., a number of which had formed new private associations to handle marketing.[42] Many growers joined together to form CADO, the California Avocado Development Organization, which compiled crop estimates and other data to improve maturity standards and marketing efforts. The Independent Avocado Packers Association published advertisements in Southern California newspapers in 1970 urging growers to "withdraw from Calavo now. Go with the people who perform instead of talk."[43] The CAS focused more of its attention on marketing, bringing in experts and members of the California Avocado Advisory Board to demonstrate how the board's annual assessments funded marketing studies and promoted California's avocados nationwide.[44]

Hank had more than marketing on his mind. He agreed with Zentmyer that *Phytophthora cinnamomi*–resistant avocado rootstock had tremendous potential, but no one had yet figured out how to replicate it on a commercial scale. Topworking scions onto rooted trees produced new fruit; how, Hank wondered, do you create new roots? The old methods were laborious and time consuming. Commercial growers needed an efficient, reliable alternative, and they needed it fast. Hank read widely, thought like a scientist, and was open to trying new techniques, but he felt like he was working in the dark.

Darkness turned out to be the answer. By the early 1970s, a technician in the department of agricultural science at UCLA, Edward F. Frolich, and a subtropical horticulturalist in the agricultural extension at UC Riverside, Robert G. Platt, had taken an interest in Zentmyer's research. Using cuttings from several hundred of Zentmyer's specimens, they tried a technique known as etiolation, or more simply, "producing tissue in the dark."[45] They started with large avocado seeds—nurse seeds, often from Lulas or Zutanos—and planted them in quart-sized cans. Once a good-sized shoot grew, budwood from one of Zentmyer's varieties, prized for its fungus-resistant roots, was grafted to it. When the graft began to bud, they moved the can into a pleasantly warm, dark room, essentially tricking the plant into thinking it was underground. There, the shoot grew rapidly, looking for light, and unable to produce chlorophyll without sunlight, the shoot grew long and white. Returning it to daylight, they covered the shoot with peat moss or sand and wrapped it in a "tarpaper collar," leaving only the tip exposed. The covered shoot began to bear roots, while the tip exposed to light bore leaves, and a clone was born. Frolich and Platt soon figured out how to graft a scion (from a fruiting variety) onto the cloned rootstock, but the resulting trees were often flimsy and unproductive. Although not a complete success, the breakthrough showed it was possible to create a fully cloned avocado tree, roots and all.

Hank studied the etiolation report carefully. The process seemed too cumbersome to produce cloned avocado rootstock at any scale, but it was a major step forward in understanding how to protect California's orchards against a deadly enemy. Hank appreciated a challenge, and the innovation fueled his passion for the industry. Every time he drove through Southern California, he could see the orchards expanding. Many of those farmers were his customers. The California avocado craze was booming. The state had more than 21,000 acres of avocados, and new plantings in San Diego County and Ventura County created demand for thousands of new trees.[46] A recent report by UC Riverside had also cast this rising star in a new light. Strangely enough, according to horticulturalist William B. Storey, the avocado was a berry! The thin covering around the pit, a soft film known as the endocarp, in combination with its pulpy flesh and outer rind, all added up to place the avocado in the same category as botanical berries like the banana or the cranberry.[47]

Botany aside, Hank had something else to celebrate. In 1973, Hass surpassed Fuerte as the California industry's favorite avocado. Hass orchards now covered 11,000 acres compared to the Fuerte's 10,224, and farmers were planting new Hass trees at a record pace.[48] Uncle Harold, it turned out, had been right all along.

On a cloudy Saturday morning in late September 1973, Hank had an appointment on West Road in La Habra Heights. There, by an old house near the edge of the windy road, a bronze plaque had been set in concrete at the base of an avocado tree. The tree, now fifty years old, nearly two feet thick, and soaring forty feet into the sky, was the original Hass, the mother tree, still producing delicious avocados. Now the president of the avocado society, Hank knew a plaque at the discovery site—the term anthropologists use to describe the location of significant artifacts—would let future generations know that something extraordinary had emerged from this ground. It felt like an American story: a "lucky chance seedling," a mistake, underestimated and against all odds, had emerged victorious. An American flag fluttered in the breeze beside the tree, surrounded by members of the CAS and local historical societies. As Hank read the dedication, two people standing beside him leaned down together to unveil the plaque: to his left, Elizabeth Hass, Rudolph Hass's widow, and to his right, brimming with pride, Harold Hazzard Brokaw, Hass's biggest champion.

Calf's Liver with Avocado

(An adaptation of recipe from The Four
Seasons Restaurant)

1 small, firm but ripe avocado
Juice of half a lemon plus 2 tsp. lemon
    juice
6 tbsp. flour
Salt to taste
6 slices calf's liver, about 1 3/4 lb.
10 tbsp. butter
3 tbsp. chopped chives or shallots
3 tbsp. grated parmesan cheese

Quarter the avocado. Discard the pit and
skin. Cut the flesh lengthwise into eight
wedges. Put them in a bowl and add about
two teaspoons lemon juice to prevent
discoloration. Dredge the avocado wedges
in flour and sprinkle with salt. Sprinkle
the liver slices with salt and dredge in
flour. Heat two tablespoons butter in a
large skillet and add the liver slices.
Brown about 30 seconds or longer to a side.
Heat two tablespoons butter in another
skillet and add the avocado slices. Cook,
tossing and stirring, about two minutes.
Remove the liver to a serving dish. To the
skillet add the remaining six tablespoons
butter and add the avocado slices. Add the
chives or shallots, parmesan cheese and
remaining lemon juice. Pour this over the
liver and serve. Yield: 4 to 6 servings.

--Craig Claiborne, 1979

12 • The Battle

WITH GUATEMALA CITY RECEDING BEHIND THEM, George Zentmyer and Eugenio Schieber, one of Guatemala's foremost experts on plant diseases, headed into the countryside. The February 1981 sojourn was the latest in Zentmyer's thirty-year quest to find wild avocados resistant to *Phytophthora cinnamomi*. Californian avocado farmers were not the only ones depending on him. The fungus had devastated orchards in South Africa, too, and on a recent trip there, he concluded that the region's heavy summer rains and high-temperature, low-calcium soils all conspired to help the fungus thrive.[2] The Guatemala excursion included Schieber's assistant Martín Cumes Sajvin, nicknamed Martín Grande to distinguish him from his colleague, the small-statured Martín Cumes Morales. Both Martíns were experienced Mayan guides from Santa Catarina Palopó, a village overlooking scenic Lake Atitlán, and for the past seven years, Cumes Sajvin had been indispensable to Zentmyer's aguacateandos, his term for the professor's wild avocado hunts.[3] Together they traveled east toward Esquipulas, a city where Christian pilgrims converged to see *El Cristo Negro*, an image of the crucified Jesus carved from gleaming black wood and housed in a sixteenth-century shrine.[4] The pilgrims believed the Black Christ answered prayers. A few miles before the shrine, Zentmyer's group left the paved road and turned onto an abandoned gravel one lined with cacti, a "desolate region," Zentmyer noted later, in sharp contrast to the green western highlands they had left behind.

The avocado hunters were not looking for miracles. Zentmyer was a scientist fighting a battle, and his wanderings through the remote regions of Central America were part of a long war against the devastation caused by *Phytophthora cinnamomi*.[5] Zentmyer had discovered how its spores swam through water to attack fragile avocado roots, how temperature and drainage influenced the spores' movement, and how organic material like alfalfa meal slowed them down. The work helped farmers limit the fungus with careful irrigation techniques and orchard management, and it would lead to his election to the prestigious National Academy of Sciences in 1979.[6]

His expeditions, funded in part by the California Avocado Society, were not without danger. There were poisonous snakes, torrential rainstorms, treacherous drives on curving mountain roads, and occasionally, as on the evening they passed *El Cristo Negro*, drunken men wielding guns in the night. On a journey through the La Lucha cloud forests of Guatemala in 1977, Cumes Sajvin led him to the elusive *Persea steyermarkii* and learned a few days later that the army had found a guerrilla camp less than a mile away.[7]

This was a world few California avocado growers had seen, and Zentmyer included photos of remote village marketplaces, towering trees, and dramatic mountain vistas in his communiqués back home. With an anthropologist's eye, he shared Indigenous words for various kinds of wild avocados, local foods and recipes, medicinal uses for Persea seeds and pulp, and Indigenous methods for using wild-avocado hardwood to make houses and dugout canoes. He bemoaned the logging companies that were clear-cutting Latin American forests and related numerous sightings of the elusive quetzal, a solitary, sacred mountain bird with iridescent blue-green feathers, a flaming red breast, long delicate tail feathers, and white wing tips that spread like fingers in flight. Zentmyer and Schieber spotted the extraordinary

Fred Popenoe at West India Gardens,
Altadena, Calif. *(From Wilson Popenoe,*
Manual of Tropical Fruits, *1920)*

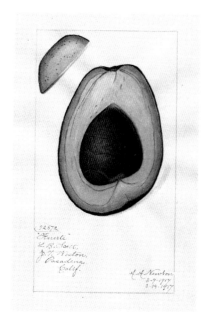

"Fuerte," Amanda Amira Newton, 1917.
USDA Pomological Watercolor Collection.
(Courtesy of National Agricultural Library,
Agricultural Research Service,
U.S. Department of the Interior)

California avocados are loaded onto an airplane headed for
East Coast markets, 1927. *(Courtesy of Calavo Growers)*

CALAVO
THE ARISTOCRAT OF SALAD FRUITS

ABOVE: Aztec pictograph of the avocado tree. *(From Wilson Popenoe,* Manual of Tropical Fruits, *1920)*

LEFT: Advertisement for Calavo California avocados, 1930. *(Courtesy of Calavo Growers)*

Avocado show, Whittier, 1933. *(Courtesy of Eyre Powell Chamber of Commerce Photo Collection, Los Angeles Public Library)*

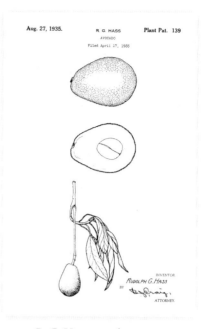

Calavo advertisement from the California Avocado Association 1928 yearbook. *(Courtesy of California Avocado Society)*

R. G. Hass avocado patent, filed April 17, 1935. *(Courtesy of United States Patent and Trademark Office)*

Judge F. D. Halm (*left*) and Puebla governor Maximino Camacho (*right*) unveiling the bronze tablet at the parent Fuerte tree in Atlixco, Mexico, April 17, 1938. California Avocado Association Yearbook, 1938. *(From the collection of the Lenhardt Library of the Chicago Botanic Garden)*

Wilson Popenoe at Casa Popenoe, Antigua, Guatemala, n.d. Wilson's children, Marion Popenoe de Hatch and Hugh Popenoe, donated Casa Popenoe to Universidad Francisco Marroquín in 2007. The university manages the property and offers guided tours of the house museum. California Avocado Society Yearbook, 1942. *(From the collection of the Lenhardt Library of the Chicago Botanic Garden)*

LEFT TO RIGHT: Carl Crawford, J. R. Padgett, W. C. Cooper, R. H. Cintron, Adolfo Rodiles, Wilson Popenoe, J. Eliot Coit, Knowles Ryerson, and C. A. Schroeder at Hacienda Xahuentla, August 1948. California Avocado Society Yearbook, 1948. *(From the collection of the Lenhardt Library of the Chicago Botanic Garden)*

Calavo debuts patented frozen avocado pulp in 1965, making guacamole available year-round to U.S. customers. *(Courtesy of Calavo Growers)*

Harold Hazzard Brokaw, Hank Brokaw, and Elizabeth Hass with the Hass mother tree, La Habra Heights, Calif., September 1973. California Avocado Society Yearbook, 1973–74. *(Courtesy of Brokaw Nursery)*

University of California plant pathologist George A. Zentmyer *(right)* searching for wild avocados in Guatemala with a local guide. California Avocado Society Yearbook, 1979. *(Courtesy of California Avocado Society)*

UC Riverside professor Bob Bergh poses in a Southern California orchard with his wife Gwen, namesake of his "Gwen" avocado variety, patented by the University of California in 1984. *(Courtesy of University of California, Riverside)*

Representatives of Mexican trucking company Frio-Express and Barrenechea Customs Brokers in Morelia, Michoacán, on November 5, 1997, two days before Mexican avocados could be exported to nineteen U.S. states. The date on the photo is incorrect. *(Courtesy of Ramón Paz-Vega)*

Ramón Paz-Vega, former chairman of the board of directors of Avocados From Mexico, at the brand's tenth anniversary celebration in Dallas, October 2023. *(Courtesy of Ramón Paz-Vega)*

University of California professor Mary Lu Arpaia, coinventor of the Luna UCR avocado, with a Luna tree at the South Coast Research and Extension Center, Irvine, Calif. *(Stan Lim, courtesy of the University of California, Riverside)*

ABOVE: Botanist Raquel Folgado examines an early-twentieth-century avocado tree, a remnant of one of the first avocado orchards in California, at the Huntington Library, San Marino, Calif., 2023. *(Courtesy of The Huntington Library, Art Museum, and Botanical Gardens)*

TE ESPERAMOS

VEN Y CONOCE SOBRE EL AGUACATE FUERTE

HISTORIA - TALLERES - DEGUSTACIONES

Día municipal del

AGUACATE FUERTE

MARTES 20 AGOSTO 12:00PM

CONFIRMA TU ASISTENCIA AL
2441214873

CASA DEL AGUACATE O CASA DE LA CIENCIA
3 PONIENTE 1102

LEFT: A poster from the 2024 Municipal Fuerte Avocado Day, an annual celebration in Atlixco, Puebla, established by local leaders in 2021. *(Courtesy of Beatríz Zafr*

birds in Guatemalan cloud forests of northern Quiché, in the Cordillera Diriense range of Nicaragua, in the soaring Esesmiles mountains of El Salvador, and in Cerro Punta in the rugged Panamanian highlands, noting that they ate small, smooth-skinned *Persea donnell-smithii* and tiny purplish-black avocado relatives with flat sides, thin shiny skin, and bright-green flesh that Indigenous Nicaraguans call *guaslipe*.[8]

Zentmyer carefully chronicled the types of wild avocados they found, where they found them, and how they looked, smelled, and tasted. In La Antigua near the Gulf of Mexico, in the courtyard of an ancient fortresslike house built for Spanish conquistador Hernán Cortés, Mexican agriculture professors introduced Zentmyer's team to eight unique varieties of avocados, including one with fruit seven inches long, a buttery consistency, and "excellent flavor."[9] In the Miramundo region of Jalapa, Guatemala, "an unknown Persea was found . . . about 18 to 25 feet in height, with smooth leaves, with a bluish color underneath," a purple trunk and small fruit "round to pear shape, with color ranging from yellow-green to yellow and occasionally reddish." In the northern Quiché region, he collected "xun-oj . . . a tree with leaves having a bluish color underneath and very dark green above, with a strong anise odor" and tiny purple fruit less than two inches long.[10]

As their truck bumped along the rural roads of Guatemala in 1981, Zentmyer hoped to add more specimens to his collection. Zentmyer's lab at Riverside attracted a steady stream of graduate students and scholars from six continents. Like Zentmyer, Eugenio Schieber had built a career around plant diseases. Born in 1912 on a Guatemalan coffee farm to German parents, he had studied in the United States before returning home to serve as director of plant pathology at the Instituto Agropecuario Nacional, Guatemala's agricultural experiment station.[11] His Mayan assistant, Martín Grande, had a keen eye for interesting trees and promising fruit. In a village market in the central highlands in 1975, Martín noticed long-necked coyous, avocado-like fruit with chocolate-brown flesh and long, pointed seeds, and brought them to Schieber to ship to Zentmyer at UC Riverside. Several of the specimens sprouted healthy seedlings in the university greenhouse, with one labeled G755C showing special promise. It resisted *Phytophthora cinnamomi* well and accepted grafts from both Hass and Fuerte scions. Transplants on farms in Carpinteria, Camarillo, and Fallbrook were looking strikingly vigorous.[12] Zentmyer was watching G755C closely.

After spending the night about twenty miles from the El Salvador border, the avocado hunters climbed back in the truck and set out for the village of Quetzaltepeque, where they heard interesting trees grew on the slopes of a nearby volcano. Although disappointed to see that loggers had cleared much of the forest, they found several useful varieties, including a large and vigorous specimen of the tree *Persea schiedeana*, an ancestor of the commercial avocado; aguacate de mico, an avocado-like tree similar to *Persea tolimanensis*; and the elusive *Persea drymifolia*, a sweet avocado with tender, edible skin. Zentmyer collected bags of budwood and seeds to ship to Riverside. A few months later, he received tragic news from Guatemala City: Schieber's assistant, Martín Cumes Sajvin, had been kidnapped, most likely by federal police. In the early 1980s, 200,000 Mayan Guatemalans disappeared during a brutal police campaign to silence leftist rebels.[13] Schieber found his body three days later.[14] Zentmyer's report to the California Avocado Society that year included a dedication to his exceptional guide Martín Grande and a photo of him dressed in a cowboy-style shirt and felt fedora.[15] "We owe him so much," Schieber wrote. One day, they hoped to find a lasting way to honor him.

From his home outside Mexico City, Salvador Sánchez Colín read Zentmyer's reports with interest. Sánchez Colín—federal agriculture official, state governor, college president, author, and publisher, a man with so many titles it had grown cumbersome to list them all—was not surprised that American scientists were seeking the avocado's salvation in the soil of Latin America. His passion for agriculture was rooted in this same ground. But Zentmyer focused on bringing budwood and seeds back to California, in part because U.S. agriculture officials banned imports of Mexican avocados. Sánchez Colín knew they underestimated Mexican farmers. Mexico had rich soil, ample rainfall, millions of acres of land to cultivate, tens of thousands of rural farmers, and government officials devoted to their success. Mexico also had the avocado. Growing wild on mountainsides, in orchards, and in dooryards of homes across the nation, the avocado was a prized natural resource that should be a source of national pride. If Sánchez Colín's vision proved true, one day everyone would know that avocados are from Mexico.

Born into poverty in 1912, Sánchez Colín came of age during an agricultural revolution in Mexico and became a soldier for the cause.[16] He was accepted to the Escuela Nacional de Agricultura in 1928. Housed on the grounds of a grand former hacienda in Chapingo, the public university's motto was "Enseñar la explotación de la tierra, no la del hombre": "To teach the exploitation of the land, not the exploitation of man." A few years before Sánchez Colín enrolled, government officials hired a rising artist named Diego Rivera to paint elaborate frescoes inside the hacienda's former Jesuit chapel. Rivera's vibrantly colored paintings celebrated socialist politics and the vigor and ingenuity of the Mexican farmer, and they contained monumental nude earth mothers, heroic peasant farmers, and cornfields rising from the graves of revolutionaries.[17] During lectures inside La Capilla Riveriana, Rivera's chapel, Sánchez Colín and his classmates stared skyward in awe, craning their necks to see each detail. Some called it "the Sistine Chapel of the twentieth century."[18]

Sánchez Colín entered government service, and in 1944, the year Zentmyer joined the faculty at UC Riverside, Mexico's agricultural ministry sent the thirty-one-year-old to study the citrus industry in the United States. For four months he toured orchards in Florida, Texas, and California, pledging to return with new tools and practices to share with Mexican farmers.[19] With war raging in Europe and in the Pacific, Sánchez Colín's mission was part of larger international collaboration between the United States and Mexico. A committee to further the cause was established at the USDA in Washington, D.C., with Knowles Ryerson, Wilson Popenoe's old high school friend and now a dean at the University of California, Davis, serving as chairman. The committee, which included Nelson A. Rockefeller and a range of university and federal officials, sought to advocate for instruction of Spanish language and Latin American history in American public schools, expand and improve educational exchange programs for Latin American scholars and graduate students, and establish agricultural schools in Central and South America.[20]

In 1942, the United States and Mexico signed a bilateral agreement to send seasonal Mexican laborers to U.S. farms to make up for wartime labor shortages and relieve political pressure in Mexico, where impoverished, out-of-work farmers were agitating against the government.[21] By 1943, Mexico had supplied the United States with almost 1 million tons of lead and copper to help with the war effort, Mexican Americans were serving heroically in the armed forces, and Roosevelt had famously declared Mexican founding fathers Benito Juárez and Miguel Hidalgo "men of the same stamp as Washington and Jefferson." The labor agreement, known as the Bracero Program from the Spanish term for manual labor, was part of Roosevelt's "Good Neighbor policy" with Mexico. As he began his tour through the American Southwest, which had been Mexican land less than a century before, Sánchez Colín was aware the president's message hadn't trickled down to the streets of Texas. Mexican newspapers published accounts of Texas business owners and educators barring their Mexican American neighbors from jobs, schools, public swimming pools, restaurants, and theaters. The situation was so notorious back home that Mexico's foreign minister refused to include Texas in the Bracero Program due to "the number of cases of extreme, intolerable racial discrimination."[22] Sánchez Colín wore a coat and tie as he traveled cautiously through the citrus orchards, managing to win over a newspaper columnist in the border town of McAllen, Texas. The "engaging young emissary from Mexico" had "soaked up enough English to come to the U.S. and intelligently carry on a conversation about an industry as highly technical and specialized as citrus," the columnist remarked, admitting that "not many of us could do as much by Spanish."[23]

Sánchez Colín first met Wilson Popenoe in the summer of 1948, when he led the energetic avocado hunter and an American contingent on a tour of Mexican avocado groves. He appreciated that Popenoe shared his passion for agricultural education, spoke fluent Spanish, and valued both the indigenous avocados that grew wild in the mountains and the hybrid varieties growing in neat rows in Mexican orchards.[24] But later, when he read accounts of the trip in the avocado society's annual yearbook, some of the criticism stung. Coit noted rotting avocados in markets and turned up his nose at fine Mexican guacamole. "There is nothing in Mexico comparable to the avocado industry in California," one of the visitors wrote later in the CAS yearbook. In a report that featured a photo of Sánchez Colín and Coit standing soberly together at the Mexico City airport, Coit noted that some in his party had "expressed concern" that the Mexican avocado industry might one day "expand to a point to give California growers competition in United States markets." Coit's report continued: "Both Wilson Popenoe and Carl Crawford have assured me this is impossible, and I fully agree with them."[25] Sánchez Colín was determined to prove them wrong.

In 1953, five years after the Americans' pilgrimage to Mexico, his vision began to bear fruit. Sánchez Colín rose to be governor of the state of Mexico and planted Mexico's first government-sponsored avocado research station: seventeen acres of Fuerte avocados in a scenic valley seventy-five miles south of Mexico City. An experienced horticulturalist, he planted the orchard not for himself but for his nation. He christened the grove Las Ánimas, the Spanish word for souls, and encouraged Mexican farmers to see the avocado's potential, use modern farming techniques, and build an industry. His research station's avocados were the first in Mexico to be packed in cardboard boxes, not cumbersome wooden crates, and in the Las Ánimas orchard, he started grafting and breeding new cultivars. In addition to doubling down on the Fuerte, Sánchez Colín was confident that Mexicans could breed a better avocado in their own native soil. He envisioned a unique avocado variety that would produce abundantly in his country's various climate zones, and his avocado research station became the center of breeding studies to develop a dwarf avocado tree that could blanket Mexico's hillsides in tight, high-density rows. The most promising was named in his honor, Colín V33, a small, picturesque tree with shiny dark-green leaves and ample fruit that remained green when ripe. Unlike most avocado cultivars, the flowers of the dwarf tree had a lovely scent that was especially attractive to bees. Sánchez Colín believed it had promise as both a fruiting scion and a *Phytophthora*-resistant rootstock, and he sent budwood and seeds to Zentmyer at UC Riverside to add to his collection.

Mexico established its first commercial Hass orchard in 1963, planting more than 18,000 seedlings from budwood acquired from a nursery in California.[26] Six years later, Sánchez Colín opened Mexico's first commercial avocado-oil factory and

established a second grove not far from Las Ánimas.[27] From
Puebla to Chiapas and everywhere in between, growers were
planting seedlings, topworking old trees, and grafting on budwood from promising Mexican and Californian cultivars.[28] The
Californians began to take notice. Don Gustafson, a University
of California extension officer based in San Diego County, took
a contingent to Mexico in 1968 to meet with Mexican growers.
They toured groves north of Guadalajara, paid a visit to three
large haciendas in Puebla, and toured flourishing young Hass
and Fuerte orchards in the new growing area of Uruapan in the
state of Michoacán. Gustafson's group came away convinced that
the region "could be one of the better areas for avocado growing
and developing of an industry."[29] In Atlixco, the Californians
remarked that a grower had developed a black Fuerte hybrid, and
southwest of Mexico City, in Tacámbaro, a group of Mexican
doctors had planted more than 1,300 acres of avocados, setting
aside five acres to test thirty-five varieties that looked promising.
All along the way, the hosts showered them with food, drinks,
and kindness. "The warm hospitality of the Mexicans was evi-
dent everywhere," Gustafson said.[30]

The California Avocado Society invited Sánchez Colín to join
its governing board as a "distinguished Director-At-Large" in
1972. They welcomed him with a full page in the society's annual yearbook, where he was described as a man with a "long and
brilliant history in serving all aspects of agriculture."[31] Sánchez
Colín's résumé was extensive by that time, and in addition to his
passion for avocados, he was known to be the founder of Mexico's
agricultural extension service, which operated test orchards and
trained tens of thousands of rural farmers in modern farming
practices.

By the time Sánchez Colín joined the CAS board of directors in 1972, avocado fever was sweeping Mexico.[32] A ubiquitous
tree that grew in household courtyards across the nation, with

delicious fruit free for the plucking, was steadily producing a valuable commodity. Mexican markets typically received avocados in fifty-pound crates wrapped in heavy paper, each box a jumble of fresh and rotten fruit, different hues, shapes, tastes, and sizes and costing only a few cents each. The Mexican government encouraged struggling farmers to turn their cornfields into avocado groves, and the coffee industry, faced with fluctuating prices and competition, doubled down on the avocado to diversify its crop.[33] By the late 1960s, the government-run Mexican Institute of Coffee had planted nearly a half million avocado seedlings and grafted many of them to select varieties, including Hass and Fuerte. The number of avocados under cultivation had doubled in a generation, to more than 1.5 million trees, and avocado production exceeded 130 million pounds, with the states of Puebla, Veracruz, Chiapas, and Guanajuato leading the way.[34] When the United Nations surveyed global avocado production in 1976, Mexico had 51,434 acres of avocado trees under cultivation, more than any country in the world.[35]

Californians weren't far behind. Bearing avocado acreage reached 44,369 by the 1979–1980 season, and farmers were planting thousands of new trees each year.[36] Many factors fueled this avocado frenzy. Zentmyer's research on *Phytophthora cinnamomi* allowed careful farmers to manage the fungus. The promotions and advertising campaigns by the California Avocado Commission, the state-backed marketing entity funded by growers and handlers, had steadily raised the avocado's profile across the nation. Meanwhile, favorable tax laws lowered taxes on farmland and allowed developers to depreciate expenses quickly, luring large companies like Kaiser Aetna to carve Southern California hillsides into ranchettes with home sites and avocado orchards.[37] Thanks to new plastics technology, farmers were replacing heavy galvanized irrigation pipes with less expensive, lightweight PVC pipe, opening up steep hillsides to avocado plantings for the first time. San Diego County farm adviser Don Gustafson introduced drip irrigation systems to California in 1969 after spending a sabbatical year in Israel and studying their new water-saving technology.[38] And in Ventura County, Hank Brokaw was working on a project at his nursery that would forever change how farmers grow avocados, in California and far beyond.

The avocado seed had to die. The question was how? As Hank knew all too well, cloning avocado rootstock was tricky. A cloned avocado tree was actually three trees in one: a seedling that grew from a seed packed with energy, a grafted rootstock, and a grafted fruiting scion. After getting the seedling started, Brokaw needed to find a tree with rootstock that could resist the cinnamon fungus, perhaps one from Zentmyer's breeding program. Then he would take a pencil-sized stick from an outer branch, making sure it had some nice fat buds on it. After snipping off the top of the little seedling tree and grafting on the Zentmyer budwood, the waiting began. If it took, more budwood could be grafted from an avocado tree with a great fruit like the Hass to create a fruiting scion. Frolich's technique worked, but as long as the grafted rootstock was attached to the avocado seedling, the tree was a sluggish grower. This was in part because the rootstock didn't know its job yet; with that nurse seed still attached, it thought it already had roots. To make the clonal tree root vigorously and grow strong, Hank figured, that avocado seed had to die.

Scientists knew it was possible. At Zentmyer's urging, Frolich at UCLA had built avocado trees with clonal rootstock under controlled conditions. Frolich managed to produce hundreds of cloned trees for Zentmyer's test orchards—but it was slow and unpredictable. Hank credited Zentmyer for urging this work to move forward—he called it one of the plant pathologist's "crowning achievements"—but for a nurseryman, slow and unpredictable wasn't good enough. Brokaw Nursery was a business, and it needed to be quick and reliable to fill its customers' orders for high-quality avocado trees. Hank spent hours in his nursery trying to work this out. He grew seedlings in the dark to accelerate their growth and moved them into the light so they would grow hardy and green. He grafted on budwood and grafted again, wrapping a rubber band around the sticks to hold them tight. Snip, splice, join, wrap. Snip, splice, join, wrap. Over and over, he planted seed after seed after seed in plastic tubes filled with soil, watered them, and waited. Over and over, he grafted budwood onto rootstock and waited again. He tried cutting the seed, scraping off the seedling's bark, surrounding the rootstock in plastic-wrapped soil, turning lights off, moving the pots into the sun. Seeds rotted; leaves withered; the rootstock didn't root; grafts didn't take.

The solution seemed almost too simple: an open metal ring, costing only a few cents at the local hardware store. Careful not to damage the bark, Hank gently squeezed the ring around the base of the rootstock near where it met the seedling shoot. He packed a tube of soil around the rootstock, and as the tree grew, the ring squeezed off the connection to the nurse seed, and little by little, the seed began to die. Cut off from its original energy source, the rootstock took over the job. Thin, white roots began to shoot out of the budwood, water and sap began to flow through its tubelike tissues, and above, the Hass scion soaked in the sun and began to grow. A hardy, double-cloned tree was born. Test plantings proved that the Brokaw trees grew vigorously, and the technique was so simple that it could be replicated on a grand scale. Hank patented the method on March 22, 1977. That year, Brokaw Nursery sold 4,000 Hass, Pinkerton, and Bacon trees on a clonal rootstock named Duke 7. Ironically, the most promising rootstock at the time was not from Zentmyer's travels through the cloud forests of Central America. He found it in an orchard in Northern California. Like the Hass, it was a chance seedling, and although its origins were a bit fuzzy, some said the seed came from the collection of Albert Rideout.

The avocado has many more nutrients,
is more versatile as a food, and,
to most people, tastes better than
olives. Some enlightened, upscale
restaurants have reportedly replaced
high-saturated table butter with
carafes of olive oil. A good idea,
but why not replace it on bread with
a still more nutritious, interesting
and flavorsome treat, avocado!

--B. O. Bergh, Department of
Botany and Plant Sciences,
UC Riverside, 1992[1]

13 · The Breeders

BERTHOLD O. "BOB" BERGH GREW UP ON THE SAS-
katchewan prairie, far from the avocado orchards of California.
But with a doctorate in genetics from the University of California,
Berkeley, he brought a scientific expertise when he stepped in to
lead the avocado-breeding program at the Riverside campus.[2] His
laboratory work extended out into hundreds of acres of orchards,
both at the university's research stations and on private land owned
by farmers who let him borrow a few acres for the sake of scientific
study. Determined to breed fruit that could weather California's
tumultuous climate and satisfy the American consumer, Bergh
began by listening to the farmers, learning of their challenges and
preferences—from the Fuerte's frustrating tendency to underpro-
duce every other year to concerns about water costs, insects, and
root rot. Based on their feedback, and mindful that the university
served the California taxpayers, he set out to build profiles of the
dream avocado and the ideal avocado tree for California. He soon
learned there were plenty of opinions to go around. Even as Hass
edged ahead of Fuerte plantings in the early 1970s, many still
feared it was too black and too bumpy for shoppers to embrace,
and others, despite pressure from packinghouses to standardize,
envisioned California offering a collection of tasty and productive
varieties in all four seasons.

The university system's avocado research began in 1930, led by
Robert Hodgson's studies of varieties and pollination, followed
by geneticist J. W. Lesley's work at the Citrus Experiment Station
in Riverside.[3] Botanist Walter E. Lammerts expanded the efforts

in 1939, when he became the first director of a controlled-breed-ing program centered at the UCLA campus in Westwood.[4] He quickly learned that genetically, at least, avocados behave more like humans than tomatoes.[5] Plant a tomato seed, and it will emerge a carbon copy of its parent; plant an avocado pit, and all bets are off. There's no way of knowing which traits will get passed on and which will lie dormant. Then there was the av-ocado's extraordinary way of discouraging self-pollination: the unusual sex-switching blossoms A. B. Stout had described in his report "Clocking the Avocado" back in 1923. Lammerts knew that avocado trees fell into two types, A and B, and that depend-ing on the time of day and the type of tree, millions of tiny buds switched in concert between female and male, transforming the tree into a feathery spectacle of yellow-green fluff as each blos-som winked open and closed twice before dying. Bees and other pollinators moved among the fluff, and if all went well (and it usually didn't), an avocado began to grow. The blossom-to-fruit ratio was dismally low—1 million flowers would produce fewer than two hundred fruit. Lammerts was determined to improve the odds.[6]

Lammerts tried to control the delicate process; he covered pot-ted trees with fine-mesh nets, brought in beehives to stimulate breeding, and hand-pollinated thousands of the tiny blossoms. Encouraged by Harlan Griswold, he tried repeatedly to cross Fuerte and Hass in hopes of creating an offspring that would ex-hibit the ideal traits of both, spending days on end with his nose in the blossoms. Up close to the flowers, he discovered there's not much to see—or smell, for that matter. The avocado's flowers, each no wider than a paper clip, are nearly odorless. They grow in clusters known as panicles, and even when in full flower, they barely look like flowers at all: the three petals enclosed by three leaflike sepals blend in a monochromatic yellowish green.[7] Lam-merts lasted just two years, from 1943 to 1945, before resigning and leaving the university to focus on breeding roses. A devout Christian, he later established the Creation Research Society, an international organization for scientists who are biblical creationists, but his efforts as a rose breeder made him world famous.[8] In his goodbye speech to the California Avocado Society, he reported on a number of successful efforts at crossbreeding, including two young trees growing from Hass seeds that had been pollinated by a Fuerte. Sixteen more Hass-Fuerte crosses grew in small pots in his greenhouse. He bemoaned the many losses, however, including sixty trees killed by root fungus. "I have never worked with a plant that was quite as cantankerous and difficult to handle from all points of view," he told the society.[9]

Bob Bergh learned from Lammerts's failures. The new South Coast Field Station had twenty-nine acres set aside for avocado research. Here Bergh planted seedlings from Hass, Mayo, Bacon, and Ganter trees that he hoped would cross-pollinate and provide interesting progeny.[10] By 1958, he was working with dozens of varieties of avocados, creating hybrids and studying the effects of interplanting. At a ranch in the Pauma Valley in San Diego County, he noted that Topa Topa trees produced twice as much fruit when a Fuerte was planted nearby. In the same orchard, Hass trees near Fuertes produced almost 60 percent more fruit than Hass trees planted alone. He hoped to gather more evidence and encouraged growers with diverse orchards to offer them for study.[11]

Bergh soon concluded that hand-pollinating the trees was too expensive and a waste of time.[12] Given how difficult it was to breed avocados, and how eager the California industry was for new, superstar varieties, there was no time to waste. Unlike roses or tomatoes, avocados take three to five years to mature into a productive

tree, and the trees' reproductive process is notoriously slow, with
a dismal success rate of less than two-hundredths of 1 percent.
The whole process can be shut down by a cloudy day, a hot wind,
a chill breeze, or even a distracted bee. If there's a citrus tree or a
more colorful, fragrant flower nearby, some bees will abandon the
avocado.

To manage the breeding program, Bergh focused on working with young trees in greenhouses, in "field cages" that isolated
bees and pollinizing insects inside mesh net houses, and in orchards where clear plastic sleeves encased flowering branches and
kept pollen from nearby trees at bay. He also planted thousands
of trees, putting similar varieties side by side and, after learning that bees tend not to roam beyond a hundred-meter radius,
planting a few of his favorites in isolated clusters to encourage
cross-pollination with a neighbor. The latter method he found to
be the most cost-effective and useful for breeding. He occasionally
grafted two varieties on the same rootstock to see if he could get
them to cross-pollinate. The flowers switched from female to male
to keep self-pollination at a minimum, but now and again the
tree's own pollen, carried by an insect or a favorable breeze, would
slip through and fertilize an open stigma.[13]

Bergh's trees eventually produced thousands of avocados. He
kept charts analyzing the quality of them all—taste, appearance,
texture, color, skin type, and stringiness of the pulp. When he
found ones that seemed promising, he'd pop out the seeds, plant
them by the bucketful, and watch what happened, observing the
characteristics passed on from the parent trees, attributes worth
preserving, and trees worthy of being grafted and studied over
time. Many of his hybridizing experiments involved Hass and
Fuerte, but he also planted a range of other varieties.[14]

Bergh's efforts soon outgrew the university system's land—by
1974 there were 4,800 trees at the South Coast Field Station—
so Bergh sought out farmers willing to loan some California real

estate for the sake of science.[15] Such partnerships came with risk. Avocado breeding takes years, and researchers occasionally drove to a test orchard to find a farmer had plowed it under. Once, after a torrential rain, Bergh arrived at a hillside ranch in Camarillo and found a mudslide had destroyed part of a test plot.[16]

Bergh learned a tremendous amount from Stout and Lammerts and built on their work to discover why Hass and Fuerte trees did so well when planted side by side. Hass, an A tree, displayed female flowers just as the male flowers from Fuerte, a B tree, shed their pollen. In warm, sunny weather with plenty of bees and other pollinators present, the trees cooperate, and the rate of pollination goes up markedly. One study of a Fuerte orchard interplanted with A trees showed that the Fuertes produced more than three times the fruit, from 6,000 to 20,000 pounds of avocados per acre.[17]

Wilson Popenoe watched the surge of avocado research with interest. After retiring from the United Fruit Company's agricultural school in Honduras, which offered a free education to promising students throughout Latin America, he relished the opportunity to share his enthusiasm for avocados. An experimental orchard at the school featured forty-five avocado varieties, including one Wilson believed showed great promise. The tree produced a small, tasty avocado with cream-colored flesh and shiny purple skin. He had grafted it with budwood clipped from the Rodiles orchard, christened it Nena, "baby girl" in Spanish, and written to the CAS that while the "California boys" had discounted the potential of thin-skinned Mexican avocados, Nena had the potential to push Fuerte "right off the map." After all, he added, "thirty million Mexicans can't be wrong."[18] Later, during his retirement in Guatemala, Popenoe continued to correspond with growers and researchers, travel widely, and scout out promising avocado varieties from Europe to South America. Scientists and nursery owners on five continents cited his work, published his letters, and exchanged seeds and budwood with him. Zentmyer frequently consulted Popenoe during his long quest for rootstock, writing in his unpublished memoir that Popenoe's insights were invaluable, and the two colleagues enjoyed "a fascinating and profitable relationship."[19] Popenoe died in Antigua, Guatemala, in June 1975 at the age of eighty-three. The California Avocado Society dedicated a page in its annual yearbook to his memory. Acknowledging his "great gifts to humanity," Jack Shepherd noted that his *Manual of Tropical and Subtropical Fruits*, published in 1920, is "still a major reference work in its field" and called Popenoe a "humble, dedicated, and personally delightful great man who walked this earth in the service of mankind," adding, "Goodbye, dear friend."[20]

Meanwhile, Bergh looked to the future, sharing his findings with members of the California Avocado Society and presenting papers on avocado breeding and production at the first international gathering of avocado experts, hosted at the University of Florida in Gainesville.[21] Bergh soon earned a reputation as a keen scientist and generous collaborator, traveling to consult and speak at international conferences from Australia to Japan and Israel, where colleagues affectionally knew him as ha-madan ha-gadol, the "great scientist," or simply, "the avocado man."[22] He also developed an extensive list of qualities of the quintessential avocado. Bergh's "avocado breeding objectives," developed in partnership with CAS members, listed twenty different characteristics for fruit quality, such as long shelf life, "ovate shape," small seeds, attractive color, and pleasing flavor; fifteen shoot quality attributes, including heat and salinity tolerance, regular bearing, and high productivity; and thirteen "rootstock qualities" that allow for easy grafting and encourage the tree's resistance to salinity, drought, and of course, *Phytophthora cinnamomi*. Bergh's research also showed that the Fuerte, the tree that fathered the California avocado industry, was a terrible parent. The Hass, on the other hand, was easier to breed and produced some remarkable offspring.[23] This knowledge came in handy when industry representatives approached him with a challenge: to produce a green-skinned version of the Hass, an avocado sure to win the hearts of American grocery shoppers and create a windfall for the California industry.

More than twenty-five years after arriving at Riverside, Bergh was getting closer to avocado perfection. Together with members of the university's breeding program, including a freethinking surfer named Gray E. Martin, who joined the team as a research assistant after graduating from Cal Poly Pomona, Bergh had produced a collection of new hybrid avocados. Among their successes were the Teague, a hybrid of the Duke and Fuerte, a fall-bearing B-type avocado with small seeds, and a promising rootstock he christened Zentmyer. At the 1982 meeting of the California Avocado Society, Bergh announced that the "University of California's avocado breeding program is reaching pay dirt" and described three new patent applications, saving his favorite for last: the Gwen, named after his wife and high school sweetheart from rural Saskatchewan. Considered a grandchild of the Hass, the fruit was a "nutty"-flavored avocado with pebbly green skin and a pleasing oval shape. Panels of taste tasters said it was delicious. Moreover, the fruit stayed on the tree longer than a Hass, extending the possible harvest window, and was a powerhouse producer. Early indications suggested the Gwen could produce twice as many avocados as a Hass tree in similar conditions. Bergh was thrilled. Not one to boast, however, his triumphant announcement was riddled with qualifiers. Data showed that the Gwen was great but not perfect. He noted that some might find its flavor "too rich," that overmature fruit had a dull appearance, and that the pulp-to-seed ratio was "unusually variable."[24]

Bergh followed up on his announcement with a public information session at the South Coast Field Station. Only two people bothered to show up, and one of them was Hank Bro-kaw.[25] Most California growers had learned they could win consumers over to a black-skinned avocado and were already committed to Hass.[26] But as fond as Hank was of the Hass, he believed it was risky for the industry to depend on a single variety. He also warned growers that it was dangerous to rely on a single rootstock to solve the problem of *Phytophthora cinnamomi.* If the fungus or another disease genetically mutated and adapted to overcome the trees' defenses, "it might wipe out the entire industry." The sweet orange industry learned this painful lesson in the 1930s and '40s, when the tristeza virus mutated and killed millions of trees.[27] Hank was at heart an innovator. His idea to plant avocado seedlings in reusable plastic tubes rather than tar paper ones had become an industry standard. He also designed a special funnel that enabled a nursery worker to fill six tubes with soil mix at the same time.[28] And like his uncle Harold, he kept a lookout for promising new varieties. He was curious to learn more about the Gwen. Perhaps, Hank thought, Bob Bergh was onto something.

The University of California patented the Gwen avocado on October 23, 1984. Four years later, Bergh reported that test plots showed the Gwen to be remarkably productive. One orchard yielded a whopping 63,356 pounds over the 1986 and 1987 seasons, more than seven times the Hass production in the same orchard. To top it off, Gwens averaged a robust 10.2 ounces per fruit, while the average Hass weighed 8.9 ounces. Bergh and Martin also grafted limbs of three B avocado trees—Bacon, Fuerte, and Whitsell—onto Gwen trees in two groves near Fallbrook to see if the pollinators would help Gwen set even more fruit.[29] Enthusiasm for avocados was growing in California, especially in Fallbrook. The community first celebrated the avocado during an annual "Pioneer Days" event in the 1950s and 1960s. In 1987, the Fallbrook Chamber of Commerce organized the state's first avocado festival, which they hoped would draw attention (and plenty of tourists) to the rural community.[30]

When Bergh retired in 1991, leaving behind thousands of seedling trees for his successors to evaluate, the California Avocado Society honored him for establishing a germplasm bank at the South Coast Field Station and for his "arduous work" developing important varieties and furthering the world's knowledge of the avocado. He shared honors that year with Rudolph G. Hass, who, nearly forty years after his death, received an official commendation from CAS for giving the world the Hass avocado.[31] A resolution delivered to his family noted that Hass was not only the principal commercial variety in California but also gaining importance in avocado-growing regions around the world. The resolution, offered "with gratitude and heartfelt appreciation," noted that "Rudolph Hass was taken from our midst before receiving the full honor from the avocado industry that he well deserved." His son, Charles Hass, later reflected that "for coming up with the greatest avocado in the world, my father's royalties totaled 4,800 bucks over the life of the patent." But Rudolph had been proud of his legacy, and he believed a higher power gave him a part in avocado history. "My father always said it was an act of God."[32]

Gray E. Martin continued Bergh's work, turning his attention to a delicious avocado with attractive golden speckles that grew on a compact, productive tree. A daughter of the Gwen, the tree was born in 1985 and the seedling planted on rancher Bob Lamb's land in Camarillo. Late one evening while filling out a patent application, Martin was inspired to christen the new variety GEM, after his own initials. He soon left his job at the university to focus on breeding dragon fruit.

It would be up to Mary Lu Arpaia to watch over the trees and keep the breeding program alive. She would end up doing that and much more.

Arpaia never intended to focus on avocados.

She studied horticulture as an undergraduate at Berkeley and, after a year teaching English with the Peace Corps in Sierra Leone, earned her doctoral degree in botany from UC Davis. Her dissertation analyzed postharvest physiology—everything that happens to a fruit from the moment it's harvested to the moment it arrives on a kitchen counter. Her mentor at Davis, F. Gordon Mitchell, pioneered experiments with forced-air cooling that revolutionized the produce industry, allowing fruits and vegetables to be shipped longer distances and stored at temperatures that slowed ripening and decay. Arpaia focused on the kiwi and transformed how the fruit is stored and shipped around the world. She also coauthored a study that determined when navel oranges are sweet enough to go to market.[33] Her work on avocados involved not only Bob Bergh's domain—test orchards at the South Coast Research and Extension Center in Irvine, at the Riverside citrus station, and on private farms around the state—but also a laboratory at the university's research station in the San Joaquin Valley equipped with a row of walk-in coolers connected to an elaborate control panel regulating temperature, humidity, ethylene, oxygen, and carbon dioxide.

In 1990, her title was extension subtropical horticulturalist, a farm-adviser role, and she was determined that her research would be useful to California farmers as well as consumers. Arpaia learned the intimate details of Bergh's "mother blocks" and other orchards, and she enthusiastically shepherded forward patent applications for promising varieties. Her research that year included a study of the Gwen, and she published studies that focused on nearly every part of the avocado tree. In one rootstock study of Duke 7, a promising rootstock discovered in Northern California, she climbed ladders to measure the size of the tree canopy, collected and cataloged leaves, and hauled crates of fruit back to the laboratory for further analysis.[34] Her postharvest study involved storing avocados at twenty, thirty, or forty degrees Celsius for one, six, twelve, or twenty-four hours, followed by storage at five degrees Celsius for up to six weeks. She also conducted an experiment to hasten ripening by exposing avocados to varying amounts of ethylene gas. When they were cut open, she noted which showed the most decline. In her reports to the avocado society, as well as her conversations with packinghouse executives and farmers in the field, she urged the industry to take postharvest work seriously. Colleagues around the world credited Arpaia with helping ensure that avocados could travel farther, taste better, and last longer than ever before. Her work on how avocados ripen and rot at various temperatures and conditions helped smooth the journey from farm to table and ensured more consumers would bring home undamaged, high-quality avocados.

In 1991, Arpaia joined Hank Brokaw as chair of the second World Avocado Congress, an international meeting of avocado researchers, farmers, and distributors held every four years. The event deepened Arpaia's connection to avocado breeders and researchers worldwide, and she later led Avocado Brainstorming, an international forum for avocado scientists founded by Reuben Hofshi in 1999. Political battles were brewing in the industry, and these collaborative meetings were a welcome respite. Mexico wanted the quarantine lifted, but scientists in Mexico and California continued to work together to share research on avocado pests, tree health, and a range of other important topics.

Arpaia helped inaugurate a global avocado community at a time of proliferating interest. There was almost no limit to avocado-related inquiry. A South African researcher, inspired by a groundbreaking paper coauthored by a biologist and a geoscientist, argued persuasively that the better scientists understood the avocado's evolution, the better they could understand how to cultivate it in the future. The paper suggested that megafauna— massive Pleistocene-era ancestors of horses, rhinos, and elephants that roamed the earth more than 10,000 years ago—swallowed fruits with large pits whole and spread the seeds in their dung.[35] The theory could help explain why avocados are so difficult to propagate yet have endured for so long.[36] The megafauna weren't the only ones shedding light on the avocado's past. During an archaeological dig of Mayan sites near Guatemala City, anthropologist Marion Popenoe de Hatch, Wilson Popenoe's daughter, came upon a clay oven dating to 700 CE. "In the hearth, can you believe it, were little burned avocado seeds which apparently were embers for roasting food," said de Hatch, adding that each seed was about the size of a lime. A subsequent experiment with fresh avocado pits showed that when burned, the avocado's oil-filled seed can smolder all night long. Her father had passed away by then, but she felt as if her discovery honored his memory.[37]

In addition to conducting notable research on the effects of storing avocados at various temperatures prior to shipping, Arpaia hosted tasting panels with members of the public, whose feedback helped her know which avocados had commercial appeal and at what stage of maturity they tasted best. Even the most devoted fan of Hass avocados may prefer the taste of a Fuerte in February or a Reed in October. A dedicated tasting center was built at the University of California research station in Tulare County, a few yards from her postharvest laboratory. Tasting isn't all a matter of opinion. Arpaia collaborated with USDA plant physiologist David M. Obenland on a study to explain what chemical components contribute to the avocado's unique flavor. Using a special device that replicates the olfactory sensors in the human nose, Obenland analyzed the data collected at Arpaia's tasting center and compared it to flavor profiles of other familiar fruits and vegetables. The result surprised him: based on chemical composition and feedback from the tasting lab, avocados taste a lot like mushrooms.

Arpaia also confronted a question that had plagued avocado growers and marketers for decades: When is an avocado ready to harvest? Since the fruit ripens off the tree, the external appearance and texture offer no clues. In 1925, California legislators had passed the Avocado Standardization Bill, which declared that an avocado was mature when its oil content reached 8 percent. The standard was viewed as a compromise that didn't account for the wide range of oil content in different varieties. (One California agriculture inspector remarked that a Fuerte with 8 percent oil content tasted like "low grade laundry soap.")[38] Measuring oil content required time-consuming laboratory tests, and a toxic solvent (Halowax) to get an accurate reading.[39] In 1983, California growers abandoned the oil content measure in favor of a complementary "dry weight" maturity standard. Inspired by a successful effort by the Australian avocado industry, Riverside botanists C. W. Coggins Jr. and Seung-Koo Lee showed that the avocado's water content decreased as the fruit matured.[40] To test dry weight, multiple thin slices of avocado were weighed, microwaved, and weighed again to compare the difference between the avocado's fresh and dry weight.[41]

Arpaia simplified the weighing process through research that led to more accurate readings of fruit maturity. Using Fallbrook grower Reuben Hofshi's "plugging machine," a custom-designed tabletop tool that punched a hole directly through the avocado at its equator, Arpaia helped develop a new technique for testing the dry weight of an avocado. Weighing and heating uniform cores of more than 1,000 avocados, she found the new method saved time, reduced the need for sharp knives, and resulted in more consistent readings of avocado readiness. Based on her recommendation, the State of California adopted the new protocol in September 2002.[42]

The Hass mother tree died that same year.

The tree, the lone remnant of a once-lush orchard, towered six stories above a ranch house on a quiet, two-lane road in the Los Angeles County hills. In less than an hour, chain saws reduced one of the most storied trees in the world to a tangle of dead wood. Logs were piled into a truck and the stump ground to dust. An hour and a half later, the wood was unloaded ninety miles up the coast, at Hank Brokaw's farm. Everyone agreed that it made sense for Hank to take the wood. He had been her caretaker and champion. Ten years before her death, she was still prolific—producing five hundred pounds of fruit in a good year—and when her leaves began to shrivel with the telltale signs of the root rot, he injected her trunk with fungicides (a technique he learned from researchers in South Africa) and cleared the ivy from her roots so the soil would drain. Still, Hank couldn't help but feel like he had failed the tree. "I felt responsible," he said. "People kind of depended on me to care for the tree."[43] Nobody blamed him.

Hank stacked the dead wood on the edge of his nursery, shoulder-high and shrouded beneath a black tarp. He believed the Mother Hass had something more to offer and let interested visitors take wood as souvenirs. People wanted a piece of her, not because her wood was rare or especially beautiful but because of what she gave to the world. Over time, pieces of the tree began showing up in odd places. A slab of her bark is displayed at the former estate of one of the world's richest men. Another collector had a limb encased in glass. At a party in Kansas City, shot glasses of avocado-chocolate pudding topped with butter crumbles were carefully arranged on a branch. Mother Hass gavels were awarded to industry leaders. The California Avocado Society arranged for these souvenirs, some given as gifts, others sold on the society's website: one hundred dollars for a pencil holder, two hundred dollars for a slice of a branch preserved in Lucite, $150 for a slice on a stand. Slices three or four inches wide are sanded down and stamped with the Aztec ahuacatl pictograph, along with the Mother Hass's dates, 1926–2002. The stockpile of limbs is getting smaller. One day, the wood will be gone.

Mexican Guacamole
(*Makes 4 cups*)

3 large, ripe Mexican avocados
3 tomatoes, peeled, seeded and diced
1 medium onion, finely chopped
Juice of 1 large lemon
1/3 cup fresh cilantro, finely chopped
2 green hot chili peppers, seeded and chopped
1/2 teaspoon salt

In a medium bowl, mash one of the avocados.
Chop the other two into 1-inch pieces. Add
the pieces to the mashed avocado. Mix in
the tomatoes, onion, lemon, cilantro, chili
pepper and salt and serve.

California Guacamole
(*Makes 2 cups*)

2 ripe California avocados
3 tablespoons fresh lime juice
1/2 teaspoon salt
2 tablespoons minced fresh cilantro
1/2 cup diced onion
3 tablespoons chopped tomato

Cut the avocados in half and remove the
seeds. Scoop out the pulp and place in a
bowl. Drizzle the pulp with the lime juice.
Mash the pulp until only small chunks
remain. Add the salt, cilantro, onion and
tomato, mix well and serve.

> --Recipes submitted by the Mexico
> and California avocado industries
> for the article "Face Off at the
> Border," *The Washington Post*,
> January 21, 1998[1]

14 • The Avocado Wars

THE NOOSE CAME AS A SHOCK, DANGLING IN BLACK-and-white ink halfway down a page in the March 11, 1996, edition of the *Los Angeles Times*. "Dear Mr. President," the caption warned, the U.S. government "is about to sign the death warrant for a billion-dollar American industry." The California avocado industry's typical promotions featured inventive recipes, a Super Bowl guacamole challenge, and sultry-voiced radio announcers urging, "Make it with an avocado." But this advertisement heralded the beginning of a public xenophobic campaign, with which the California Avocado Commission asserted it was fighting for a fledgling American industry. The ad warned that an influx of pest-infested Mexican avocados threatened to destroy California's orchards.

The commission, a state-backed marketing entity that represented some 6,000 growers, was the successor to the California Avocado Advisory Board, voted in by the growers in 1959. Unlike the California Avocado Society, a nonprofit association run by volunteers with a focus on agricultural education, the commission's mandate was economic. Overseen by the California Department of Food and Agriculture and funded by mandatory assessments, the CAC was run by an elected board of fourteen growers and avocado handlers who settled on the annual assessment rate and how to spend it. Farmers paid up to a few cents on every dollar sold to packinghouses. Over the years, the CAC spent millions to support the avocado market and persuade Americans to love avocados.[2]

Initially, the commission encouraged this love through cook-books, imaginative supermarket displays, nutrition studies, and festive magazine ads. There were commercials featuring sexy models, including actress Angie Dickinson, and cross-promotions with brands like Jose Cuervo tequila and Kraft mayonnaise. Be-hind the scenes, the CAC also served as a fierce advocate for California-grown avocados, keeping an eye on changing laws, trade deals, and competition, both foreign and domestic. To the commission, the noose ad of March 1996 was an act of self-defense against a grave threat. After more than eighty years, USDA officials were inching toward ending the 1914 quarantine of Mexican avocados, arguing that the agriculture officials from the two nations could find a way to control avocado pests and keep U.S. orchards safe.

The commission funded a series of ads in *The Wall Street Journal*, *The Washington Post*, and *The Hill*. "THERE'S A SMOKING GUN," read one showing a revolver with smoke rising from the barrel. In another, the state of California slid into a sewer drain labeled "Mexico" beneath the question, "Dear Mr. President, Are you really willing to risk California?" A third hinted at current political feuds over Mexican immigration: a flashlight shone down into darkness illuminated the letters "USDA," casting ominous shadows on the sand. "Caught in the Spotlight," the caption read. The messages, directed at President Bill Clinton as he campaigned for a second term, accused Mexican and USDA officials of strik-ing a secret deal, ignoring evidence of pest infestation, shutting down public commentary, and failing to investigate a mysterious "foreign agent." For the first time, avocados were at the center of a heated international battle featuring criminal allegations, death threats, and intense emotions. It would not be the last.

The commission's board hoped the inflammatory ads would slow down the USDA's plans and draw the attention of power-ful business leaders beyond the Southern California avocado belt, people who could use their clout in Washington to protect an American industry. "A lot of big businesspeople don't necessarily read the *Fallbrook Times*," a grower recalled later. "But they read the *Wall Street Journal*." Leaders of the Mexican avocado industry read the *Journal*, too. Soon after the ads ran, the controversy boiled over onto the news pages, tempers flared at public hearings, and accusations flew. Journalists christened it the "avocado wars." "*La guerra del aguacate*," read a headline in *La Opinión*, a Spanish-language daily based in Los Angeles. "The tactics are beyond contempt," said Xavier Equihua, a lobbyist for the Mexican avocado industry and a former junior aide to a Texas congressman. California Avocado Commission leaders called him Agent X and accused him of negotiating an unspecified secret deal to drop the quarantine. Equihua fired back, declaring the allegation a "desperate, last-ditch effort to stall the USDA rule-making process."[3] His former boss, U.S. Representative Eligio "Kika" de la Garza of Texas, was firmly behind dropping the quarantine: "If we can send a man to the moon, we can get a bug out of an avocado," he told a reporter for the *Los Angeles Times*.[4]

Whether or not they all supported the commission's tactics, the state's growers bankrolled the effort through their assessments, and most were anxious for their orchards and their futures. Hank Brokaw wondered how Californians could compete with Mexican farmers, who faced fewer government regulations and paid far less for labor and water, and he doubted the USDA staff could keep the avocado pests out of California.[5] The lines in the public avocado war, however, were not as clearly drawn as the newspapers implied. Mexican avocados were already moving through the United States in sealed trucks on their way to Canadian markets, and the USDA had opened Alaska to Mexican avocados in 1993. Michael Browne, the CEO of Index Fresh of California, an avocado distributor that imported Chilean avocados to the United States in the California offseason, urged the CAS membership to consider creating a regional avocado market across the Americas. A year later, in 1994, Browne moderated a panel on the topic at the CAS annual meeting.[6] The California Avocado Commission's xenophobic ads were the public face of the avocado war, but the society's meetings featured a more nuanced picture. They continued to showcase international research, include reports from avocado regions around the globe, and highlight Mexico's vital role in avocado history.

A little over a year later, the Californians appeared to have lost the war. On November 5, 1997, Mexican government officials waved flags and television crews gathered in Plaza Central in Uruapan, Michoacán, as five semitrucks drove out of town with Hass avocados bound for Texas. One truck carried white cardboard boxes from Joaquín Barragán Ortega's San Lorenzo packinghouse, which planned to ship twenty tons of Alejandrina-brand avocados to East Coast markets. By the end of the season, more than 13 million pounds of Mexican-grown avocados made it to American restaurants and grocery stores, and *The Washington Post* food section held a "Dueling Guacamoles" contest, with recipes submitted from the California and Mexican industries.[7] The Mexicans won that battle, too.[8] The festivities on November 5, however, were largely ceremonial: four of the five trucks were empty and had joined the caravan for the photo op on their way to the loading dock.[9] More importantly, the victory was incomplete: the USDA would open only twenty states and Washington, D.C., to Mexican avocados, and only between November and February.[10] Farther south, residents of towns along the U.S.-Mexico border had been able to enjoy Mexican avocados for generations. In 1925, University of California professor Robert Hodgson noted that residents of Brownsville, Texas, would regularly cross the Rio Grande into

Matamoros for avocado sandwiches made with fruit from a local grove.[11] Other shops along the frontera sold avocado pulp that flowed freely across the border for that day's guacamole.[12] Calavo's new guacamole processing plant in Mexicali did the same thing on a grand scale.

Nevertheless, the crowd gathered in Uruapan's Plaza Central on November 5 had much to celebrate. For the first time since 1914, the USDA was permitting tons of Mexican avocados to reach millions of U.S. citizens. Mexican TV stations broadcast the story on the evening news, and a report about the festivities in Michoacán ran the next day in dozens of U.S. newspapers, even in states that wouldn't benefit from the new bounty. *The Desert Sun* of Palm Springs, California, proclaimed, "'Avocado accord' with Mexico brings U.S. more guacamole." And in Waterloo, Iowa, the headline in the Sunday *Courier* read simply: "Welcome back, avocado."[13]

In Chicago, chef Rick Bayless had scrambled for a decade to find a steady, quality avocado supply for the guacamole-loving patrons of his hit restaurant Frontera Grill. He'd fallen in love with the flavor and texture of Mexican avocados while living in Mexico City early in his career. He was so thrilled when the quarantine lifted that he threw a launch party at Frontera Grill for people in the Mexican avocado industry.[14] The chef would still struggle to find enough California fruit to satisfy his customers in the summer, and he looked forward to the day when Mexican avocados would be available year-round.

The California Avocado Commission's advertising strategy had shifted from tostada recipes and bikini models to sewers, guns, and nooses, while the Mexican industry, proudly touting the avocado as its own, was shipping trucks loaded with Hass, a variety born in the foothills of Los Angeles. Few understood the contradictions more keenly than Ramón Paz-Vega, a Michoacán avocado grower who, on November 5, 1997, watched the avocado trucks roll out of Uruapan's Plaza Central, then caught a plane to fly seven hundred miles north to Laredo, Texas, to greet them as they made the historic crossing onto U.S. soil. Paz-Vega knew avocados well. He also knew the war wasn't over.

Paz-Vega liked to tell people he was nearly born beneath an avocado tree. Indeed, his grandfather, Rafael Paz Hernandez, owned a fifteen-acre orchard in Uruapan a short walk from Paz-Vega's childhood home, the trees towering high over coffee bushes that thrived in the avocados' shade. Most of his grandfather's trees were seedlings native to Mexico, criollos with licorice-scented leaves and small, tasty fruit with large seeds and thin skins. Avocados had deep roots in the region. They grew wild in the volcanic soil of the Cordillera Neo-Volcánica, the Trans-Mexican Volcanic Belt mountain range, and had been an important ingredient in local diets for generations. In 1896, Vicenta Torres de Rubio's *Cocina Michoacana*, the first Mexican cookbook to be published by a woman, included elaborate recipes for avocados stuffed with sardines, avocados with walnut salsa, and guacamole made with vinegar, onion, oregano, and fried chiles.[15]

By the time Paz-Vega turned ten in 1970, Mexicans' annual avocado consumption had increased 56 percent in just five years.[16] When he was a teen, his father expanded the family orchard and topworked the old trees to Hass, the variety selling well in Mexico City markets. Paz-Vega left home to study agriculture and agribusiness at the Instituto Tecnológico y de Estudios Superiores de Monterrey, a university about six hundred miles northeast of Uruapan, then returned to help oversee the family orchards, manage packinghouses, market avocados, even establish a credit union to help locals plant new orchards. The state forest commission in Michoacán encouraged the industry's growth, offering young avocado trees free to small growers. "The industry grew a lot in Michoacán," Paz-Vega said. "We began to sell in the domestic market, which was eager for more and more fruit. So, we planted more, and they wanted more."[17] Other, less savory, industries were growing in the region, too. Michoacán's volcanic soil and secluded valleys made it a prime spot for marijuana and opium groves, attracting drug traffickers who wanted easy access to the state's busy seaport.[18]

With plenty of rain and deep, mineral-rich soil, the mountains of Michoacán were a perfect place for avocados to thrive, rivaling other avocado-growing regions like Puebla, Sinaloa, and Jalisco. While Hass gradually became the dominant variety, farther east in the state of Mexico, Salvador Sánchez Colín in 1982 established a research station known as CICTAMEX—the Centro de Investigaciones Científicas y Tecnológicas del Aguacate del Estado de Mexico—charged with developing new hybrid varieties well suited to Mexico's various climate zones and soils. Sánchez Colín planted a germplasm collection—a living library of domestic and imported avocado varieties—and continued the quest for even better varieties. He also planted a new orchard of a promising dwarf variety named in his honor, the Colín V33, a small, productive tree that bore delicious fruit and could be planted in dense rows to maximize the harvest.

He shared his research with Hank Brokaw and University of California plant scientists, who took an interest in the promising variety.[19] Sánchez Colín had faith that indigenous criollos were a valuable resource for Mexican farmers and opened an avocado-oil processing plant that could process a ton of these native avocados per day. The plant shut down in 1973 as criollo avocados became harder to find in sufficient quantities. Mexican consumers had developed a taste for California varieties, and farmers, including Paz-Vega's father, saw they could earn more topworking their trees to Fuerte or Hass.[20]

Uruapan became the center of a bustling avocado business.[21]
A farmer named Leopoldo Vega set up the first mechanized
packinghouse in Michoacán in 1970, and with his son Ricardo
Vega López named their company the Purépecha Group, after
the region's Indigenous people.[22] While continuing to supply his
local customers in Monterrey and Mexico City, Leopoldo Vega
became a pioneering exporter of Mexican avocados. In the early
1970s, with the help of a friend who worked at Mexico's largest
private bank, he shipped two freight containers containing forty
tons of avocados to Rotterdam in the Netherlands. He knew
Europeans had a taste for avocados—the Israelis had been shipping them to Europe since 1962—and Vega's fruit, believed to
be the first official export of Mexican avocados, weathered the
long journey across the Atlantic and fetched a good price at auc-
tion in Rotterdam.

The avocados didn't always arrive unscathed. Most of the
Michoacán packinghouses were rustic buildings without ade-
quate storage facilities. Hand labor slowed the sorting process,
and mismatched packing boxes didn't help matters. The Mexican fruit shipped to France sometimes decayed on the two-week
trip through the Panama Canal and across the Atlantic. In the
early 1980s, a recession sent avocado prices plummeting and unprecedented numbers of Michoacán residents fleeing north to the
United States to look for jobs and decent wages. Some found their
way to the California avocado industry, including a young mother
named Consuelo Mendez, who left her small children with family
and found a job with Brokaw Nursery in Ventura.

Back in Michoacán, the pioneers of the avocado industry knew
they also had to look beyond Mexico to survive. In a watershed
moment in the early 1980s, three industry leaders from Uruapan—
Salvador García, Adolfo Barragán, and Carlos Illsley—traveled
to Israel to study how to modernize their orchards and packing
houses. The three Michoacán entrepreneurs took note of the

cooling systems in the Israeli packinghouses, as well as their electric scales, coordinated harvest times, uniform plastic harvesting bins, and careful statistical analysis of each grove's productivity.[23] Thanks to Salvador Sánchez Colín's connections to agricultural officials and researchers abroad, Leopoldo Vega met Israeli avocado exporters eager to supply even more avocados to their European customers, an eagerness that turned to urgency when record heat waves devastated Israel's avocado harvest.[24] The Michoacán growers stepped in, and by 1985 Mexicans were shipping more than 2.1 million pounds of avocados to Europe and Japan, and commercial avocado groves in Mexico had swelled from less than 10,000 acres to nearly 130,000.[25] The ties between Mexico and Israel caught some by surprise, especially in 1988 when Amiram Nir, an Israeli counterterrorism expert connected to the Iran-Contra arms-for-hostages scandal, was killed in a plane crash in rural Michoacán. News reporters, incredulous that Nir had been in Uruapan to inspect an avocado packinghouse, nicknamed the episode "guacamole-gate."[26]

Meanwhile, the California Avocado Commission kept a watchful eye on Mexico's growing industry. When the USDA briefly permitted California packinghouses to ship Mexican avocados to Japan from ports in California, California industry leaders protested, and the permits were pulled. Ramón Paz-Vega, who acted as a sales manager for Mexican avocado exports to Japan, could see the Californians were passionate about their industry and likely genuinely concerned about the risks posed by competition. Paz-Vega wasn't daunted. By the age of twenty-nine, he had risen to a leadership position in a Michoacán avocado association and traveled the world negotiating contracts. Following in the footsteps of Mexican avocado pioneers like Sánchez Colín, he furthered his education by joining the California Avocado Society. There, he met Warren Currier, an independent-minded California grower who had just joined the society's board. Currier was looking for an

insider to speak to the society about the Mexican avocado industry. Paz-Vega knew cooperation would be good for business. He
seemed like the perfect man to broker peace.

In October 1989, Paz-Vega stood at the front of a conference room
at the DoubleTree Hotel in Ventura, California, facing an audience of fellow members of the California Avocado Society. The
mood was cordial but tense. Mexicans continued to press their
case to open the U.S. market, and Paz-Vega knew the Californians were predicting a disaster. He came prepared. His speech
had seventy-four footnotes, citing sources ranging from his own
academic research in Mexico's avocado-export businesses to a paper on trade protections in the *Harvard Business Review*. The society had a tradition of inviting avocado experts from around the
world (the year before, Salvador Sánchez Colín's address praised
the society's importance to the world avocado community), but
Paz-Vega's speech was different. He'd titled it "Mexican Avocados:
Threat or Opportunity for California?"[27]

Paz-Vega invited the audience to picture the lush mountains of
Michoacán, a region he called "Avocadoland," with tens of thousands of acres of Hass avocados growing across eleven different
climate zones, their roots winding through mineral-rich soil and
soaking up ample rainfall, between forty-three and sixty-seven
inches per year. "Can you imagine what this area looks like?" Paz-
Vega asked, inviting them to picture the 40,000 people employed
by this industry and the nearly 900 million pounds of avocados
produced by Mexico's groves. The avocado was "one of the wonders that Mexico gave to mankind," he noted proudly, and "our
country is the largest producer of avocados on earth, with a crop
in 1988 of 1.5 billion pounds," nearly half of all avocados grown in
the world. Thanks to the popularity of the Hass variety, Mexicans
by 1989 were consuming eighteen pounds of avocados per person

each year, more than double what they ate in 1965. The rest of the world was hungry for avocados too. That year, Europeans would import 89,000 tons, Canadians 5,800 tons, and Asia nearly 3,000 tons, most headed to Japan.[28]

Paz-Vega knew from experience that Californians and Mexicans could work in partnership. He invited his audience to imagine a future where Americans would have access to Hass avocados year-round. California didn't produce enough avocados to meet the untapped demand, and their groves produced Hass avocados only through spring and summer. Chileans, whose groves didn't contain quarantined pests, had already begun selling avocados in the United States in the California offseason. Paz-Vega was frank about the challenges, too. As passionate as the men and women from Uruapan were, they faced obstacles that made it difficult to export their avocados at great scale: few cold rooms to keep fruit from ripening too fast and spoiling, packinghouses lacking modern technology, inexperienced growers who weren't focused on quality control, and many more. "Under the current situation," Paz-Vega told the CAS, "Mexican avocados definitely are not a threat to your industry." Yet no other country was in a better position to supply Americans with avocados, he added, noting that some California packinghouses were already working in Michoacán and urging the Californians and Mexicans to extend their partnerships. "Forget about seed weevils; they will not come." Together, he added, "we both can have a much stronger team. I invite you today to join forces." The room was silent.

Paz-Vega's words would prove prophetic. California-based companies were already exporting avocados overseas, and Calavo was the first to find partners in Mexico to keep the avocados flowing during the California offseason. Mission Produce, founded in Oxnard, California, in 1983 by twenty-nine-year-old Steve Barnard, a Santa Paula native who got his start driving a forklift at a celery plant, turned to Mexico out of necessity. Already supplying Dole's Japanese customers with California avocados in September and October, he and an employee flew to Hong Kong to meet with the head of Dole in Asia. "We want this business year-round," Barnard said. The executive leaned back in his chair, smiled, and said, "All right, on one condition: Don't ever let me run out." "Not a problem," Barnard replied. "We got it." On the elevator ride down, the two Mission executives looked at each other and said, "Holy Toledo! What the hell do we do now?" They found the answer in Mexico. One of Mission's Mexican-born employees helped Barnard make contacts in Uruapan, and in 1985, Mission and its Mexican partner, Socoaac, a Uruapan-based cooperative that was the first to export avocados year-round, began exporting Mexican avocados to Japan.

Despite the concerns of California growers, the lifting of trade barriers powered an unprecedented boom in the industry, fueling the rise of avocados as one of America's favorite fruits. But lifting a plant quarantine is no simple matter; the expensive process involves many years of scientific study, cooperation between governments, new training, and new farming, packing, and shipping practices. The avocado wars put it all under a microscope. Over the next eighteen years, from the time Paz-Vega left the Double-Tree Hotel in Ventura in the fall of 1989, to early 2007, the USDA and Mexican agriculture officials studied Mexico's avocado pests like they'd never been studied before.

Negotiations surrounding NAFTA, the North American Free Trade Agreement, drafted by the United States, Canada, and Mexico, brought the quarantine issue to the table in the early 1990s. Leaders of the Mexican industry were optimistic but wary. They'd had their hopes dashed before. In 1972, the USDA had denied a request from Mexico to drop the quarantine, but the following year, U.S. government entomologists working for

APHIS, the Animal and Plant Health Inspection Service, spent a combined 4,000 hours combing the commercial orchards of Michoacán's mountains, looking for avocado pests. After finding only two fruit flies, the agency began working on a protocol that would open some U.S. states to four varieties of avocados from Michoacán. And just in case a seed weevil snuck past the inspectors, the plan prioritized states with winters cold enough to kill Mexican insects and steered clear of states where avocados were grown—California, Florida, and Hawaii. After seed-weevil adults and larvae were spotted on a return trip to Michoacán in 1976, the USDA expanded its study, joining Mexican officials to test more than 10,000 trees in three Mexican states. Inspectors reported finding no threatening pests.[29]

The efforts to drop the quarantine languished until the early 1990s, when Mexico brought it back to the negotiating table during NAFTA talks. This time, USDA inspectors flew to Mexico City, where a new Mexico-U.S. Phytosanitary Working Group formed to tackle the problem. The California Avocado Commission, facing the prospect of both pests and plummeting prices, kept a close eye on the USDA's work. Agricultural economists at UC Davis reported that the quarantine had served to keep avocado prices high in the United States. Mexico had been selling avocados to Canada for years, trucking their fruit in sealed trucks along USDA-prescribed routes across the continental United States. "As a result of the ban on Mexican avocados in the US, a box of US-grown avocados in the US sells for about $30," a University of California report noted, "while a box of Mexican-grown avocados in Canada sells for about $8."[30]

The first state to open to Mexican avocados was Alaska. The USDA, noting that cold weather and distance made it unlikely avocado weevils would survive the trip, opened Alaska to Mexican avocados in July 1993. The USDA received three hundred letters opposing the idea, mostly from California growers who feared the state known as the last frontier would be the first step along a slippery slope.[31] The Mexicans weren't thrilled, either. ("Alaska?" a Mexican agricultural official huffed. "Nobody buys fresh avocados in Alaska.")[32] By then, avocados were growing across 260,000 acres in seventeen Mexican states, with Michoacán leading the way; its "Avocadoland," including Ramón Paz-Vega's family orchard, covered 225,000 acres, 90 percent of which were Hass trees. "The orchards filled every valley, covered almost every hilltop," California Avocado Society member H. Leonard Francis reported after a reconnaissance trip. He marveled at the beauty of the area, the mountain pine forests, and the generosity of his hosts, which included executives from Mission Produce.[33]

As part of its investigation, the American agricultural inspectors identified 116 avocado pests in Mexico and narrowed in on five they said posed the greatest risk to U.S. avocado groves: three seed weevils, one stem weevil, and a seed moth. Two of the seed weevils flew around orchards at night, feasting on avocados and leaves until the females, ready to lay their eggs, burrowed into immature fruit. The hatched larvae gnawed away at the seed until they reached maturity, at which point they burrowed out of the avocado, headed for the soil, and entered a caterpillar-like pupa state. The more damaging seed weevil entered the pupa stage inside the avocado pit, and the adults that emerged devoured everything in sight: buds, leaves, sprouts, and fruit. The stem weevil wreaked havoc on the tree itself, boring into stems and branches to lay eggs and leading to withered trees vulnerable to bacteria and viruses. The seed moth, which the USDA affirmed was not found in Michoacán, lived among the leaves until attacking the fruit to lay eggs in the seeds and pulp.

Working with Mexican agricultural officials, the USDA came up with a new pest-control protocol to ensure no contaminated avocados crossed into the United States. The comprehensive system that included insect traps, computerized tracking of each avocado back to its home orchard, periodic shaking of tree branches, and visual inspections of millions of avocados failed to win over the California Avocado Commission. At public hearings, in writing, and in the series of inflammatory newspaper advertisements, the CAC worked hard to keep the quarantine in place. At one USDA hearing in Southern California, representatives of a national restaurant chain spoke in favor of Mexican avocados, noting that they'd love to have avocado on their menus year-round. A furious California avocado grower stood up, pulled the chain's loyalty diner card out of his wallet, and ripped it to shreds.

Despite the opposition, on July 15, 1997, Mexico and the United States agreed to allow Mexican avocados to enter nineteen states for part of the year in a region that spread from Washington, D.C., and Virginia north to Maine and west to Wisconsin. A new organization, the Association of Avocado Exporting Producers and Packers of Mexico, known by the acronym APEAM, formed to administer and fund the USDA-required inspection process. That December, growers and lawmakers in Southern California met to christen a section of Interstate 15 between Temecula and Escondido as the Avocado Highway, staking their claim on a twenty-two-mile strip that snaked through Fallbrook and 30,000 acres of avocado groves. At a "sign unveiling and cake-cutting ceremony," avocado commission officials announced that California was still on track to produce 90 percent of the nation's avocados—320 million pounds—and infuse about $1 billion into the state economy.[34]

The following year, Calavo opened a packinghouse in Uruapan, and on November 1, 2001, six weeks after the September 11 terrorist attacks, the USDA lifted the Mexican avocado quarantine in thirteen more states. While the Department of Homeland Security added names to terrorist watchlists, detained suspects, and enforced new screening measures at airports, DHS border agents armed with knives sliced open thousands of avocados and eyeballed them for insects. In June 2003, after four separate risk assessments, the USDA released a ninety-two-page report that recommended lifting the quarantine year-round in all fifty states.

The California Avocado Commission, seeing the writing on the wall, sued the USDA in federal court ahead of the report, frightening Calavo executives, who warned investors that if the commission prevailed, its Michoacán plant would shut down.[35] But the Mexicans, at long last, had won. After six years of monitoring exports from Michoacán, inspectors had cut open and examined more than 10 million avocados, slicing open 8.8 million in orchards, 1.4 million in packinghouses, and 100,000 at border inspections to look for larvae. The safeguards in Michoacán were working, the report said, and the "redundancy of the systems approach mitigations" had convinced the USDA that California orchards would remain safe. Most importantly, it noted, "examination of over ten million fruit has not revealed even one pest."[36]

Despite lawsuits, allegations of new pests, and more heated debate, the avocado wars were ending. Mexico proved victorious. On February 1, 2007, more than 20,000 Michoacán growers—including Paz-Vega and his family—began shipping avocados to all fifty U.S. states.[37]

Not long after Ramón Paz-Vega addressed the California Avocado Society, and just as government officials in the United States and Mexico began to seriously discuss lifting the quarantine, Hank Brokaw drove to La Habra Heights to visit the Hass mother tree. He'd brought his clippers and snipped thin pieces of young budwood. Back at his nursery, he nestled the clippings in dirt and tended them. Using the technique he had perfected and shared with the world, he coaxed roots out of them in a darkened room and brought them into the light to grow. The result was an exact clone of the original tree. In 1991, at the second World Avocado

Congress in California, Hank presented one of the mini Mother Hass clones as a gift to a representative from each country, about twenty in all, neatly packaged in a protective brown cardboard tube to carry home. The avocado wars would drag on for more than a decade, but that act of goodwill would come to represent the spirit of cooperation defining the international avocado community—a timely reminder of common interests as a new threat loomed on the horizon.

State Dinner Herb Green Ceviche

Hawaiian opah fish
Lime juice
Roasted garlic
Roasted green chile
Cilantro
Parsley
Hass avocados
Sesame-cilantro crackers

Finely chop herbs. Combine lime
juice, garlic, chile, cilantro, and
parsley to form a marinade for the
fish. Decorate with small chunks of
avocado before serving.

--Rick Bayless[1]

15 · Cartel

ON MAY 19, 2010, PRESIDENT BARACK OBAMA HOSTED
President Felipe Calderón of Mexico for a state dinner at the
White House.[2] The Obamas invited Rick Bayless, a James Beard
Award–winning chef from Chicago, to fly in and prepare the
meal. Through his cookbooks, three popular restaurants, and
seven seasons of his PBS show, *Mexico: One Plate at a Time*,
Bayless celebrated a flavorful spectrum of regional Mexican cuisine and exposed Mexican cooking techniques and ingredients
to new audiences. "America is enriched by *el sabor de Mexico*,"
Obama said in a predinner toast.[3] Bayless was honored, but he
was disappointed that he couldn't use his favorite avocados, the
Alejandrina-brand Hass grown in Calderón's home state of Michoacán. His ceviche drew special compliments from Mexico's
first lady, Margarita Zavala, but the chunks of avocado on top
were made in America.[4] "Everyone's lobbying to have their food"
included in a state-dinner menu, said Bayless, who put Hawaiian
fish and Oregon beef on the table that evening. "They had to have
California avocados."[5]

Americans, however, were hungry for Mexican avocados. As
the presidents sat down to eat, more than 335,000 tons of avocados were being trucked into the United States annually from Michoacán.[6] In just seven years, USDA-certified acreage had nearly
tripled, from 52,880 acres in 2003, to more than 155,000 acres in
2010, with no signs of slowing.[7] As avocados went north, money
flowed in. Between 1994 and 2007, the value of Mexican avocado
exports surged from $34.5 million to $620.8 million.[8] With the

money came jobs, economic prosperity, and new opportunities for local farmers. Success also drew something more sinister: the attention of Mexican drug cartels. Some used avocados to hide their contraband. In 2003, Chicago police found hundreds of two-kilo bricks of cocaine carefully wrapped and frozen inside buckets of avocado pulp. Police officers smashed more than nine hundred plastic buckets and dug through a river of thawing green mush for six hours to get it all, 312 kilos of high-grade cocaine worth about $39 million. The packets were marked with a stamp of a Mexican drug cartel, most likely from Jalisco, police said. "Holy guacamole—what a drug bust," read the *Chicago Tribune* headline the next day. A police officer remarked, "I don't want any guacamole for a long time."[9] At the White House, Obama mentioned the drug-fueled violence in Mexico and emphasized joint responsibility, vowing to curtail illegal weapons trafficking from the United States.[10]

Much of the notorious crime in Michoacán resulted from feuds between rival gangs, like an incident in September 2006, when twenty masked men walked into the Sol y Sombra, a Uruapan nightclub not far from busy packing plants operated by Mission and Calavo of California. The men fired guns into the air, rolled five freshly severed heads onto the dance floor, and left a note. The killings were "divine justice," it read. "The family . . . doesn't kill innocent people. Only those who deserve to die." Journalists from the United States flew to Uruapan to report on the brutality. Some pointed out that the nightclub's name translates to "sun and shadow," strangely apt in a community that embodied all that is wonderful and all that is bleak about the avocado's native home.[11] "We live in fear," a local said.[12]

"The family" the note referenced was La Familia Michoacana, a gang of drug traffickers. The five severed heads were allegedly retaliation for the rape and murder of an employee of the bar. The episode was one among many in a time when violence seemed to have no limits. In addition to chopping off heads, the Family and its fiercest rival, a quasi-religious gang called Los Caballeros Templarios, the Knights Templar, hung bodies from bridges, dumped them in public squares, ambushed public officials, and shot journalists at their desks in the middle of the day. They kidnapped farmers and demanded ransom. The Knights Templar harbored ambitions beyond drug trafficking; they followed the money and diversified into mining and agriculture. Avocado growers weren't the only ones impacted; mango and lime had run afoul of them as well. According to Ramón Paz-Vega, "these guys would just show up and say, well, now this property is mine, sign here." It didn't matter what people owned—homes, taco restaurants, avocado orchards, a plot of land—the narcos could show up with guns and take it away.[13]

Michoacán political candidates and mayors were detained, gunned down, and held hostage as gangsters competed over territory housing marijuana plantations and methamphetamine labs. In 2006, President Calderón sent thousands of troops and federal police to the region, essentially putting Michoacán under federal government control. The effort helped reduce the impact of the narcos, but it had its own negative effects. "When those organizations are dismantled, you create a lot of unemployed people, and people that are used to making big money without working and who are already willing to kill or to steal," Paz-Vega said.

The drug war in Mexico began long before avocado orchards blanketed the volcanic mountain slopes of Michoacán. Like the avocado wars, it had roots in the early twentieth century. In 1914, the same year that the United States banned avocados from Mexico, the U.S. Congress passed the Harrison Narcotics Tax Act, a law that required all sellers of coca or opium products to register with the government, maintain detailed records, and pay a tax. In a country that had permitted soft drinks like Coca-Cola, home remedies, and cigarettes to legally contain derivatives of opium or cocaine, the effort was aimed at protecting consumers and battling a growing addiction crisis.[14] But just as the prohibition of alcohol in 1919 lured bootleggers into the shadows to control a lucrative underground industry, some argue that the Harrison Act ushered in the new era of illegal drug trafficking. Mexico became fertile ground for opium and marijuana plantations, and traffickers found U.S. customers eager to pay. Later, cocaine, methamphetamines, and fentanyl followed. By 1975, Mexico was supplying about 95 percent of the marijuana consumed in the United States and at least 70 percent of the heroin.[15]

The 1980s were a time of deep recession and high unemployment throughout Mexico. Rural areas were hit especially hard.[16] Free trade agreements like NAFTA, which sent cheap U.S. corn flooding into Mexico, further destabilized Mexican farmers and supercharged a lucrative drug trade. The gangs that flourished in Mexico involved an ever-changing cast of characters and kingpins, with enduring rivalries and family vendettas. Like the million fleeting blossoms of an avocado tree that wink open and close before dying, the ubiquitous criminal groups seemed to be forever changing: they formed new alliances and rebranded with new leaders, a phenomenon known as the "Hydra principle" after the mythological creature that grew two heads to replace every one that was severed.[17] Some labeled their enterprises cartels, although some experts in the evolution of crime in Mexico, noting that the narcotraficantes don't eliminate competitors or control prices, prefer the term "transnational criminal organizations."[18]

Michoacán had a lot to offer the drug trade: secluded valleys in which to hide illegal businesses, a strategic coastal highway, and Puerto Lázaro Cárdenas, a large deepwater port. While most avocado farmers ran small operations and did their best to steer clear of the narcos, a family nicknamed the "avocado kings" allegedly managed at least six avocado farms in the 1980s and early 1990s and opened several packinghouses as a front for illicit marijuana and poppy plantations.[19] When they expanded into the cocaine business and rebranded as the Milenio Cartel, they moved to the neighboring state of Jalisco, where they allied with Joaquín "El Chapo" Guzmán and his powerful Sinaloa Cartel.[20]

Veteran Mexican journalist José Reveles has placed the blame on the Mexican government, arguing it had abandoned farmers and failed to enforce the rule of law. Ten of Mexico's thirty-two states, including Michoacán, were battlegrounds for police and criminal drug gangs. Seventy thousand people had been killed in the violence, and another 10,000 were missing.[21] By granting prosecutors more legal authority and relaxing rules around government spying, Reveles argued that Calderón had helped create an "ominous force" that threatened to transform Mexico into "an intimidating militarized state." Marco Lara Klahr, a Mexican researcher and activist, declared that extortion had become part of everyday life in Mexico, as had mistrust in government authority.[22] Despite Calderón's draconian methods, only a small percentage of criminals were brought to justice.

In Michoacán, the Knights Templar set up an extortion racket so pervasive that some residents began to grimly accept it, including a Uruapan municipal official, who told local researchers, "If it happens to you, it happens to you, and if it happens to others, what can you do? The only thing is to tell them, 'I give you my condolences . . . because I cannot do anything.'" Avocado harvesters, truck drivers, wealthy landowners, high-ranking military officials—everyone had to pay.[23] Even the world's largest steel company was not immune from the violence. In April 2013, a top official of ArcelorMittal, which operated a massive steel plant in Michoacán, was found shot to death a few miles from Puerto Lázaro Cárdenas, allegedly after reporting the Knights Templar to authorities.[24]

Just over a month later, on May 16, 2013, a clear, pleasant night beneath a rising crescent moon, the body of a sixty-year-old man was found a few miles south of Uruapan. News reports said the body, lying in the middle of a road a few yards from his black Ford

Expedition, bore signs of trauma; a broken fragment of a Chevrolet nearby suggested he was run over by a truck. Local officials identified the man as Ezequiel García Uves, the general manager of Empacadora Aguacates Misión de México, the packinghouse operated by Oxnard-based Mission Produce, one of the world's largest avocado distributors.[25] García Uves was well known in the community and a pioneering figure in avocado history. In 1984, he helped make connections that enabled Mission to open for business in Mexico. Two days after his death, a local newspaper published memorial advertisements from his colleagues and friends, some of which called the tragedy an irreparable loss.[26] Many in the avocado business were shaken by his death. Some still speak of it in whispers, wondering what went wrong.

García Uves's death didn't make the U.S. newspapers, but other stories about the region's turmoil began to capture global attention. Following a tip from José Reveles, Jan-Albert Hootsen, a Dutch journalist based in Mexico, traveled to Michoacán for a November 2013 report called "Blood Avocado: The Dark Side of Your Guacamole."[27] Published in a new digital magazine called *Vocativ*, the story featured an image of a Hass avocado smeared with red paint and hanging from a tree. The title wasn't Hootsen's choice. Editors at *Vocativ* were known to pair serious reporting with sensationalist headlines to compete with established edgy news sites like *VICE*. "Blood Avocado" was an allusion to the blood diamonds produced by enslaved Africans. Despite the clickbait headline, the situation in Michoacán bore little resemblance to the diamond trade. Hootsen's story began in the beautiful colonial city of Morelia, a place of "almost Mediterranean charm" in Michoacán's avocado covered hills. Between 2012 and 2013, nearly $1 billion in avocados was exported to the United States from the region's idyllic orchards, leading locals to call the fruit *oro verde*—green gold.

Hootsen described a region under the control of the Knights Templar, a place where the most vulnerable residents sometimes had to flee for their lives. He interviewed a local farmer named Jesus, whose sons had been kidnapped by gangsters extorting him for ransom. "The extortion," Hootsen wrote,

> usually occurs by phone. The narcos call farmers and tell them how much they must pay: 10 cents for every kilogram of avocado they produce, $115 for every hectare of land they own. Those who export the fruit are charged up to $250 per hectare. The Templars collect the money—cash placed in a bag at an agreed upon drop off—once a year, usually in January. The extortion fees are non-negotiable, says one farmer, who asked to remain anonymous for fear of reprisals.

The farmer told Hootsen: "If you lie to them, they'll kill you or one of your family members."

Jesus's sons were kidnapped after he refused to turn over his farm. He sold his house and cars to pay the ransom. "Every link in the avocado production chain is a cash cow for the cartel," Hootsen wrote, from the employment agencies who had to pay the gang members a few dollars per day for each avocado harvester they hired to "those who buy, develop and sell plantations."[28] The cartel employed lawyers and notaries who falsified documents to push people off their land. Federal police and Mexican Army soldiers patrolled the state's highways, attempting to keep a fragile peace.

Hootsen's story drew attention worldwide. It was republished in German, he earned a guest slot on a news show produced by Al Jazeera's U.S. news bureau, and more journalists followed. *The Wall Street Journal* ran a front-page story in January 2014, in advance of that Sunday's Super Bowl parties. "The Violent Gang Wars Behind Your Super Bowl Guacamole," by reporter José de

Córdoba, described heavily armed vigilante teams fending off the drug lords who were seizing orchards, kidnapping, burning down packinghouses, and demanding thousands of dollars in so-called protection fees. A farmer named Alfonso Cevallos said that, two years earlier, "the gang killed three of his brothers, his father and two uncles, driving his family from their land." He had since reclaimed 297 acres of his avocado groves. "'Six people they took away,' Mr. Cevallos said. 'I would return those properties if I could get those lives back.'"[29] Even the pope noticed. On February 16, 2016, Pope Francis visited Morelia, Michoacán, to expose the violence to the world and comfort the brokenhearted left behind.[30] The coverage managed to accomplish what the California Avocado Commission had attempted twenty years earlier through its graphic advertising campaign: paint Mexican avocados as dangerous. Only this time, the danger wasn't seed weevils threatening to kill California's avocado trees, it was violent gangsters wreaking havoc. *Rotten*, a Netflix documentary series, covered this other avocado war. The documentary depicts avocados as a "magnet for money-hungry cartels" and a water-hungry luxury food produced in drought-plagued regions from California to Chile.[31]

The avocado industry and its employees responded to the violence and crime in Mexico in various ways. Some locals moved out of the area. Some who stayed avoided driving at night. Occasionally, the problems hit close to home. In 2023, the U.S. Department of Justice reported that employees of U.S.-based guacamole maker Yucatan Foods L.P. were found to have bribed Mexican officials in Guanajuato while seeking wastewater-management permits. Such actions run afoul of a U.S. law called the Foreign Corrupt Practices Act. Similarly, in early 2024, Calavo Growers noted concerns raised in an internal audit and asked the U.S. Justice Department to investigate a potential FCPA violation related to its operations in Michoacán.[32] Meanwhile, managers of U.S.-owned packing-houses travel in bulletproof cars. Armed guards protect the Mission packinghouse in Uruapan, which now resembles a prison with high walls edged in razor wire. Executives keep their travel schedules private, avoid major airports, and leave quickly. APEAM, the association of Michoacán avocado packers and growers, has responded by beefing up security, supporting local efforts to deter cartels, investing in local schools, building a $12 million office complex to house APEAM and USDA officials, and highlighting the industry's strengths and positive contributions through studies and media campaigns. They've also hosted guided tours through the region for social media influencers, food-industry executives, chefs, and international visitors. In 2017, twenty California growers visited Michoacán on a trip cosponsored by APEAM and the California Avocado Society. A Carpinteria farmer who attended said he felt safe and was impressed by the lush scenery, the hospitality, and the expansive packinghouses that boxed Hass avocados round the clock.

A total of 1,338 people were killed in Michoacán the following year.[33]

In 2019, Mexican papers reported that USDA pest inspectors were accosted while driving through Michoacán. The USDA issued a warning: if any of its employees were threatened again, the flow of avocados would stop.[34]

In September 2020, USDA pest inspector Edgar Flores Santos, a thirty-year-old biologist and a Mexican citizen, drove to the outskirts of Tijuana to inspect for fruit flies and other pests that could impact American agriculture. Like the inspectors watching over the orchards in Michoacán, Edgar, a father of two young children, worked for APHIS, the USDA's Animal and Plant Health Inspection Service. APHIS employed hundreds of people in Mexico, many of them scientists and veterinarians. Trade agreements required Mexico to pay for the inspectors' salaries in exchange for opening the U.S. border to Mexican produce. As part of its recruiting efforts, the agency portrayed its staff as heroic guardians of the American food supply.

On that September day in 2020, Santos was shot nine times. His body was found in a desert east of Tijuana with bullet wounds to the head and torso, not far from his USDA-issued Chevy Silverado with consular license plates. American news outlets covered the Santos story, and the media coverage had an immediate impact. The USDA issued a press release expressing condolences, and the State Department took the unusual step of convening an Accountability Review Board, a high-level investigative committee composed of former diplomats and consultants who look into politically sensitive cases, including crimes against top American officials on foreign soil. Prior to the Santos case, an ARB convened in 2012 after the attack in Benghazi, Libya, that killed a U.S. ambassador and three others—and became a rallying cry for opponents of Hillary Clinton during her failed run for president. Mexican officials arrested two men from local drug gangs, and the ARB's final report concluded that Santos had simply been in the wrong place at the wrong time. Advising APHIS to beef up its security protocols in Mexico, the U.S. State Department closed the case.[35] Perhaps because he was murdered 1,500 miles from Avocadoland, Santos's murder didn't stop any produce from crossing the border.

Then, on the eve of the Super Bowl, in February 2022, the world learned what it takes to stop the avocados. In a period when American football fans typically consume 144 billion Hass avocados, APHIS's top inspector in Michoacán received an anonymous threat on his cell phone. The caller was furious that an inspector had halted a valuable truckload of avocados heading to the United States. This time, USDA officials in Mexico City followed through on their threat and ordered an immediate halt to all avocado exports. The move triggered a media frenzy. As news anchors warned of an American guacamole shortage, avocado prices soared. Ten days later, after Mexican officials promised to improve security, the USDA reopened the border. Once again, truckloads of avocados were moving north to American restaurants and grocery stores. Paz-Vega learned later that an illegal shipment of avocados from Puebla, a state that although famous as the birthplace of the original Fuerte tree was not certified to ship avocados to the United States, had been stopped at a Michoacán packinghouse after an inspector realized that the shipment didn't match his records. News reports from Puebla hinted at a rivalry between avocado growers in the neighboring states. A report from Puebla a few days earlier claimed local growers had been trucking avocados into Michoacán to sell to American football fans. "Súper Bowl 2022. El aguacate de Puebla se usará en el guacamole gringo," read a headline in *El Universal Puebla* above a story describing the practice.[36] In January, another newspaper published a story under the headline, "El origen del aguacate no se encuentra en Michoacán, sino en Puebla, revela estudio"—"The origin of avocados is not found in Michoacán, but in Puebla, study reveals." The study, published two decades earlier, was coauthored by Salvador Sánchez Colín.[37]

To Paz-Vega, the lesson was not about Puebla-Michoacán rivalries, cartels, or Mexican gangs. Rather, he believed the unfortunate incident showed that the system was working: the presence of the USDA in Michoacán deterred criminals. "One single phone call was enough to stop the whole program," he said. "They learned that they cannot mess with the USDA. The whole thing stops. The whole thing. It's not one shipment, one packing house, one orchard. No. The whole program."

At a news conference in late 2022, Mexican president Andrés Manuel López Obrador accused competitors of trying to besmirch the Mexican industry for their own gain. "The avocado is very good, and it is not linked to the drug trafficking industry," he said, challenging a Canadian journalist who had interviewed gangsters in Michoacán. Obrador focused on the farmers, describing them as "successful producers who provide jobs."[38] Two years later, in June 2024, the USDA again halted Michoacán avocado exports after two APHIS inspectors were reportedly assaulted and detained while traveling through the state. Mexican industry leaders argued the shutdown, which sent the wholesale price of Hass avocados soaring as much as 54 percent, cost them more than $3 million a day.[39] "The mother of all monkey wrenches got thrown into the US avocado market last week," the California Avocado Society reported in a member newsletter, "and it's wedged deep in the cogs of the machine."[40] This time, the tension threatened to rekindle the avocado wars. APEAM pushed back, arguing the incident was unrelated to avocado inspections and that it was time for the Mexican industry to take greater control over the inspection process. The California Avocado Commission responded on behalf of California's roughly 3,000 avocado growers, pushing the USDA to "uphold their mission and retain control of the Mexico avocado inspections" to protect California farmers from "the threat of an invasive pest."[41]

The tension and temporary shutdown followed a 2024 study commissioned by the European Green Party, which blasted Mexican officials for failing to address the problems in Michoacán. The report recommended new trade policies that would develop niche markets—similar to those implemented in the cacao, soybean, and coffee industries—and reward best practices.[42] Without new policies, "the unsatiable global demand for avocados threatens the region and its inhabitants," the report concluded.

Despite the problems in Michoacán, industry leaders hoped to avoid a boycott of Mexican avocados. There were 40,000 avocado growers in the state of Michoacán, and 70,000 people working in the industry full-time. And Michoacán is no longer the only source of Mexican avocados for U.S. customers: in 2022, the USDA permitted growers in the neighboring state of Jalisco to export avocados to the United States. Ramón Paz-Vega, now a consultant, warned that if consumers stopped buying avocados, people working in the Mexican avocado industry would head to the United States to look for jobs, fall into poverty, or be ensnared by organized crime. The violence in Avocadoland was fueled by corruption on both sides of the border. "You buy the drugs, and with that money, our guys buy your weapons, and then we kill each other here," he said. Paz-Vega has witnessed the U.S. government's power to monitor and regulate global trade. "I know how difficult it is to ship 40,000 pounds of avocados from an orchard here to Chicago. All the problems of logistics, trucks, borders. It's very complex. How in the world do all the drugs get to the U.S.?"

At the White House in 2010, President Obama told President Calderón that "the promise and the perils of our time are shared."[43] Paz-Vega's take was similar: "It is a problem that is really binational, and we should be working together to solve it." The avocado shouldn't be blamed for these problems, Paz-Vega argued. The avocado is the antidote.[44]

Bar Mezzana's Smoothie Moves
(Avocado Toast Cocktail)

To serve 10-12, blend 1 liter of
Prairie Organic Vodka with two ripe
avocados and strain through a single
layer of cheesecloth. For kale syrup,
pulse 1 cup of destemmed kale into
crumb-sized pieces and combine with
1 cup simple syrup, then strain
through single layer of cheesecloth.
Chill.

Combine in shaker:
2 oz. avocado vodka
3/4 oz. kale syrup
3/4 oz. fresh lime juice

To serve, rim a cocktail glass with
mixture of 1/4 cup salt, 1/4 cup
unseasoned breadcrumbs, 1 Tbsp Maras
chile or Aleppo-style pepper, and
1 tsp cayenne.

--Adapted from *Bon Appétit*,
March 13, 2018[1]

16 · Icon

THREE DAYS BEFORE THE PHILADELPHIA EAGLES AND the New England Patriots faced off in the 2018 Super Bowl, a crowd of football and guacamole fans gathered at El Vez, a trendy restaurant in Philadelphia's Center City. The Avocados From Mexico marketing team had chosen the venue for a memorable pregame event. AFM had more than $52 million to spend on advertising and promotions in 2018, and for the fourth consecutive year was airing a multimillion-dollar television commercial for the big game. The event at El Vez, complete with music and a guacamole bar, was part of a strategy to generate pregame buzz. In a video later posted on YouTube, the camera zooms in on a perfectly ripe Hass avocado with an "Avocados From Mexico" sticker before the screen goes white and fills with a single sentence: "WHAT YOU'RE ABOUT TO SEE IS REAL."

A party host offered a challenge: anyone willing to "look like an avocado for a little while" could win a year's supply of avocados. A few people seemed excited, until they were shown a photo of a woman with dyed green hair, the top of her head shaved as bald as an avocado pit. "Yeah, I don't know about that," one guy says. "How do you expect me to do that?" a woman says. The host tosses in free Super Bowl tickets to sweeten the deal, and the video jumps to a barber taking a razor to the long, voluminous brown curls of two young women, only one of whom knows about the tickets. The stylist gives the crowns of their heads tight buzz cuts, dyes them an avocado-pit brown, keeping long sidelocks that are blow-dried smooth and dyed a vibrant mint green. The camera cuts to the host sitting with the two friends, one of whom seems on the verge of tears. "Because you showed what you would do for your love of Avocados From Mexico," he hands them an envelope with Super Bowl tickets "to make it worth your while." The friends joyfully embrace: "Thank you for being an avocado with me," one says. The screen goes blank, and a question appears: "WHAT WOULD YOU DO FOR AVOCADOS?"[2] Three days later, AFM's Super Bowl ad featured a cameo from the actor Chris Elliott and a crowd of avocado fans clamoring for chips inside a domed paradise called GuacWorld. The commercial led all other big-game advertisers in social media mentions and hashtags, and out of all Super Bowl–related social media posts that day, the most commonly used word wasn't the name of a star quarterback or the championship team. It was *guac*.[3]

In 2024 on the religious holiday of Epiphany, known in Spanish as El Día de Los Reyes Magos, some avocado-marketing associations honored the occasion on Instagram with cartoon Hass avocados playing the role of the biblical three kings, wearing tiny crowns and carrying gifts to the infant Jesus. Later that year, El Rio Grande Latin Market, a Dallas-based grocery store chain, staged a Cinco de Mayo avocado extravaganza for customers at its newest location, a neighborhood previously designated a food desert. Working with Mexican Hass avocado importers from Fresh Del Monte and Stonehill Produce, store produce director Lou Rotell orchestrated the delivery of 301,000 avocados weighing 86,764 pounds to set the Guinness World Record for the largest avocado display in history, breaking a record set in 2019 by a Louisiana market. "Folks wanted their pictures taken in front of it," social media influencers filmed the event, and children stared, mouths agape, Rotell said. "It was a hoot." He later sold the bounty at five for a dollar and gave unsold fruit to a food pantry.[4]

Marketing schemes like these capitalize on two significant demographic shifts. The first was the coming of age of the millennials, a cohort of more than 72 million people—the first generation in the United States to be raised with the avocado as a mainstream product. The second shift was the dynamic growth of the Hispanic/Latino population in the United States, a population that increased by 44 percent between 2000 and 2010, and was on track to surpass 62.1 million by 2020.[5] Few were in a better situation to assess the impact of this dual phenomenon than Emiliano Escobedo.

Born in Mexico City in 1981 to a French mother and a Mexican father, Escobedo is a millennial Latino—part of a cohort that represent close to half of the U.S. Hispanic population.[6] When the first trucks filled with Mexican avocados arrived in California in 2007, he was twenty-six years old and working for the Mexican avocado industry. Mexico shipped a record 237,000 tons of avocados to the United States that year. Soon, the first young adults to purchase iPhones began to notice avocados everywhere, from fast-food franchises and Michelin-star restaurants to rural Walmarts and corner bodegas.

Avocado social media memes swarm the internet; avocado toast pops up on Pinterest boards and Instagram feeds. Before long, avocado beer appears on a London pub menu, and an Australian coffee shop begins selling an avocado latte that goes viral; a Los Angeles craft brewery produces an avocado-infused ale, and an avocado-themed restaurant opens in Brooklyn.[7] Searches for guacamole trend on Google. Oscar-winning actress Meryl Streep is among more than 50,000 people with documented cases of "avocado hand," a bloody casualty of poor avocado-slicing technique, a problem so prevalent it warrants a university study.[8] A mesmerizing stop-motion short film called *Fresh Guacamole*, where the filmmaker uses grenades, dice, green clay, and golf balls as stand-ins for traditional ingredients, is nominated for an Academy Award. Avocados play a starring role on television. In the sitcom *Mr. Mayor,* Ted Danson leads a panicked Los Angeles through an avocado shortage. *The Masked Singer* includes a costumed avocado, and *Ted Lasso* introduces a charismatic soccer star turned avocado farmer, whose parting gift to the team is a Hass-shaped avocado as large as a human baby. *The Great British Baking Show* sparks public outrage when a contestant peels an avocado like a potato and mispronounces *guacamole.* Pop star Miley Cyrus tattoos an avocado on her left arm. Actress Gwyneth Paltrow, whose rising Goop empire fueled millennial interest in health and wellness, includes an avocado-toast recipe in her popular cookbook. *Sesame Street*'s Elmo debuts a dance number called the Guacamole while Chipotle coins the phrase *guac is extra.* In 2017, *VICE* announced that the avocado has slid into a "guacamole of chaos, confusion, and pop culture absurdity."[9]

Escobedo not only watched the chaos unfold, but as part of the APEAM marketing team, he helped make it happen. The story of how America's interest in avocados transcended food to become a stand-in for aspirational living can't be explained by demographics alone. It also defied previous American food obsessions. Unlike McDonald's hamburgers, Coca-Cola, or mom's apple pie, the avocado didn't rely on brands or special recipes. While "amber waves of grain" conjured the American heartland and citrus signified Florida and California sunshine, the avocado's image floated freely, seemingly uprooted from place and time. The moment was simply ripe for the avocado. Escobedo, on behalf of the Mexican avocado industry and armed with a $7.5 million marketing budget, capitalized on the zeitgeist to promote avocados to as many consumers as possible. He got avocado news coverage in *Martha Stewart Living, Good Housekeeping,* and *O, The Oprah Magazine,* scheduled appearances on the Food Network, ran promotions on Facebook and Twitter, launched a breakfast campaign called "good morning avocado," booked celebrity chefs on the *Today* show to demonstrate avocado recipes, and gave away colorful pop-up boxes that expand the avocado's real estate in grocery store produce sections.

Together with APEAM's outside marketing agency, he teamed up with DreamWorks Animation to promote its hit film *Puss in Boots*, a *Shrek* spin-off starring Spanish actor Antonio Banderas. The co-branded ads featured the swashbuckling feline posing beside a glowing half of a Hass avocado towering over a guacamole-filled molcajete, a traditional volcanic stone bowl from Mexico.[10]

Escobedo saw that avocados were more than a pricey item on the menu or in the produce section; avocados *meant something* to people. The image of the Hass avocado carried symbolic weight. It became a stand-in for powerful ideas: joy, healthy living, fleeting pleasure, safe harbor, self-indulgence, quirky individuality, millennial aspirations, the impermanence of life, and for some Mexican American millennials, a sense of pride. When an Australian economist famously claimed that millennials couldn't buy houses because they were spending too much on pricey avocado toast, a flurry of comic memes launched across social media, pillorying his analysis and defending the avocado.[11]

Like all symbols, the image has a dark side. Rotting avocados illustrate articles debunking fad diets, warning of climate change, or mourning millennials' thwarted dreams. Avocados on the half shell ooze bullets alongside reports on cross-border epidemics of drugs, guns, and crime. But whether the coverage was favorable or negative, Escobedo recognized the truly remarkable thing about it: at long last, the avocado was an American icon. Twentieth-century avocado pioneers in Southern California and Michoacán helped build a hunger for avocados, as did Escobedo's mentor, a former Brooklyn homemaker and public relations genius named Anita Fial, legendary for introducing unfamiliar foods like mangoes, avocados, and radishes to American palates. The first person to see the avocado as a true celebrity, however, may have been Ralph M. Pinkerton, a former Fuller Brush salesman from Spokane, Washington.

In 1961, the California Avocado Advisory Board hired Pinkerton to be its first president.[12] A former navy pilot with experience selling mops and Washington apples, he proved to be a dynamic salesman.[13] Pinkerton (also known as Pink) was a snappy dresser and by all accounts charming company. He helped growers and packing companies maximize returns by collecting and sharing data on fruit volumes and price changes, and in 1965 he collaborated with the California Avocado Society to establish the Nutrition Research Advisory Board, the state's first committee dedicated to studying the health benefits of the avocado.[14] Pinkerton squeezed Hass and Fuerte avocados side by side into ads for big-name brands like Kraft Foods, Spice Islands, Jose Cuervo tequila, and Frito-Lay and published an avocado cookbook funded by growers' mandatory assessments.

The forty-eight-page recipe booklet titled *The Avocado Bravo*, named in homage to the Río Bravo, the river that marks Mexico's northern border (and also, perhaps, one of his favorite John Wayne movies), sold for fifty cents in supermarket produce departments. On the cover, Hass and Fuerte avocados overflow in a bowl near a wrought-iron candelabra and a vintage flintlock pistol. Inside, Pinkerton credited Mexico with giving California the avocado, but rebranded it as a European delicacy—"Spain's legacy to California cuisine"—and left Mexico off the map on the inside cover. Recipes included salami and avocado chunks on skewers with mustard dip and "avocado Alaska," a baked dessert featuring two pureed avocados and two quarts of French-vanilla ice cream. Fourteen versions of guacamole, plus five "traditional recipes" from Mexico to be eaten with "corn chips, potato chips or crackers," were made with ingredients ranging from cottage cheese and capers to anchovy paste and hard-boiled eggs.[15]

Pinkerton may have also benefited from the avocado's cachet in art and fashion circles. Around this same time, famed surrealist artist Salvador Dalí published an avocado-toast recipe in his 1973 cookbook, *Les Diners de Gala*. His version of avocado toast included mashed "avocado pears" mixed with boiled lamb brains, spread across rye toast and garnished with minced almond and a splash of tequila.[16] In addition, a fashion trend that began in the late 1920s was picking up steam: avocado-green shoes, dresses, suits, and household decor were proving increasingly popular from New York City to Nashville, Miami, Arkansas, and beyond. Perhaps inspired by a similar shade called "green almond" on the streets of Paris, the renowned California-born fashion designer Bonnie Cashin designed avocado-colored clothing for high-end department stores in the 1950s.[17] Fashionable wallpaper company CW Stockwell of Los Angeles, famed for its bold banana-leaf patterned design installed in the Beverly Hills Hotel in 1949, partnered with Calavo to create an avocado-themed wallpaper as part of the company's Trend of the Times collection.[18] Calavo printed the pattern inside matchbooks as a clever cross-promotion. Paint colors, textiles, and furniture followed. By 1966, when General Electric included avocado green in its new line of home appliances, a companion to a toast-colored harvest gold, the color had officially entered the mainstream. Soon, consumers could buy cars in avocado green, too: 1968 Dodge Chargers, 1969 Opels, 1970 Cadillac Eldorados, 1973 Ford Gran Torinos, and 1974 Volkswagen Things.[19]

Studies showed that Americans considered avocados fattening, and many consumers didn't know what to do with them. To combat these perceptions, Pinkerton sent newspapers and produce departments easy recipes and kitchen tips and a bright-yellow Styrofoam "avocado merchandiser" to display fruit in grocery stores. He also pushed the avocado's sex appeal by promoting California avocados as "the sensuous food" and commissioning radio ads with soap-opera-style drama and sultry-voiced women who coaxed listeners to "make it with an avocado."[20] A 1977 full-page ad in *Cosmopolitan* magazine showed a thin blonde woman in an avocado-print bikini lounging on a beach, her ribs protruding, her eyes closed, her face tilted back soaking up the sun. Readers who mailed a "sliver of avocado skin (wiped dry and flattened between two pieces of paper)" along with a check or money order for $10.95 would receive their own slice of paradise from the California Avocado Advisory Board: an avocado-print "California Avocado Bikini" in one of two styles, "halter tie" or "sliding triangle," available in cup sizes A–D.

Over the next decade, as more and more acres of avocados emerged on Southern California hillsides and the California Avocado Society swelled to a record 2,023 members, Pinkerton argued that marketing was becoming increasingly crucial to the industry's success.[21] Hundreds of new acres meant thousands of new trees, and thousands of new trees meant hundreds of thousands of avocados hitting the markets. Who would buy them? "Only 25 percent of Americans even know what an avocado is," Pinkerton told *The New York Times* in 1978.[22] In response, the California Avocado Commission rolled out a national ad campaign featuring the svelte actress Angie Dickinson, star of the hit TV drama *Police Woman* and John Wayne's love interest in *Rio Bravo*. In a television ad, smooth jazz played in the background while the camera lovingly panned along her bare legs and she purred, "This body needs good nutrition, including vitamins A, B1, C, E, potassium, niacin, iron, and this body gets them all in California avocados, for just one hundred and fifty-three calories in a luscious half shell. Mmm!" Print versions of the ad depicted Dickinson in a white bodysuit and shimmery high-heeled sandals, holding a piece of avocado aloft on a fork. They ran in twenty-three magazines with the caption, "Would this body lie to you? California Avocados. Only 17 calories a slice." Pinkerton proudly told the CAS that a survey of *Reader's Digest* subscribers declared it the most memorable ad in the August 1981 issue.[23]

Southern California's Japanese chefs also began to incorporate avocados into their cuisine. In November 1979, a *Los Angeles Times* restaurant reviewer visited a tiny strip mall sushi bar in Tarzana called Niikura, where he enjoyed a "California roll" with shrimp, avocado, and rice rolled in sesame seeds, topped by a flower carved from cucumber. "The place is about as big as Buddha's bicuspid," wrote the critic, who called chef Masayuki "Nick" Niikura a "sushi sculptor" and a "star."[24] A few sushi chefs claim credit for inventing the California roll, including Ichiro Mashita, a pioneering Little Tokyo sushi chef, and Ken Seusa, who opened his restaurant Kin Jo in 1979.[25] Both Japanese chefs found the avocado had a texture similar to toro, the costly fatty tuna belly flown in from Japan. The rice-covered roll made with local avocados was less expensive and designed to appeal to American tastes. The innovation, now ubiquitous at sushi bars across the United States, was a tougher sell in Japan, where perfect, blemish-free avocados were prized as a healthy delicacy but rarely incorporated with sushi.[26]

In 1982, the avocado got a huge boost from another innovation. For decades, hard green avocados fresh from the orchard, fruit needing five to fifteen days to ripen, were shipped directly to supermarkets. Curious if ripe avocados would sell, UC Riverside botanist Seung-Koo Lee and plant physiologist Charles W. Coggins Jr. exposed boxes of unripe Hass avocados to ethylene gas, a natural plant hormone that causes ripening, and brought several boxes to an Alpha Beta supermarket in Riverside. Ripe avocados outsold their green counterparts two to one. Follow-up surveys were unanimous: 100 percent of shoppers preferred having ripe avocados available to purchase. Written comments on the surveys hinted at the avocado obsession to come: "People need to be able to have avocado when they need it, not have to plan ahead," one shopper said. "Sometimes I need them immediately," said another. "It's about time."[27]

Lee and Coggins's study was a game changer for the industry. Gil Henry of Henry Avocado Corporation in Escondido became the first packer to embrace the program, preripening avocados in ethylene-infused ripening rooms and selling them, initially to the King Soopers supermarkets in Denver, Colorado, which had been trying, unsuccessfully, to ripen avocados in banana-ripening rooms. Henry's evangelism for the "ripe program" and his willingness to experiment led to a new California Avocado Commission marketing effort, "Ripe for Tonight." Mission Produce's Steve Barnard conducted his own experiment at an Oxnard grocery store and became the first to pitch the concept to a national chain and build a series of state-of-the-art avocado-ripening centers across the country. Barnard also convinced grocery stores to stop piling avocados in deep bins, a habit that hastened the ripening (and rotting) of fruit low down in the pile. Through careful management of ripening rooms, cold storage, and grocery store displays, the industry leaders hoped to guarantee customers never encountered a bad avocado and would not have to wait more than three days for their avocados to reach perfection.[28]

In 1989, first-time filmmaker J. F. Lawton made a low-budget movie on the Riverside campus. Titled *Cannibal Women in the Avocado Jungle of Death*, the campy comedy starred former *Playboy* Playmate of the Year Shannon Tweed as a feminist professor in a world where avocados were in short supply. The plot involved a lost tribe of man-eating women fighting over guacamole and their future. At least one scene was filmed in the university's experimental orchards. Eric Focht, a doctoral candidate in Mary Lu Arpaia's avocado breeding program, believed Lawton likely picked up on a bit of avocado-industry drama from his father, who founded the university's creative-writing program. Lawton went on to write more successful films, including *Pretty Woman* starring Julia Roberts.[29]

Ralph M. Pinkerton retired in 1994 after twenty-three years as the CEO of the California Avocado Commission. One of his successors was Mark Affleck, who, in addition to leading the commission during the long fight with Mexico, took up Pinkerton's mantle as an energetic advocate for the health benefits of the avocado. But while Affleck was often in the spotlight, he did not make the avocado a celebrity. The avocado became iconic thanks, in part, to Charley Wolk, a white-haired farmer and ranch manager in jeans and cowboy boots who helped get the federal government to back the Hass avocado.

Wolk, a U.S. Marine Corps veteran, was elected chairman of the avocado commission in 1994, stepping into leadership just as the USDA was considering ending the quarantine against Mexican avocados. He urged the commission to champion the health benefits of the avocado, which it did by inviting health researchers to all-expenses-paid weekends at swanky California resorts and sponsoring studies on the avocado's healthy fats and vitamins. These efforts resulted in the essay "The California Avocado: A New Look," in the May 1994 edition of the journal *Nutrition Today*.[30] As a public relations coup, the article was groundbreaking. Aimed at a broad readership of influential nutrition experts, the report outlined the nutrients in the avocado, emphasizing its healthy fiber, high folate content, and monounsaturated fats.

In addition to supporting health research, Wolk joined Mark Affleck as a public face of the avocado wars. Privately, however, he knew the war was lost. One way or another, Mexican avocados were coming into the United States, and it was in everybody's best interest to build demand for them. Too many avocados on the market with too few customers would result in rotting fruit and dropping prices. Someone had to convince the American public to buy avocados. "We have people who don't have the foggiest notion what an avocado is," Wolk told the *Los Angeles Times* in October 2000. "It's a marketer's dream."[31]

Wolk went on to help write the Hass Avocado Promotion, Research and Information Act, and to convince Congress to pass the new law. President Bill Clinton signed the act on October 23, 2000, authorizing the USDA to establish a federal marketing program funded by California avocado growers and importers from every country that imported Hass avocados. The move guaranteed a steady stream of cash to market avocados to the American public. "It became a matter of necessity," Wolk said. "The challenge was convincing the California growers that they had to do this."[32] The growers didn't want to see more bureaucracy, pay more fees, or deal with the federal government any more than required. Wolk sympathized, but like Ralph Pinkerton before him, he knew that demand didn't always follow supply. The only way to get consumers to buy avocados was to market them effectively and that required money. By law, industry stakeholders had to vote to approve marketing orders. In June 2002, more than 86 percent of California's 6,000 growers and one hundred avocado importers voted in favor.

The new order took effect on September 9, 2002—the year the Hass mother tree died. Overseen by the USDA, the order required every country exporting avocados to the United States to set up a U.S.-based association to market avocados to the American public. The newly created Hass Avocado Board, known as HAB, would collect 2.5 cents for every pound of avocados sold and return 85 percent of the fees to the various associations in amounts proportional to their sales. By 2004, HAB collected more than $17 million and used its share to fund its own marketing efforts on behalf of imported and homegrown avocados.[33] To keep California growers from paying double for state and federal marketing programs, the avocado commission agreed to lower its assessments. In essence, just as a wall of Mexican avocados was about to enter the United States, Wolk ensured that Mexico would pay to build an audience of avocado-hungry American consumers.

Some in the Mexican and Chilean industries were fuming, wary of a program conceived of and administered by the same California growers who fought to keep Mexico out of the market. A few tried to tank the whole enterprise, arguing that the HAB assessment amounted to a hidden tariff. Two avocado importers sued, alleging that a forced marketing order violated free speech protections enshrined in the U.S. Constitution, an argument mushroom growers successfully made to the U.S. Supreme Court in their fight against a similar marketing order.[34] The challenge failed. The California Avocado Commission, meanwhile, was embroiled in its own scandals. In 2008, Mark Affleck, the state's most visible avocado champion, resigned his post. A state audit found evidence of excessive spending by CAC on hotels, clothing, renovations, and other items. Neither Affleck nor CAC leadership were charged with wrongdoing, the board vowed to tighten its oversight, and Affleck reportedly reimbursed some expenses.[35] That same year, HAB collected more than $27 million in annual assessments.[36] Wolk weathered the controversy and looked on the bright side. He saw the creation of HAB as a win for everybody. "All boats float with the tide," he said. "California could not survive being the only marketing organization" promoting avocados in the United States. Wolk's former opponents also managed to win his respect. Reflecting on the battle years later, Wolk said, "The Mexican grower community had a lot more savvy than they were given credit for."

Heart-Healthy Oven-Roasted Salmon with Avocado Citrus Salsa

1 ripe, fresh avocado, halved, pitted,
  peeled and diced
3 Tbsp. fresh lime juice
1 ripe navel orange, peeled and diced
1/2 cup seedless cucumber, diced
1/4 cup scallions, finely diced
1 jalapeño pepper, seeded, finely diced
2 Tbsp. fresh cilantro, chopped
1/2 tsp. salt, divided
4 skinless salmon fillets (approximately
  2 oz. each)

In a medium bowl, combine avocado, lime
juice, orange, cucumber, onion, jalapeño,
cilantro and 1/4 tsp. of the salt and set
aside. Heat broiler. Season salmon with
remaining 1/4 tsp. salt. Arrange fillets
on a lightly greased foil-lined rimmed
baking sheet. Broil salmon 4 inches from
heat source until cooked through, 8 to
10 minutes. To serve, place fillets on a
platter and top with salsa.

--*Love One Today*, Hass Avocado Board

17 • Avocados From Mexico

WHILE U.S. AND MEXICAN OFFICIALS NEGOTIATED over the quarantine, Emiliano Escobedo graduated summa cum laude with a degree in food and resource economics from the University of Florida, where he specialized in marketing and agribusiness. He next landed a public relations job with publicist Anita Fial. Her company, Lewis & Neale, represented the Association of Avocado Exporting Producers and Packers of Mexico, or APEAM. Fial convinced APEAM to fly her and a cohort of U.S.-based food influencers—cookbook writers, chefs, journalists—to tour the Michoacán orchards. The APEAM team was so impressed by her trilingual junior associate that they offered him a job. Avocados were already slipping into the zeitgeist; in 2006, the superstar grunge band Pearl Jam put a photograph of a half avocado on an album cover. The idea emerged during a brainstorming session in Seattle, and bandleader Eddie Vedder went to a local grocery store to choose the avocado himself. "I didn't realize it was Super Bowl Sunday," he said in a podcast interview, chuckling at the memory of the puzzled onlookers in the produce section, wondering why the Grammy-winning rock star was holding avocados to the light, "auditioning" them to find the perfect specimen.[1]

As a marketing strategist for APEAM, Escobedo understood the quest for perfection, and he dove into the world of avocados. He visited warehouses; walked through Hunts Point Produce Market, a twenty-four-hour wholesale market on 113 acres in the Bronx; spoke (in English or Spanish) with the packinghouse's workers and representatives of import companies large and small—Calavo,

Mission, Index Fresh, and more. He was friendly, he was observant, and he learned fast. In 2008, the leaders of APEAM tapped Escobedo as their new director of global marketing.[2]

Inspired by his mentor Fial, he convinced celebrity chef Rick Bayless, fresh from winning the first season of Bravo's *Top Chef Masters*, to lead a press tour of Michoacán, featuring a cooking class and a private tour of local food markets. He shared recipes for salsa and avocado-lime Jell-O at food trade shows, introduced Canadians to a cartoon character named "Miss Ava Cado, Mexico's sultry avocado ambassador," staged avocado giveaways outside the Toronto train station, and debuted avocado recipes with celebrity chefs in Japan. At times, he stepped in to run damage control, as in 2008 when a Texas supplier's avocados were recalled after a pepper shipment was tainted with salmonella.[3] He also had a novel idea. Intel, the Silicon Valley chipmaker, played a simple tune—five notes lasting three seconds—on radio and television commercials for tech products that used their computer chips. Escobedo approached Kari Bretschger of IMW, APEAM's marketing consultant who helped write the first avocado nutrition study for the California industry. Could Mexican avocados do something like that? Create a sound people identify with the brand? As he recalled, Kari answered: "You need a jingle."

They commissioned Curt Lyon, a Southern California audio and television producer, who had worked with Stevie Wonder and written jingles for car-rental companies, Hansen's Natural sodas, and hundreds more. With his writing partner, Lyon produced a sixty-second clip that ended with a voice singing, "Avocados From Mexico" ("Aguacates de México" in the Spanish-language version). It would prove to be a catchy tune. Years later, as Escobedo waited in line at a ski resort, some children who noticed the avocados on his water bottle spontaneously burst into song. "I'm like, 'Oh my gosh, I'm at 6,000 feet and I'm in Idaho, and these kids are singing my jingle,'" Escobedo said.[4] By 2024, a ten-minute YouTube video with the jingle on repeat had been viewed more than 1.6 million times.

In 2012, the leaders of the Mexican avocado export industry published a leather-bound coffee-table book, *Ahuacatl: Tesoro Verde Mexicano* (Avocado: Green Treasure of Mexico). Ramón Paz-Vega wrote the prologue. The book, published in Spanish, was a labor of love and pride, with full-page color photographs of Michoacán avocado orchards, farmers, and women cooking tortillas. The Aztec pictograph for ahuacatl, the same one that fascinated Wilson Popenoe, was stamped into the cover of the book. The leaders of the Mexican avocado industry also came up with a game-changing idea—combining the U.S.-based Mexican Hass Avocado Importers Association, formed to collect assessments from HAB under the auspices of the USDA's marketing program, with the exporters at APEAM, formed to fund and implement the USDA's phytosanitary protocols in Mexico. In 2013, the two groups merged to create Avocados From Mexico, a nonprofit U.S. corporation.

To head the organization they hired Alvaro Luque, an experienced marketing executive. Luque had risen up the ranks selling tortillas and chips for the Mexico-based GRUMA, owner of the Mission brand and one of the world's largest producers of tortillas and corn flour, and early in his career helped a Scott tampon brand smash the competition in his native Costa Rica. Luque brought in former GRUMA marketing executive Stephanie Bazan and proposed a novel idea: market the Mexican avocado as if it were a brand like Coke or Pepsi or a packaged good like tortillas or tampons. His board loved the enthusiasm, but when he told them he wanted to do a Super Bowl commercial, some thought he had gone too far. The California Avocado Commission had been promoting the opening of the California avocado season during the big game since the mid-1990s, inviting the rival teams to submit guacamole recipes for its annual Guacamole Bowl challenge. But the Californians never ran a national television commercial during the game. Thirty seconds of airtime during the Super Bowl costs millions of dollars, and no one had ever tried to pitch fresh produce in this way. Beer, cars, chips, soda—sure. But a piece of fruit with no brand and no packaging?

Luque persuaded them to say yes; after all, they had millions of dollars in the budget and a USDA mandate to promote the avocado. He and his team, including digital-marketing expert Ivonne Kinser, hired GSD&M of Austin, Texas, the advertising team that coined the "Don't Mess with Texas" anti-litter campaign, and with weeks to go before the big game purchased the rights to the catchy "Avocados From Mexico" jingle from Curt Lyon. The commercial, "First Draft Ever," aired on February 1 before a television audience of more than 114 million people. In the spot, a Noah-like figure with a long beard and a robe stands at a mic dryly leading a football-like draft for plants and animals from various modern nations—a tuft of wheat from America, a kangaroo from Australia, a sloth from Brazil. While former pro football players Doug Flutie and Jerry Rice weigh in, Mexico contributes the avocado, a perfect-looking ripe Hass, "grown with love since the beginning of time." The commercial closed with Lyon's jingle. The ad was shared on social media and earned Avocados From Mexico the number two spot among all Super Bowl advertisers. The commercial won a Clio, advertising's highest award.

Luque credits the ad's success to what he called the avocado's "Mexicanity." The term builds off the concept of mexicanidad, the unique mixture of cultures and qualities that is a deep source of Mexican pride and inspiration. He believed that the fruit held a special position in the American imagination. It evoked positive memories of Cinco de Mayo parties, football games, and special-occasion fiestas with piñatas, tequila, friends, and family. If these were stereotypical images, or if there was any irony in a Costa Rican defining for Americans what it meant to be Mexican, Luque didn't worry too much about it. He and his team also steered clear of stories of violence or extortion in Michoacán; instead, they focused on building a wholesome, positive image around the Mexican avocado industry. They produced an

English-language video series called *Avocadoland*, hosted in part by Ramón Paz-Vega, that introduced viewers to Michoacán avocado farmers and the industry's public service work in Mexico. The Mexican Hass Avocado Importers Association and APEAM also funded studies by researchers at Texas A&M University that showed the positive impacts of Mexican avocado imports on the U.S. economy. The report found that, in the 2021–2022 season alone, avocado imports from Mexico added $6.1 billion to the gross domestic product, created more than 58,000 U.S. jobs, and generated $1.3 billion in taxes. California reaped more benefits than any other state: according to the study, more than $476 million worth of economic activity in 2021 and 2022.[5]

When the USDA halted Mexican imports on the eve of the 2022 Super Bowl after an APHIS inspector received a death threat, Luque canceled some media interviews and let leaders of the export industry do the talking. He left taunts from President Donald Trump unanswered. When the president called Mexican immigrants "bad hombres" and threatened to shut down trade with Mexico, AFM didn't comment. When the anti-Mexican rhetoric from the White House boiled over before the Super Bowl one year, Luque convened his PR agency in his Super Bowl "war room" to help with damage control in case Trump sent out a negative tweet. Much to his team's relief, the president didn't comment on their Super Bowl ad.

"I want to keep the brand safe and out of those conversations. We are not here for the controversy," Luque said. "My job in this country is to make you happy and healthy and celebrate with you the best of your events and the best times of your life. That's my job, and that's my purpose in life."[6]

In 2020, *Hispanic Executive* magazine credited Luque with coming on the scene "at the exact moment when the population of the United States collectively realized there was an avocado-sized hole in their lives."[7] The following year, *Fast Company* named Avocados From Mexico the year's most innovative brand and one of the world's most innovative companies, praising its Super Bowl digital campaigns and its "nontraditional marketing avenues," including using NFTs (non-fungible tokens) and blockchain. By 2022, Luque was making more than $1 million a year and preparing to bring his brand to the college football season, buying a digital billboard in New York City's Times Square in time for New Year's Eve and launching a catchy new 2023 campaign.[8] Called the "Avocados From Mexico Jingle Challenge," it asked avocado lovers to record themselves delivering bad news to the tune of their catchy and ubiquitous popular jingle. The promotion's tagline: Avocados From Mexico "Make Everything Better."

Emiliano Escobedo had fond memories of sitting in the recording studio where the jingle was created. He enjoyed seeing the social media memes, the Super Bowl ads, the Instagram feeds filled with avocado toast. But Escobedo, recruited to lead the Hass Avocado Board beginning in January 2012, didn't think any of this explained how the avocado became a juggernaut. Rather, it was the avocado's unique qualities, fueled by a spirit of international collaboration, that helped build the avocado's iconic status.

Working together hadn't happened easily. When Escobedo stepped in to lead, HAB had collected $37 million in assessments, most of it from Mexico, yet board seats were dominated by Californians who either grew or imported avocados.[9] Representatives of countries of origin that exported avocados to the United States—Mexico, Chile, and Peru—felt outnumbered and outvoted. Many didn't trust each other, and some didn't trust Escobedo, a Mexican-born former employee of the Mexican avocado industry. Yet, under mandate from the USDA, the board had to pull together to decide how to market the Hass avocado to America, no matter which country the fruit came from. Working with a board member named Bob Schaar, a California grower, Escobedo set about to build trust. He proved to be a good listener and a persuasive leader.

Escobedo and HAB knew that people still had a lot to learn about the avocado, most importantly its health benefits. But where Ralph Pinkerton had hired a sexy actress and sold avocado-print bikinis in *Cosmopolitan* magazine, Escobedo hired a PhD with an expertise in nutritional sciences. Over the next decade, Nikki Ford, who held a doctoral degree from the University of Illinois, led a team that funded independent studies about the health benefits of the avocado. About 20 percent of the research focused on Hispanic Americans. Between 2010 and 2023, HAB invested $20 million in peer-reviewed nutrition studies conducted by researchers from top universities, including Pennsylvania State University, Tufts University, Wake Forest University, and UCLA. The first of these studies to capture broad attention showed that people who ate a whole avocado a day lowered their cholesterol levels, regardless of diet.

The study was published in the *Journal of the American Heart Association* on January 7, 2015, less than a month before Avocados From Mexico aired its award-winning Super Bowl commercial.[10] Stories about the report went viral. "It was huge," Escobedo said. "It hit every single news channel, throughout the day for a couple of days. I attribute that study and the American Heart Association getting behind it. That really put avocados on the map." The following year, the FDA designated the avocado as "heart-healthy," a status that affects how foods are listed on menus and recommended by doctors and nutritionists. At the same time, avocados rode the wave of so-called "superfoods," a new surge of fruits and vegetables from quinoa to blueberries, all marketed for being extra rich in nutritional qualities.[11] Americans embraced the avocado's health benefits.[12] By 2017, Mexico shipped 1.5 billion pounds of avocados to the United States, and Americans were eating an average of 6.2 avocados per year, almost twice what they ate just a decade before.

Miguel Barcenas grew up in Uruapan, studied computer science, and moved into marketing, joining the Mexican avocado industry in 2012 after stints at Procter & Gamble and PepsiCo. He considered the avocado a marketer's dream, "a product you can only talk good about." He tailored his marketing efforts to the nuances of the avocado's image. In Japan, for example, where there is affection for manga and adorable mascots, he hired an award-winning graphic designer to create a mascot for the brand. She came back with an avocado family—grandparents, parents, and children—who communicated different messages that resonated with the Japanese customer: nutritious diets for babies, a longing for travel, an appreciation for ancestors. In the latter case, the avocado's origin story was important. They also had to change the avocado's image: nine in ten avocado buyers in Japan were women, so the brand hired male celebrities and sports stars and lobbied to get avocado chunks inserted in the popular onigiri, handheld rice balls popular with office workers. In Canada, where consumers were spread out geographically and divided by language, Avocados From Mexico hired two marketing agencies to create unique campaigns in English and French and sponsored high-profile Canadian athletes, including entire hockey teams and tennis star Leylah Fernandez.

The deepest nuance, however, emerged in Barcenas's home territory.

Mexican-born chef Pati Jinich had hosted a cooking show on PBS since 2011. Avocados From Mexico was an early sponsor of *Pati's Mexican Table*. In addition to making Avocados From Mexico–branded YouTube videos highlighting avocado recipes and cooking tips, she made annual visits to Michoacán to help lead tours for American chefs and food-industry influencers as an Avocados From Mexico ambassador. In each episode of her show, Jinich visited a different region of Mexico, introducing viewers to recipes and techniques as well as the diverse cultures and people of her native country. The Emmy-nominated show has won three James Beard Awards. Jinich held a master's degree in Latin American studies and had work experience at the Center for Inter-American Policy and Research, a policy-research center in Washington, D.C. Her status as a cultural ambassador led to an invitation to cook at a White House Cinco de Mayo celebration for President Obama. In a second Emmy-nominated PBS series, *La Frontera with Pati Jinich*, she explored the food and culture of the U.S.-Mexico border communities, a region that about 15 million people call home. With locals as her guides, she compared burritos in the shadow of the border fence and watched cattle herded across international boundaries off-limits to people. The series won a James Beard Media Award in 2024.

Her show, her website, and her cookbooks featured dozens of recipes using avocados, which she called "iconic symbols of who we are." Her sponsor, AFM, was focused on the Hass avocado, but Jinich noticed that while Mexico City shoppers seemed to prefer the Hass in markets, their tastes were varied. "We delight in the different kinds of avocado," Jinich noted, including large "lizard-like" avocados or tiny criollo varieties that are eaten like wild plums, with skin and all. "You can just smash it in a warm tortilla, squeeze the pit out, and eat the whole thing." She continued,

> I aways say that the food of a place is a lot like its people, and I think the avocado is really a lot like Mexicans: it is exotic, beautiful, accessible, adaptable . . . You can put it on sushi, you can put it on pizza, and that's how Mexicans are. We will adapt. We will get the job done. We will sleep in the Four Seasons, or we will sleep on the floor. If you want a Mexican to make tacos, a Mexican will make tacos. But if you want us to make pasta and we don't know how to do it, we will figure it out. Avocados show that accessibility and resiliency.[13]

Chile Verde Guacamole/Guacamole de Chile Verde from the Arizona/Sonora Borderlands

1 serrano chile finely chopped
1/2 cup coarsely chopped cilantro leaves and upper part of stems
1/4 cup finely chopped white onion
3/4 tsp kosher or sea salt or to taste
3 ripe avocados, halved, pitted, meat scooped out
1 chile verde, such as Anaheim, Fresno or New Mexico, roasted and charred, stemmed, peeled and diced

Combine the serrano chile, cilantro, onion, and salt in a bowl or a molcajete and mash and mix together. Add the avocado and mash and mix together. Add the roasted, diced Anaheim chile and stir and mash until the ingredients are nicely incorporated. Taste, adjust salt, and serve.

—Pati Jinich[1]

18 · Global Avocado

CALAVO'S BUSIEST U.S. PACKINGHOUSE SITS BY THE railroad tracks on the edge of Santa Paula, a farm town in a fertile river valley about sixty miles northwest of downtown Los Angeles. The low, beige building blends in with the dusty roads, the only pop of color a Calavo sign, its green letters lined with gold. Inside, past a row of small offices, the packing floor is roughly the size of a hockey rink. Beyond the packinghouse door is a wall of sound: rock-hard avocados rumbled by on conveyor belts, cardboard boxes thunked down chutes, beeping forklifts zipped back and forth, dumping fruit into a sorting machine with a thunderous roar. Out back, trucks lined up at the loading dock, brimming with bins filled with that morning's harvest, each holding close to 1,000 pounds of fruit. It was late April, avocado season in California, and Cinco—industry shorthand for the Cinco de Mayo holiday—was only a few days away. The holiday marks the Mexican army's defeat of French forces at the Battle of Puebla in 1862, and while not observed widely in Mexico, Mexican Americans embraced it as a cultural celebration in the mid-twentieth century, and advertisers soon followed. Beer sales outpace Saint Patrick's Day during the holiday, and except for Super Bowl weekend, Americans eat more avocados at Cinco fests than at any other time of the year.[2]

The packinghouse was built in 1955, but a renovation that began in 2018 put in new lighting, flooring, and a state-of-the-art stainless steel sorting machine. Every second, eighty-eight avocados are photographed on all sides by a line of computerized cameras suspended above the moving belt. This optics technology calculates quality and size and sends the fruits on to twenty-eight different intersections that determine their fate. Upon arriving at the facility, avocado bins are held in cold storage. Forklift drivers then weigh the bins on an industrial scale before emptying them into a hopper. From there, the avocados proceed onto a track of moving rollers.

On that day, two women in matching smocks stood on a raised platform on either side of the flow, their fingers quickly searching for rejects. A computerized camera catches whatever they miss: any avocado with a scar, rodent bite, sunburn, or insect blight larger than a thumbnail isn't allowed to move on. Avocados that are small but otherwise pristine are ejected and sold to specialty buyers. The fruit sorted that day came from Sal Dominguez, whose family farm outside Santa Paula is one of the largest in the state. There were very few culls, proof of his expertise as a farmer. Amid the bin of culls was a five-inch-long beige avocado with the texture of sandpaper, a victim of thrips, tiny, winged insects that feed on avocado foliage and young fruit. Ironically, the avocado inside was probably delicious. Thrips stunt the fruit's growth. As a result, according to some, the oil content becomes more saturated in thrip-infested avocados. Still, it stayed in the reject bin. Nobody would buy a beige avocado.

On a busy day, the packinghouse crew can sort and pack close to 1 million pounds of avocados. Perfect avocados travel to boxes stamped "Calavo." Near-perfect avocados, the fruit with small blemishes or scars, flow down ramps into boxes stamped "Bueno." These are routed to the food-service industry. Places like Chipotle pay less for fruit with cosmetic imperfections. Computer optics also sort the fruit by size: 48s, the industry standard; 60s, 70s, and 84s, the small ones; and 40s, extra-large. Before it hits the box, each avocado receives one of three stickers with numbers noting its size along with a computerized barcode that contains the avocado's home orchard and harvest date, information that allows the fruit to be traced in case of a food recall down the chain. The boxes receive barcodes, too. Once filled, the boxes are loaded onto pallets, cooled, and driven to one of fourteen ripening rooms, where they will be ripened with ethylene for three or four days, depending on the customer. Chipotle likes riper avocados; Vons markets prefers them a bit greener. After ripening, the avocados are cooled again and sprayed with a plant-based coating to preserve shelf life.

Pallets of ripened fruit are then loaded onto semitrucks heading to supermarkets, warehouse stores, and produce-distribution hubs, most likely within the state. Californians are the biggest avocado consumers in the nation, and the Santa Paula packinghouse packs almost all of Calavo's California harvest. In 2022, bearing avocado acreage in California (a tally that does not include new immature plantings) was less than 46,000 acres, the smallest since the late 1970s. The orchards are shrinking for many reasons—rising water costs in a state plagued by drought, costs of labor, and high land prices make growing the crop untenable for many farmers. Still, new farming techniques, including sophisticated water-management tools and carefully tended dense-planting schemes, have helped make some of the remaining orchards more productive than ever. Overall, California produced 215 million pounds of Hass avocados in 2023, and a bumper crop in 2024 brought in close to 330 million pounds. Still, even at its most productive, California can't begin to satisfy the hunger for avocados in the United States. The state produces fewer than eight out of every one hundred avocados Americans eat.[3] To satisfy demand, and to fill orders on its more than eighty retail accounts around the United States, Calavo and its largest competitor, Mission Produce, rely on their packinghouses in Uruapan. They also buy fruit from Chile, Colombia, and Peru.

These days, more than 80 percent of Calavo avocados are from Mexico, although surveys by the California Avocado Commission have shown that customers in the United States are willing to pay more for California-grown fruit. CAC advertising emphasizes the fruit is locally grown by California farmers. At the CAC's annual meeting in spring 2024, Henry Dominguez, one of the state's largest growers, echoed a strategy first implemented by industry pioneers a century before. He had commissioned a prototype for a custom box that would promote California avocados as a premium product sold at premium prices. While some growers still grumble about Mexico, the commission's advertising no longer demonizes Mexicans or their avocados. Mark Affleck, the former commission president who signed the inflammatory ads of the late 1990s, has set aside the rivalry and devoted his life to Christian ministry. Still, the avocado wars occasionally flare. In September 2024, when the Mexican press reported that APHIS would step back and Mexican agricultural officials would inspect their own orchards for pests, the CAC fired off an angry letter to USDA secretary Thomas J. Vilsack. Without USDA oversight, the CAC warned, people would "game the system" and pests could destroy California orchards.[4] A USDA spokesman noted in October 2024 that APHIS continued to supervise orchard inspection according to "the framework of the Operational Workplan" between the two nations. He described the news as a safety measure: "APHIS inspectors traveling to avocado orchards have faced crimes, including assault, theft, and kidnapping while performing their duties."[5]

Calavo's stock price has plummeted in recent years, and its avocado business fluctuates; the company sold more than $645 million worth of avocados in the 2022 season and nearly $75 million worth of packaged guacamole.[6] In the 2023 season, its avocado revenues were $466 million and guacamole revenue had dropped to $70.6 million.[7] Hass dominates the supply, although other varieties are gaining in popularity. In 2023, California avocado farmers harvested about 4.5 million pounds of GEM and 6.4 million pounds of Lamb Hass, two varieties bred from Gwen seeds and patented by Bob Bergh and Gray E. Martin at UC Riverside.[8] GEM acreage, in particular, is growing; fans note the compact trees are easier to harvest, and some studies show they're more productive than Hass. The Brokaws have planted thousands of GEM trees, and at the University of California's taste panels, GEMs rate highly with consumers. Martin, who pulled a GEM avocado out of his pocket at the 2022 CAS meeting, believes it's the avocado of the future. But Hass is the only variety Mexico is permitted to sell in the United States, and while avocado exports lag behind beer, tequila, and berries, in 2023 Mexico shipped more than 1.5 million tons of Hass avocados to the United States; production reached an all-time high. Americans ate more than 3 billion pounds of avocados in 2023, an average of 8.8 pounds per person.[9] Mexicans are hungry for more avocados, too. Between 2021 and 2023, average annual consumption in Mexico increased from eighteen to twenty-four pounds per person. Demand was so high that Mexico, the world's largest avocado producer and exporter, imported avocados from Peru and Colombia to meet local demand.[10] In Mexican markets, as in the United States, Hass avocados fetch premium prices. No matter how good Bob Bergh's varieties are, Hass is still king.

Consuelo Mendez sat in Brokaw Nursery's greenhouse at a small table. In her right hand was a grafting blade that resembled a delicate X-ACTO knife. Over her right thumb, she wore a protective rubber sleeve. Beside her was a pile of grass-green sticks. The sticks, each about the length of a pencil, were clipped from the "mother block," a grove of Hass trees behind the nursery that are grown for this purpose. The Hass trees in this orchard never fruit and rarely flower; instead, they are pruned back hard in the late summer, forcing them to put their energy into making new branches through late fall and winter. Come spring, the tender new shoots are sturdy enough to clip and use as budwood. Each tree helps grow about two hundred new trees. The process repeats every summer.

On plastic trays in front of Mendez, grafted rootstocks emerged from black tubes of soil like spindly green fingers. One by one, she picked up a piece of budwood, deftly cut a T into the rootstock, spliced them together, and wound a length of rubber clockwise around the junction to seal the wound. At top speed, she could graft nine hundred trees a day, while her most able colleagues managed five or six hundred. Mendez has trained them all. She trained her boss, too. Rob Brokaw was twelve years old when Mendez arrived at the nursery, and when his kids were old enough, she also showed them how to graft budwood. Videos of her grafting have been sent to Viveros Brokaw, Brokaw's sister nursery in Spain—the world's largest clonal avocado nursery—and to nurseries throughout the world that have licensed its rootstocks.

Mendez has worked at Brokaw Nursery for more than fifty years. When she began, about forty people worked there, and clonal rootstock wasn't sold commercially. In 2024, she was one of 140 employees, not including colleagues at Brokaw's nurseries in Spain and Jalisco. On the wall in the nursery office in Ventura, there is a black-and-white photo of Cesar Chavez, his eyes cast downward, a dirt-caked shovel, rake, and hoe balanced on his right shoulder. The photo was from Apple's "Think Different" campaign; below it hangs a vintage photo of a bracero work crew standing in front of a Ventura County citrus grove. The nursery was one of the first in the state to sign a union contract with the United Farm Workers of America.[11] Ellen Brokaw led the negotiations for the nursery. After Chavez showed up in person to negotiate an impasse, she was so impressed that when it was time to deliver the signed agreement, she put her young son Rob in the car and drove a hundred miles to the union headquarters, La Paz in Kern County, to deliver it in person. It turned out to be Chavez's birthday, and they accepted the invitation to stay for a church service and a barbecue.

Chavez once lived in Oxnard, a few miles from Brokaw Nursery. Although born in Yuma, Arizona, he picked avocados and walnuts there as a boy before following his family, and the harvest, north toward San Francisco.[12] Mendez followed the fruit, too, although her journey was longer. She was twenty-four years old when she knocked on Hank Brokaw's door in 1968 looking for a job. She and her husband, desperate for work, had left their small children with family in Michoacán to come north, and Mendez quickly learned she hated working in the strawberry fields. "Start tomorrow," Hank told them. Mendez watched, and asked questions, and learned fast. Hank knew every worker and every job in the greenhouse. He always worked alongside them, she said, and was dedicated to the workers. Full-time employees had medical insurance before the union came, and when the employees voted out the union nine years later, the nursery continued to offer medical, vision, and dental insurance, holiday and paid sick leave, and sometimes no-interest loans and immigration services.[13] In 2003, Ellen helped found House Farm Workers!, a nonprofit that works with public and private partners to build farmworker housing in Ventura County.

At seventy-nine, Mendez's fingers were sometimes stiff, but when Rob asked if she wanted to slow down, she said no. She was proud of her work. Smiling, she said she enjoyed urging the others to move faster.

If all goes well, two years after Mendez makes her grafts, the young trees will leave Brokaw Nursery and find a new home in a farmer's orchard. Given her pace, Rob figured it was likely that Mendez's hands have knit together more than 1 million Hass avocado trees. Together, those trees have produced hundreds of millions of avocados. "I feel happy," she said when she reflected on the impact of her work. "My hands have touched many countries."[14]

Avocados are harvested by hand. Most of the harvesters in California are Mexican immigrants who move through the state, picking avocados in Southern California in the spring and early summer, traveling north to the San Joaquin Valley to pick apples and pears in late summer and fall, and returning south to harvest citrus in the winter. Some are on temporary work visas that require employers to cover transportation and housing, and many work for labor contractors who pay based on how much each person can pick.

Angel Serrano García left Toluca, Mexico, when he was sixteen, moved in with a brother, and began harvesting avocados after working in a flower nursery. He started his own labor contracting business in 2017, helped by an investment from his brother, and five years later, he had a roster of twenty-three men who work the harvest on more than twenty avocado farms. Most of the men are from the states of Mexico or Nayarit, and they find each other through word of mouth. García, who was thirty-three in 2023, lays down firm policies: no drinking, no smoking, no messing around. He works alongside his crew and instructs them to keep the orchard clean, with no broken branches, and no fruit left on the trees or on the ground. According to García, farmers appreciate his level of care and ask for him to return the following season. People who harvest avocados can make decent money, García said; a man who is strong and works quickly with his small clippers can pick three 1,000-pound bins in a day, earning about eighty-five dollars a bin, one of the highest rates for harvesting produce. But the men carry eighty-pound bags on their shoulders, and the harvest can be dangerous work.[15]

Many avocado farmers in California plant trees in tight rows and prune them regularly to increase productivity, a method developed in Chile and pioneered in California by Brokaw Nursery. In San Diego County, a grove of 3,200 trees planted on berms in a six-by-fourteen-foot grid produced an average of 25,000 pounds per acre and became one of the most productive orchards in the state. A local Indigenous tribe, the Pauma Band of Luiseño Indians, now owns the impressive grove.[16] Smaller trees require more pruning and therefore more labor, but they are also safer to harvest. Avocados in the state's mature groves can be three stories high, requiring crews like García's to climb tall metal ladders. Labor contractors are required by law to follow safety regulations and hold regular training sessions, but the work still has its perils. García once helped a man whose ladder had touched a power line hidden in the tree canopy; he had the presence of mind to remember his safety training and donned gloves before helping the man down. His colleague survived. Since 1998, however, at least four people harvesting or pruning avocados in California have been electrocuted when their metal ladders or saws touched power lines, according to government records. Others have sustained serious injuries after falling off twenty-foot ladders or being hit by falling branches or pinned beneath turned-over tractors. In December 2010, a man clearing brush and avocado wood was killed after getting his leg caught in a wood chipper.[17] Many of these incidents never make the news.

More than a century after the California avocado pioneers met in a Los Angeles hotel to launch a new industry, their fascination with avocados now spans the globe. In April 2023, more than 1,000 people from more than thirty-two nations gathered in an Auckland, New Zealand, convention center for an event called the World Avocado Congress. New Zealand—known locally by its Māori name, Aotearoa, "land of the long white cloud"—may seem an unlikely venue for a global avocado meeting. The country's most famous trees aren't avocados but kauri trees so massive that, according to Māori legends, they are related to whales. Kiwifruit is the largest produce export by far. But New Zealand farmers have been growing avocados commercially since the 1930s, and exports doubled in the past decade, to $69 million in 2020.[18]

The first congress was held in South Africa in 1987, a

controversial choice at the time. Apartheid wouldn't end until the early 1990s. Since then, the conference has rotated among different avocado-producing nations on a four-year cycle, from Israel and Australia to Mexico, Colombia, and Peru. Originally focused on science, the event expanded with the avocado's surge in popularity and now includes sessions on avocado sales, marketing, technology, and trade. Some of the new tech displayed or discussed at the Auckland congress included biodegradable fruit stickers, automated fruit sorters, paper pots for avocado seedlings, thick plastic syringes used to plunge fungicides into the trunks of ailing trees, apps that connect with satellites to map orchards or predict weather patterns, and a new device that does bees' work, brushing pollen onto tiny avocado blossoms with the help of an electrostatic charge.

The congress's academic program lasted three days and included more than one hundred panel discussions, reports from avocado-growing countries on five continents, and presentations on topics ranging from marketing trends to genomics, avocado breeding, farming techniques, and pest control. Chilean researchers reported on an experiment in "careful harvesting," where they put newly picked avocados in small, cushioned boxes and drove them slowly through orchards in an air-conditioned van to reduce black spots on avocado flesh. Elizabeth Dann, a plant pathologist at the University of Queensland, drew a standing-room-only crowd to a conference room where she spoke on the use of phosphorous to manage trees afflicted with fungus. Arpaia, so well regarded in these circles she was introduced as a "woman who needs no introduction," spoke about her research and unveiled a new avocado from the UC Riverside breeding program: the Luna, a tasty black avocado and a type B bloomer that can make nearby Hass trees more productive. The Luna was first spotted by Bob Bergh and Gray E. Martin, who christened it Marvel, a name the university scrapped due to fear of lawsuits. University officials found that Marvel Characters Inc., owned by the Walt Disney

Company, holds the "Marvel" trademark not only for movie and comic book characters but for foods including grains, seeds, flowers, pet food, and fresh fruits and vegetables.[19] Arpaia named the avocado Luna, after her dog. The Spanish name, which translates to "moon," also pleased the executives at Eurosemillas, a Spanish company that in 2020 invested $2.25 million in the UC Riverside avocado-breeding program.[20]

Conference attendees also learned who's eating Hass avocados (Americans, mostly, followed by Europeans), who's selling them (Mexico sells six out of every ten avocados sold on Earth), and who's planting them (thousands of people on six continents). They learned that the avocado trade has been growing at six times the rate of the global fruit trade, increasing by 55,000 metric tons annually in 2012 to 880,000 metric tons a year in 2021, all to meet increasing avocado demand in the United States and European Union. In the United States, which consumes about half of the world's avocado exports, the market has swelled from $2.1 billion to $7 billion in the past decade. There was also sobering news: a ring of avocado thieves in Kenya had sent shiploads of tasteless, unripe Hass into European markets, and during the COVID-19 pandemic, avocados had rotted in Asian ports due to supply chain backups. While the Hass avocado is only the world's eighth most popular fruit export, far below the banana, apple, and orange, when it comes to the rapid growth of its market, no other fruit matches it. Global exports were valued at $6.6 billion in 2021, making avocado the world's fourth most valuable fruit export. Between 2011 and 2022, avocado exports grew 10 percent a year, five times the growth rate of fresh produce overall.

The congress is also a venue to share updates on avocado production in various nations and connect with potential suppliers or customers. Dr. Srinivas Rao, a physician whose day job was working in a clinic in Hyderabad, India, was in New Zealand to network and find inspiration for his side hustle—jump-starting India's avocado industry. Indian farmers planted 1 million avocado saplings in southern India between 2019 and 2021. Dr. Rao ordered budwood from Israel and California and set up an avocado-focused YouTube channel to train Indian farmers how to care for the trees on behalf of the company Deccan Exotics. In China, where the Hass was first introduced in an experimental orchard in the 1950s, growers planted 17,000 acres of avocados between 2018 and 2022—a 91 percent increase in acreage. Today, China imports an average of 34,800 tons of avocados each year.[21] Marguerite Wang, the general manager of a Chinese produce importer based in Shanghai, was at the congress looking to buy. A popular national chain in China had added avocado boba tea to its menu and was struggling to find enough avocados to meet the demand. Jacinta Foley, who ran a large Australian avocado farm owned by a Canadian teachers' pension fund, was looking to sell. During the COVID-19 pandemic, Australian avocado farmers had more avocados than they could eat or export; piles of fruit rotted in fields. Foley had her eyes on Japan, where she was working to find new customers. While Hong Kong remains Australia's biggest importer, avocado exports from Australia to Japan surged 161 percent between June 2022 and June 2023, to a total of 277 metric tons.[22]

French agricultural economist Éric Imbert warned congress attendees that the supply of Hass avocados may soon exceed demand. While U.S. consumption continues to increase, he noted that Japan and France, once robust avocado eaters, have been losing their appetites. Other markets are slow to develop. The average German only eats about one and a half pounds of avocados annually; Koreans typically eat only one small avocado a year. In China, a love for avocado smoothies notwithstanding, only a "small niche group" of consumers are even aware of the fruit, according to the USDA.[23] Mission Produce, the world's largest avocado supplier, is one of the few companies making a serious effort to break into China, landing a deal to distribute Mr. Avocado brand avocados through Shenzhen Pagoda Industrial Group, which operates 5,600 small produce markets in 140 Chinese cities. Imbert encouraged the delegates to listen to consumers, who are worried about the avocado's image, its use of water, and its carbon footprint. He predicted that the local-food movement will continue to grow and that shoppers who love avocados will favor ecologically and socially responsible suppliers.[24]

Not all agricultural economists see trouble on the avocado horizon. David Magaña of Rabobank predicts the industry will continue to build demand and attend to consumers' concerns about sustainability.[25] Climate impact was a focus at the congress, where Sarah McLaren, an environmental scientist who led the New Zealand Life Cycle Management Centre, warned that the global agricultural-food sector uses more than 30 percent of energy generated globally and contributes about 22 percent of greenhouse gases. "Continuing with business as usual is not an option," she said. A recent analysis of the New Zealand avocado industry, however, offered some hopeful notes, including the fact that the avocado is highly nutritious and grows on trees, two qualities that positively impact its carbon footprint. Shreyasi Majumdar, a doctoral student at Massey University, worked with McLaren on a "cradle-to-orchard gate" life cycle analysis that surveyed more than 100 farmers in the country's three avocado-growing regions. The study, which assigned a "climate change score" to each region, found that lime- and nitrogen-based fertilizers, along with gasoline-powered farm vehicles, contributed to the highest emissions and that orchard irrigation, unsurprisingly, used the most water. Surprisingly, the scores varied dramatically, even among farms in the same region. Researchers planned to expand the study to look at climate change impacts of avocado-cooling and -ripening facilities and packinghouses, with the hope of providing an environmental footprint of the New Zealand avocado industry and a model for other avocado-growing nations.[26]

The message from the congress was that for the global industry to endure, its leaders needed to address the climate impact of growing avocados. As the world's largest avocado supplier, Mexico has come under scrutiny for the avocado's environmental impact on protected forests in Michoacán.[27] Seven months after the congress, the advocacy group Climate Rights International published a report showing that between 2014 and 2023, more than 25,000 acres of forestland had been cleared in Michoacán to make way for avocado orchards, including 817 orchards planted in violation of Mexican law.[28] In addition to including emotional testimony from small farmers and climate activists in the region, the report, "Unholy Guacamole," compared Google Earth satellite images with the 50,000 USDA-certified orchards permitted to export avocados to the United States and found that neither U.S. nor Mexican officials were enforcing policies to protect the region's forests. A 2022 study by researchers at the University of Texas and the Universidad Nacional Autónoma de Mexico in Michoacán predicted that in the worst-case scenario, by 2050, deforestation in the state's "avocado belt" would grow by about 386 square miles, a 74 percent increase since 2017. This would include a 6 percent loss of the oyamel fir forest, home to the Monarch Butterfly Biosphere Reserve; an 8.5 percent loss of the rare mesophilic forest; and a 7 percent loss of pine-oak forests, or about one hundred square miles. The pine-oak forests, they noted, are more effective at storing carbon than avocados and other agriculture in the area.[29] "Virtually all the deforestation for avocados in the last two decades may have violated Mexican law, which prohibits 'land-use change' without government authorization," *The New York Times* reported in November 2023.[30]

"Unholy Guacamole" made an impact. The report and the accompanying media coverage caught the attention of several U.S. senators, who issued a public statement demanding change, and it also earned Climate Rights International representatives closed-door meetings with U.S. agricultural, trade, and State Department officials. In February 2024, U.S. ambassador to Mexico Ken Salazar traveled to Michoacán, joining Mexican officials at a news conference where officials from both nations pledged to implement regulations forbidding exports from illegal avocado orchards.[31] Later that summer, the state of Michoacán announced a certification program for farmers whose land complies with the rules.[32] And while CRI continued to pressure the leading avocado importers—Calavo Growers, Fresh Del Monte Produce, Mission Produce, and West Pak Avocado—to refuse to pack fruit harvested on illegally deforested land, for Brad Adams, who founded CRI after a long career with Human Rights Watch, the avocado report was making an impact. It was also a perfect test case for an innovative, human rights approach to climate activism. Much like the beloved polar bear, whose plight captures headlines in stories about global warming, the avocado is a "charismatic flora" with a passionate fan base. "Because of the avocado's cultural significance and its near ubiquitous consumption and its association with positivity and healthiness," study author Max Schoening said, CRI saw the avocado as a "vehicle to draw attention to broader issues" like environmentally responsible supply chain policies and the impact of deforestation.[33] Compared to much larger industries like beef, palm oil, and soy, "we know . . . the avocado industry is not a major global driver of deforestation," Adams acknowledged. But "nobody can relate to soy or palm oil." The "avocado toast brigade, of which I count myself to be a proud member," tend to care about the environment.[34]

The fact that the avocado is indigenous to Mexico was not mentioned in the CRI report. Mexico's deforestation crisis did not begin with the avocado industry. From Spanish colonizers in the sixteenth century to American railroad barons in the twentieth century to farmers wanting to clear a stand of trees to sell timber, graze animals, or grow food for their families, many have contributed to the loss of Mexico's forests. In 1997, the year that the USDA first lifted Mexico's avocado quarantine, Mexico was losing up to 2.5 million acres of forest each year, more than any other nation at the time.[35] Government officials have long turned a blind eye to illegal logging in the area and other industries in Michoacán that contribute deforestation. ArcelorMittal, the world's largest steel company, operates an iron ore mine in the region and a steel plant nearly three times the size of New York City's Central Park.[36]

In response to consumer concerns about the avocado's environmental impact, the Hass Avocado Board in 2023 debuted the Avocado Sustainability Center, a website with links to more than ninety peer-reviewed academic studies on the avocado's water needs, its carbon footprint, and the economic and social impact of avocado growing in various nations.[37] Creating the site took some negotiation among HAB's constituents, including California-based growers and avocado packers as well as representatives from nations that export avocados to the United States: Mexico, Chile, Peru, and Colombia. "Nobody wanted to talk about it," said John McGuigan, director of industry affairs for HAB. "There was a lot of fear."[38] Aware that the industry faces allegations of "greenwashing," or boasting about climate-friendly practices and ignoring more negative aspects of avocado commerce, HAB's sustainability website, approved by the USDA, is rooted in science. Several of the independent academic studies linked on the site show the negative climate impacts of certain practices, while others illustrate the environmental benefits of widely used drip irrigation, the thick beds of leaf mulch that blanket avocado orchard floors, and the avocado trees' ability to produce oxygen and store carbon dioxide. In 2024, HAB's sustainability task force was considering a more comprehensive environmental impact study of the industry.

Academic research on avocados and sustainability is growing and includes studies on pollination, biological control of pests, and orchard biodiversity. Organic farmers and others are planting a "biomass mix" of vetch, ryegrass, bell beans, and field peas between orchard rows, which both attract pollinators and pest predators but also add a boost of nitrogen and potassium when tilled into the soil. Avocados top the list of the Environmental Working Group's Clean Fifteen, a list of fruit and vegetables that have the lowest amount of pesticide residue. Fewer than 2 percent of avocados sampled by the USDA in 2012 showed any detectable pesticides, EWG reported.[39] Water is a greater concern, particularly in drought-plagued growing areas like Chile, Peru, and California. The Water Footprint Network, based in the Netherlands, estimates that it takes about 18.6 gallons of water to produce a single avocado.[40] At Brokaw Nursery in California, high-tech water-monitoring equipment, including wireless devices on tree trunks that measure if the tree is in distress, have helped decrease water use dramatically. In the 2023 avocado season, one of Brokaw's mature blocks of trees consumed only 9.35 gallons per avocado. In Mexico, where climate activists have decried encroachment on natural forests to make way for more avocado groves in Michoacán, APEAM runs a reforestation effort that has planted nearly 3 million plants and pine trees in the past decade.

Plant pathologists also play an important role in promoting a sustainable food supply. At UC Riverside, Patricia M. Manosalva, a professor of microbiology and plant pathology, has stepped into Zentmyer's role as director of the avocado-rootstock-breeding program. Her goal is to breed and identify rootstocks that will better withstand water salinity, pests, and diseases and encourage robust fruit production. Manosalva, the first woman to have the role, is Peruvian with Indigenous Incan roots. Her working-class parents scraped together money so their daughter could attend college. Maintaining a robust and sustainable industry is important to her.

On a research trip into the Andes Mountains, when she met potato farmers whose plants had been withered by *Phytophthora infestans*—the same fungus that wiped out Irish potato fields in the mid-nineteenth century and triggered a famine that killed more than a million people—she decided to become a plant pathologist. "There were fields after fields that were black," Manosalva said. "There was nothing left."[41] Everything she learns from the dozens of avocado rootstocks in her program—the rootstocks emerging from seeds in her greenhouse, the ones in the field grafted onto older tried-and-true varieties, those topworked onto established trees at the research station or planted in the orchards of California farmers willing to donate some land—is about protecting the food supply from the dangers ahead.

Some of the threats are difficult to fight. In 2018, Manosalva planted hundreds of varieties of avocado rootstocks in a field at the front of the South Coast Research and Extension Center, near Irvine Boulevard. The plan was to encourage these varieties to cross-pollinate and produce fruit with the potential to pass on important traits, from salinity tolerance to tree structure. The orchard isn't uniform. The trees in a breeding block are from different parents, and they vary widely in size and shape. A Toro Canyon spreads its limbs wide and its leaves curl slightly, while a neighbor rises twice as high in a narrow column. On one tree, smooth-skinned green avocados with crooked necks hang on a high branch, like unripe squash dangling in the shade. The fruit is often rubbery and doesn't taste great, but that's not what matters here. What matters is if they survive. Manosalva planted a younger block of open-pollinated trees beside the first block in 2020. Not long after, she learned that the University of California intended to take over the land to build housing for employees of its nearby Irvine campus. A major source of budwood for the university's research would be lost. Manosalva started over with new plantings at the back of the research station, but she feels the University of California regents have disrespected her work. "They jeopardized my trees," she said. "It's not trivial. It's five years of my work."

On a pleasant Orange County day, Matthew Elvena, one of

Manosalva's research assistants, stood near one of her new orchards, young trees grafted from the block soon to be plowed under to make way for housing. He pulled a bottle of water out of the cab of his truck. It was seventy-five degrees Fahrenheit with a soft offshore breeze blowing in from the Pacific, but in the back of the orchard the sun felt hot. He watched a coyote lope through a neighboring grove and disappear into the high golden grass. The trees were remnants of seeds and budwood collected by Zentmyer during his travels through Central America. All that remained was a cluster of trees of various sizes, some with wide, low limbs and sparse foliage, others towering four stories high. Bare branches rose up from the crown of one tree like antennae, providing a perch for crows and hawks looking for prey. Many of Zentmyer's collections, despite showing resistance to *Phytophthora cinnamomi*, proved incompatible with *Persea americana*; others that did accept grafts didn't become productive or vigorous tress.

The rootstock found in Guatemala by Martín Grande continued to show promise in certain conditions, and Manosalva was seeking patents on several rootstocks from the Riverside program. Many of the trees at the South Coast Research and Extension Center were planted on Duke 7 or a rootstock from South Africa called Dusa. Orchards in South Africa had been devastated by root fungus in the 1980s and 1990s, and while the South Africans had pioneered a phosphorous treatment that helped the trees heal, Westfalia researcher Stefan Köhne spotted Dusa's promise and sent budwood to Riverside for further study.

Then one day in the mid-1990s, "out of the blue I got a call from California . . . and it was Hank Brokaw," Köhne said. "I remember well his words. He said, 'I think we need to talk about the Dusa. I'd like you to come and visit us.'"[42] Hank encouraged him to patent the rootstock and grant Brokaw Nursery a commercial license, a gesture Köhne describes as both businesslike and gentlemanly, since many people simply took budwood and planted it without asking. As of early 2024, close to 12 million avocado trees worldwide have been planted on Dusa rootstock. While the profits went to his employer, in the world of avocado breeding, Köhne's name is as famous as Popenoe, Brokaw, and Hass. As Köhne put it, "That little call was the start of a very long story that hasn't ended yet."

Epilogue

WILSON POPENOE'S CHILDREN DONATED CASA POPENOE, the historic family home in Antigua, Guatemala, in 2007 to the Universidad Francisco Marroquín to preserve it as a museum and research center. A towering Fuerte tree in the garden, planted by Wilson, continues to bear abundantly. Wilson's daughter, Marion Popenoe de Hatch, an esteemed archaeologist now in her nineties, lives nearby, and each year when the tree is in season, she receives a paper bag of fresh-picked Fuertes she enjoys sharing with friends. Of all the avocados her father knew and named, the Fuerte was his favorite, she said. "Everybody loves it."[1]

The Fuerte's historic importance to the industry is celebrated in its ancestral home, too. On a late August day in 2024, historian Jesús Pérez Romero sat in a folding chair beneath the shade of an avocado tree in a courtyard off 3 Poniente 24 in Atlixco, Puebla, the courtyard where Alejandro Le Blanc received his medal nearly a century ago. To his left was the plaque set in concrete by the California Avocado Society in 1938 to mark the historic Fuerte mother tree. Pérez Romero, a former professor at the Meritorious Autonomous University of Puebla, sat beneath the branches of a clone of the original tree, another gift from the Californians, and told visitors the history of the Fuerte during an event known as Fuerte Avocado Day, an annual municipal celebration first marked in Atlixco in 2021 to celebrate the region's deep roots in avocado history.[2] In recent years, Le Blanc's house, affectionately known as La Casa del Aguacate Padre, has operated as a school and a university science museum. The event is the brainchild of

Beatríz Zafra, a local resident who grew up nearby and has worked to rescue the story of the Fuerte and help Atlixco reclaim its role in avocado history.[3] She designed a tourism route with stops at important avocado-related sites, an effort embraced by local chefs and artists as well as avocado producers hoping to expand local Fuerte orchards and create a larger market for the variety. "Few know about the Fuerte avocado," Zafra said. "What we're looking for is to spread the word."[4]

Three thousand miles north, on a steep hillside with a view to the Pacific, two more Fuertes grow among nearly four hundred avocado trees rooted above a narrow canyon. The orchard includes all the varieties important to California and valued samples from among the world's more than one thousand named varieties; together, the trees make an eclectic orchard: some leaves are forest green and glossy; some yellowish; some grow in tight, narrow columns; some reach their branches wide and brush their neighbors. Each tree is identified by name with a metal tag on the trunk. This is the Brokaw Nursery "library block." Grafted onto two kinds of Israeli and South African rootstock that do well in this part of Southern California, the hundreds of trees are clones of every avocado tree that's ever mattered to the U.S. avocado industry. One of the latest is the Luna, a variety launched by the University of California in 2023 with great fanfare. Funded by an investment from the Spanish company Eurosemillas, the Luna looks similar to Hass, and taste panels liked its creamy texture and flavor. Journalists loved its story, pitching it as a climate-saving superfood that would use less water and devour less acreage than the ubiquitous Hass. The Luna grew from a seed produced by a Gwen tree, but unlike its mother, Luna benefited from a well-funded marketing campaign. Its debut made headlines, including *Time* magazine's list of best inventions of the year, even though very few people have ever tried it.[5] Some growers are skeptical it will live up to the hype. Most have never tasted a Luna, and Ramón Paz-Vega says Mexican growers are not interested. Only 1,000 trees are planned for California orchards in 2025, but Eurosemillas expects that number will grow.

Other varieties in the library include the Mexicola, planted from a seed in 1910 at Coolidge Rare Plant Gardens in Pasadena, and the Nabal, one of Fred Popenoe's selections that came from Antigua, Guatemala, in 1917. The Puebla is here, too, along with a Fairchild, a Popenoe, and the wild avocados Zentmyer and Schieber collected in Central America. There's the Choquette, a large, oval, green avocado planted in 1929 on Remi D. Choquette's land in Miami. Gwen is here, along with Gray E. Martin's pride and joy, the popular GEM. There's a Hashimoto, a Hawaiian avocado that tastes rancid if picked too late; Reed, a tasty round avocado patented by James Reed in San Diego County in 1960; and Lamb Hass, a UC Riverside–patented variety bred from a tree at Bob Lamb's farm in Camarillo. The Lamb Hass turns black when ripe, and a blunt end near the stem looks a bit like shoulders. The list goes on: Don Gillogly, Queen, Iron Horse, Jan Boyce, Linda, Hollister, Hayes. The Holiday, believed to be a grandchild of the Murrieta, is also in the library block, a UC Riverside selection whose branches tend to sprawl across the ground. There's Zutano and Bacon, Kidd, Julia, and Jones. Secret avocados known only by code numbers are still being studied and await their public debut.[6]

Consuelo Fernández Noguera and Kamille Garcia-Brucher scale the slope, their eyes scanning the brush for rattlesnakes. Garcia-Brucher holds a clipboard with a map identifying the location of each tree. Every few yards, one of them pulls back a thick curtain of leaves and disappears into the tree canopy. Two copies of every tree grow here, a built-in backup system for an orchard that is itself a backup. Fernández Noguera studied agriculture in her native Chile and has worked with avocados for almost fifteen years, first at the South African produce company Westfalia, then at Brokaw Nursery, where she began in 2014 as the manager of international business and research and development. In 2022, she became the nursery's COO. The library block was planted in 2017 and is a close copy of the orchard kept by the University of California avocado breeders at the South Coast Research and Extension Center in Irvine. Like Patricia Manosalva, she was shaken to learn that the university regents planned to build on the university-owned farm.

"The whole germplasm concept is at risk," Fernández Noguera says. "Housing is coming into play. Reclaimed water is stressing the trees."[7] Fernández Noguera pulls a dark, slender leaf from a nearby branch, crushes it in her fingers, and breathes in. The scent of licorice and the fruit's smooth, thin black skin signal the tree comes from Mexico.

Not all trees in the library block are commercially useful, but they are kept alive "por amor al arte," Fernández Noguera says, using a Spanish phrase that translates "for the love of art" or creativity. Once a year, they harvest the library's fruit and invite guests, university staff, and CAS members to the nursery to see, taste, and enjoy the wild abundance. Por amor al arte, Brokaw Nursery also shared some tree cuttings with the Huntington in San Marino for two more avocado libraries. The first, planted in 2010, is filled with sixty-five trees representing thirty-three historic varieties in honor of Hank Brokaw and Jack Shepherd, a past president of Calavo and editor of the California Avocado Society yearbook for nearly fifty years. Former society president Carl Stucky oversaw the project, and a crew led by Pablo Rodriguez, an expert grafter trained by Hank, grafted the entire orchard in a single day.

A short walk from the collection of Fuertes and Ganters and Reeds, past Huntington's massive sarcophagus and the hulking remnants of the orchard William Hertrich planted here for Huntington in 1908, Raquel Folgado is growing avocados in her laboratory. Folgado, a cryopreservation research botanist who grew up on a farm in Spain, has dozens of glass jars of varying sizes lining metal shelves, each holding bits of plant tissue suspended in clear gel with a cocktail of sugars, minerals, and hormones. Illuminated by long bulbs that emit a cool, bright glow, some jars burst with bushy green tassels, others host tiny brown stumps with leaves no larger than a grain of rice. She has labeled every jar with the date and the name of the variety: "Here you can see, Lyon," she says. "This is Toro Canyon. This is wild avocado, *Persea indica*."[8] She goes down the line, sixty-six varieties in all, including Pinkerton, Bacon, and Puebla, Duke 7, Gwen, and Hass. The varieties that make progress are moved to larger jars filled with perlite, where some send out delicate roots. The roots are important. These test-tube avocados can grow leaves all day, but if you don't have roots, Folgado explains, you don't have a tree. She tweaks the cocktail, tries younger plant tissue, and sees what grows. A few of her lab-grown specimens have matured enough to plant in a nursery. It will take time to get the stubborn Hass to root, but Folgado will persevere.

For many conducting research on the avocado, the work is not about art, it's about survival. Humans need diverse ecosystems, and the food supply can be threatened by many things: diseases, pests, fires, floods, housing developments, drug traffickers. Mono-crops like the Hass avocado are particularly vulnerable. If scientists can learn to grow trees in a lab, they can deep-freeze the tissue in a national cryobank and save it for future generations. If they can find a better rootstock, they can grow more productive trees and feed more people. If they can find a way to use less water in the orchards, they can help reduce the climate impact of the industry and, like the scientists who came before them, share their knowledge with other researchers striving to save and protect the food supply.

Scientists are also continuing efforts to build a better avocado. In 2019, an international team of scientists, led by Luis Herrera-Estrella, professor of plant genomics at Texas Tech University in Lubbock and an emeritus professor at Mexico's National Laboratory of Genomics for Biodiversity, sequenced the Hass avocado's genome.[9] The analysis revealed a genetic map providing insight into the Hass's past—its lineage turns out to be 39 percent Guatemalan and 61 percent Mexican—and opened new possibilities for its future. Using avocados donated by the Salvador Sánchez Colín Foundation in Mexico, researchers sequenced the genome of sample avocados from the three known botanical types, *Persea* vars. *drymifolia*, *guatemalensis*, and *americana*, as well as some wild avocados and fungus-resistant rootstocks. The USDA is also invested in genetic research, maintaining a germplasm collection in Miami. Recent genetic studies led by researchers in Australia have delved deeper into the Hass's twelve pairs of chromosomes and roughly 48,000 genes and are helping explain why the Hass is so rich in potassium, more susceptible to certain diseases than some varieties, and so quick to brown when exposed to the air.[10]

Dr. Jeff Touchman of GreenVenus, an agricultural biotechnology company in Davis, California, is working to solve the browning problem. Touchman estimates that up to half of avocados purchased by consumers are thrown away due to browning. Studies show it's one of the top reasons people don't buy the fruit. In June 2023, he announced a breakthrough: his group had silenced a gene in the avocado responsible for browning, the same enzyme that causes lettuce, mushrooms, apples, and potatoes to brown when cut. Touchman spent six years and used CRISPR technology to coax avocado cells to grow in his laboratory. Several six- or seven-inch-high "plantlets" were planted. "We have not produced fruit yet. That will be the biggest test of non-browning, of course," Touchman said. He was confident the avocado trees would grow and bear fruit. "I think it's going to be a blockbuster."[11]

The river of avocados keeps flowing. Day and night, the fruit crosses into the United States from Mexico by the truckload, each truck carrying 40,000 pounds of Hass destined for Costco or

Walmart or regional wholesalers like JL Gonzalez Produce of Chicago. There, as he has for the past two decades, Inocencio Andrade greets the avocados at 3:00 a.m. at the loading dock behind the Chicago International Produce Market off Interstate 55. Forklift by forklift, he moves stacks of twenty-five-pound boxes into a two-story-high cold storage room set at a cool forty degrees Fahrenheit. He can squeeze five truckloads into the room—one hundred tons of avocados—and each box comes with a story, stamped on labels with the packinghouse name and encrypted codes noting the farm of origin and the date of harvest.

Most of the avocados are the Alejandrina brand from Michoacán—the gold standard, the "Coca-Cola of avocados," said Miguel Gonzalez, whose oldest brother, José, started the business in 1993. Back then, they sold less than a truckload a week, with the only supply coming from California or Chile. Today, they sell at least ten truckloads a week, two hundred tons of avocados, more than 99 percent of them Mexican. They also own a 227,000-square-foot warehouse in Texas. While most avocados grown in Mexico are not from clonal rootstock, that is beginning to change. A new Brokaw Nursery in Jalisco is selling double-cloned Hass avocado trees to Mexican farmers who prize their hardiness and resistance to drought and disease. That fruit will eventually make its way to the Gonzalezes' loading dock, too. "The demand keeps growing, and it's not only Hispanics for guacamole," Gonzalez said. "It's Asians, Indians, all cultures. They want avocados."[12]

Look in the backs of hundreds of small grocery chains, sushi restaurants, mom-and-pop stores, chain stores, and Michelin-star restaurants in Chicago, and you'll find the Gonzalez brothers' avocados. Sysco, the food-distribution giant, is a major customer; its trucks pull up to the warehouse's loading dock daily to transport avocados to restaurants, schools, hospitals, and stores throughout Chicago and as far west as the Dakotas and east to Ohio. Rick

Bayless will buy from no one else. The Gonzalez family won his loyalty because of the quality of the Alejandrina fruit and their expertise in ripening it.

The produce contracts are negotiated at a bank of computers under the watchful eye of Our Lady of Guadalupe, a portrait of the Virgin Mary who serves as a national symbol for Mexican Catholics. But the magic happens beyond her view, between the two loading docks on the spotless, gleaming concrete floors of the 85,000-square-foot warehouse, where Andrade monitors ten state-of-the-art avocado-ripening rooms. The rooms are two stories tall, simple concrete rooms with pull-down garage-style doors, high steel racks to hold the crates, and small black boxes about the size of home-computer routers affixed to one wall near the floor. The boxes emit ethylene, control temperature and humidity, and connect to a console on the warehouse wall and an app on Andrade's phone. The ripening process is an art and a science. Each step is carefully calibrated: the temperature, the timing, the percentage of oxygen and ethylene. Andrade relies on the expertise of the Mexican farmers as well as the work of scientists, marketing experts, horticulturalists, nursery owners, and business owners across many generations. He also relies on two decades of experience watching the avocados come into the Chicago loading dock day after day. He adjusts the gas and the timing depending on the season, when the fruit was harvested, and what the customers want. Some want green fruit; others want avocados ready to eat within three days, or two days, or one. All want perfect avocados.

As delicious as it is, the creamy, ripe Hass avocado is not the only standard of avocado perfection. Those who have embarked on the quest for the ideal avocado—from Fred and Wilson Popenoe to George Hodgkin, Salvador Sánchez Colín, Bob Bergh, Hank Brokaw, Mary Lu Arpaia, and others—appreciated the avocado's vast array of flavors, hues, and textures and understood its vulnerabilities. As new orchards rise up from Mexico to Chile, South Africa to Spain, China, India, and Kenya, a new generation will have the opportunity to decide what a perfect avocado should be. This is a generation that values healthy food at affordable prices and also cares deeply about responsible water management, climate-friendly supply chains, fair wages, and safe housing for laborers.

To meet the growing demand and prepare for the new challenges ahead, the Hass Avocado Board recently developed a training program to mentor young industry leaders.[13] Many who join the HAB cohorts farm avocados themselves or work for distributors with ties to avocado-producing regions in Mexico, California, Peru, Chile, and Colombia. HAB's aim is to cultivate new board members who are tech savvy, globally minded, and able to communicate with people across the industry, from family farmers and packinghouse managers to politicians, megastore executives, scientists, and representatives of the USDA. In the years ahead, these trailblazers will have the opportunity to follow the path of the avocado pioneers and embark on new quests to redefine avocado perfection. Wherever they decide to invest their money and attention, they will learn what it takes to leave us all craving more.

Notes

ABBREVIATIONS

CAA, AR   California Avocado Association, Annual Report
(vol. 1, 1915–vol. 11, 1926)

CAA, Y   California Avocado Association, Yearbook
(vol. 12, 1927–vol. 25, 1940)

CAS, Y   California Avocado Society, Yearbook
(vol. 26, 1941–vol. 90, 2007)

WPFP, HI   Wilson Popenoe (1892–1975) family papers, Archives
collection no. 204, Hunt Institute for Botanical
Documentation, Carnegie Mellon University

Introduction

1. Alvaro Luque, Stephanie Bazan, and Ivonne Kinser, "The Story Behind the Avocado with Avocados From Mexico (AFM)," interview by Jorge Ferraez, *Latino Leaders Magazine*, June 23, 2020, video, 1:07:40, youtube.com/watch?v=5EzuXAiyZQc.

2. David Magaña, Cindy van Rijswick, Gonzalo Salinas, and Pia Piggott, "Global Avocado Update 2024: Trade Gradually Shifting as Industry Expands," Rabobank Rabo Research, May 2023, www.rabobank.com/knowledge/q011429713-global-avocado-update-2024-trade-gradually-shifting-as-industry-expands.

3. Stephania Corpi and Toya Sarno Jordan, *Caliber 60*, Texas Public Radio, www.tpr.org/podcast/caliber-60-a-podcast-about-the-flow-of-avocados-guns-and-people.

1 • Dreamers

1. "Charles Monroe Sheldon/Central Congregational Church Collection," Kansas Historical Society, accessed September 5, 2004, www.kshs.org/p/charles-monroe-sheldon-central.../14115.

2. "That Experiment," *The Topeka State Journal*, March 23, 1900; "A Turmoil: Topeka Capital Sanctum Is Divided Against Itself; As Jesus Would Edit," *The Oberlin Times*, March 23, 1900; "Popenoe Affairs Involved," *The Topeka State Journal*, March 27, 1901.

3. This was also the site of the Thayer Mining and Milling Company. "Col. Johnson's Expedition," *The Topeka State Journal*, June 21, 1899.

4. "Col. Johnson's Expedition," *The Topeka State Journal*; Milton Franklin Reitz, "The Gold Mines of Costa Rica," *The Engineering and Mining Journal* 74 (August 16, 1902): 210–13.

5. Frederic Rosengarten Jr., *Wilson Popenoe: Agricultural Explorer, Educator, and Friend of Latin America* (Lawai, HI: National Tropical Botanical Garden, 1991), 1–7.

6. D. W. Coolidge, "Pasadena the Beautiful" and "Fruits and Flowers of Pasadena," *The Pacific Monthly*, vol. 15 (January 1906–June 1906).

7. "William A. Bowen House," Greene & Greene Virtual Archives, accessed August 20, 2024, gamblehouse.org/ggva/123.html; "Houses, Lots and Lands—Review of Building and Development, Continued," *Los Angeles Sunday Times*, May 5, 1907.

8. Michelle Huneven, "The Polymath Popenoes," *Altadena Heritage Newsletter*, May 2014.

9. Wilson Popenoe, "Recollections of an Agricultural Explorer," 33:23, 3, WPFP, HI.

10. Victoria Padilla, *Southern California Gardens: An Illustrated History* (Santa Barbara: Allen A. Knoll, Publishers, 1994), 257.

11. Knowles A. Ryerson, "Avocado Reminiscences: Some Egotistical Notes by a Tropical Tramp," CAS, Y 27 (1943): 72.

12. Rosengarten, *Wilson Popenoe*, 7.

13. Jana Shaker, "The Founding and First One Hundred Years of the Citrus Experiment Station," *Chronicle of the University of California*, no. 8 (Fall 2006): 3–29; Historical Note, University of California, Riverside, Citrus Research and Agricultural Experiment Station records, University Archives, UC Riverside.

14. Ernest Braunton, *The Garden Beautiful in California: A Practical Manual for All Who Garden* (Los Angeles: Cultivator Publishing Co., 1915), 51.

15. Ernest Braunton, "Thirty Years' Observation of Tropical Fruits," CAA, AR 7 (1920–1921): 17 19.

16. Wilson Popenoe, "Looking Back," CAA, Y 21 (1936): 51–59.

17. Popenoe, "Recollections," 3–4.
18. Wilson Popenoe, Scrapbook 5, WPFP, HI.
19. Popenoe, "Recollections," 4.
20. Padilla, *Southern California Gardens*, 88–92.
21. Mary June Burton, "Avocados Made to Order," *Los Angeles Times*, August 30, 1936.
22. Nelson Klose, "Dr. Henry Perrine, Tropical Plant Enthusiast," *The Florida Historical Quarterly* 27, no. 2 (1948): 189–201.
23. Perrine is credited for the first documented planting of avocados in the continental United States. Cyrus W. Butler, "Pineapples and Other Tropical Fruits," *Proceedings of the Fourteenth Annual Meeting of the Florida State Horticultural Society* (DeLand: Florida State Horticultural Society, 1901), 52.
24. R. J. Griesbach, *150 Years of Research at the United States Department of Agriculture: Plant Introduction and Breeding* (USDA, June 2013).
25. David Fairchild, *The World Was My Garden: Travels of a Plant Explorer* (New York: Charles Scribner's Sons, 1938), 286.
26. Fairchild, *The World Was My Garden*, 117.
27. Fairchild, *The World Was My Garden*, 120.
28. Fairchild, *The World Was My Garden*, 130.
29. It was thanks to Cook that Fairchild was soon known by the title *plant explorer*, rather than the eyebrow-raising *special agent*. Fairchild, *The World Was My Garden*, 117.
30. Harold T. Pinkett, "Records of the First Century of Interest of the United States in Government in Plant Industries," *Agricultural History* 29, no. 1 (January 1955): 40.
31. G. N. Collins, *The Avocado, a Salad Fruit from the Tropics*, USDA, Bureau of Plant Industry (Washington, D.C.: Government Printing Office, 1905).
32. Janet M. Hill, *The Boston Cooking-School Magazine*, vol. 9, June–July 1904–May 1905, 153, 194.
33. Janet M. Hill, *A Short History of the Banana and a Few Recipes for Its Use* (Boston: United Fruit Company, 1904).
34. Amanda Harris, *Fruits of Eden, David Fairchild and America's Plant Hunters* (Gainesville: University Press of Florida, 2015), 137.
35. Popenoe, "Looking Back," 55.
36. Popenoe, "Recollections," 4.
37. Popenoe, "Recollections," 4.

38. Ryerson, "Avocado Reminiscences," 72; Roma Coolidge Mulvihill, "Heaths Are Bonnie," *Los Angeles Times*, February 16, 1950.

39. In 1909, Coolidge budded about 150 two-year-old seedlings "in the open ground." Wilson Popenoe, "The Avocado in Southern California," *Pomona College Journal of Economic Botany* 1, no. 1 (February 1911): 9.

40. Popenoe, "The Avocado," 8.

41. Knowles Ryerson, M. E. Jaffa, and H. Goss, *Avocado Culture in California* (Berkeley: University of California Press, 1923), 584–86.

42. "Avocado Propagation," *The Tampa Daily Times*, April 24, 1916.

43. Ryerson, *Avocado Culture*, 584–86.

44. Ryerson, "Avocado Reminiscences," 72.

45. Popenoe, "Looking Back," 56; "A Streetcar Named Orange Dummy," *Los Angeles Times*, January 16, 2000.

46. Fairchild, *The World Was My Garden*, 130.

47. C. W. Beers, "Joseph Sexton—An Appreciation," CAA, AR 3 (1917): 75–77.

48. "Fruit Wealth in the Making, Experimenters Develop New Varieties Here," *Los Angeles Times*, June 21, 1914.

49. "Among Owners and Dealers," *Los Angeles Sunday Times*, July 31, 1904.

50. William Hertrich, "Early Experiences in Avocado Growing," CAA, Y 21 (1936): 158–60.

51. William Hertrich, *The Huntington Botanical Gardens, 1905–1949: Personal Recollections of William Hertrich* (San Marino, CA: Huntington Library Press, 1988), 38–39.

52. "William Hertrich, In Appreciation," CAA, Y 25 (1940), 10.

53. Ryerson, "Avocado Reminiscences," 73; Hertrich, *The Huntington Botanical Gardens*, 3; Carroll C. Calkins, ed. *Great Gardens of America* (NY: Coward-McMann Inc., 1969), 280.

54. Rosengarten, *Wilson Popenoe*, 9.

55. Wilson Popenoe, "Reflections, Reminiscences, and Observations," CAS, Y 32 (1947): 101.

56. Wilson's scrapbook also contained pamphlets outlining how to send plant samples to the USDA. "Agricultural Experts Here," Scrapbook 5, p. 13, WPFP, HI; Popenoe, "Looking Back," includes a reference to receiving government plants for testing; "Government Officials Favor Alligator Pears," *Los Angeles Herald*, August 17, 1910.

57. Rosengarten, *Wilson Popenoe*, 8–9.

58. "Inaugurate a Course in Plant Life," *Los Angeles Express*, November 25, 1909.

59. "Foreword," *Pomona College Journal of Economic Botany* 1 (February 1911): 1.

60. Charles Fuller Baker to Wilson Popenoe, December 24, 1910, 3:22, WPFP, HI.

61. Popenoe, "The Avocado."

62. Popenoe, "The Avocado," 3. The next issue of the *Pomona College Journal of Economic Botany* included an endorsement from Professor E. J. Wickson, director of the state experiment station in Berkeley, who believed Wilson's article would not only help to pump up the avocado industry but also "do our state credit through Popenoe's scientific industry and ability."

63. William D. Stephens, "Promise of Enlarged Horticultural Possibilities," *California Cultivator* 36, no. 2 (January 12, 1911): 1, 38.

64. Wilson Popenoe, "Atlixco," CAA, AR 5 (1919–1920): 24–43.

65. "New Avocado Firm," *California Cultivator* 36 (May 18, 1911): 614.

66. Padilla, *Southern California Gardens*, 83. Harvey and horticulturalist William S. Lyon were among a committee of gardeners who introduced unusual trees into Los Angeles' Elysian Park.

67. Ernest Braunton, "Juan Murrieta, 1844–1936," CAA, Y 21 (1936): 45–46.

68. Popenoe, "Citrus and Tropical Fruits, A Widening Horticultural Horizon," *California Cultivator* 36, no. 17 (April 27, 1911): 516; Wilson Popenoe to David Fairchild, March 3, 1911, 7:93, WPFP, HI.

69. Popenoe, "The Avocado."

2 • The Survivor

1. Dr. Beul F. Enyeart, interviewed by Dan Hoppy, California State College, Fullerton Oral History Project, December 2, 1968.

2. "In Memoriam, Carl B. Schmidt," CAS, Y 54 (1970–1971): 6–7; Popenoe, "Recollections," chap. 3, p. 1.

3. Popenoe, "Looking Back"; "Southern California Field Notes, October 9, 1915–February 15, 1916," Wilson Popenoe papers, University Archives, UC Riverside.

4. "Southern California Field Notes." Wilson explains the term *ahuacate de China* as of "indefinite application," but referring to high-quality thin-skinned fruit. *Papel de China*, "the term commonly used for tissue paper," appeared to describe the avocado's thin skin. He later

revised this theory, noting that superior fruits of all types were given the *de China* designation, which derived from "the early days," when "many fine things came to New Spain, as Mexico was then called, from China." Wilson Popenoe and Louis O. Williams, "Mexican Explorations of 1948," CAS, Y 33 (1948): 56. No. 13 was later named Puebla.

5. "New Avocado Firm," *California Cultivator*, May 18, 1911.

6. Wilson Popenoe, "The White Sapote," *Pomona College Journal of Economic Botany* 1 (May 1911): 83.

7. Wilson Popenoe, "The Commercial Avocado," *Rural Californian* 35 (July 1911): 208–10.

8. "General Meeting, Nov. 7, 1911," *Journal of the Royal Horticultural Society* 37 (1911/1912): ccix.

9. Wilson Popenoe, "Doctor Franceschi on the Avocado," CAA, Y 27 (1943): 64.

10. Dr. F. Franceschi, "The Ahuacate," *Rural Californian* 17 (July 1894), 328; plant catalog, Southern California Acclimatizing Association, 1894.

11. Franceschi, "The Ahuacate," 328.

12. Popenoe, "Doctor Franceschi on the Avocado," 65.

13. "Horticultural Society Meeting," *Daily Independent* (Santa Barbara), July 2, 1885.

14. H. C. Ford, "Rare Fruits, Productions of Santa Barbara Channel Region," *Los Angeles Times*, February 19, 1888.

15. Franceschi, "The Ahuacate," 328.

16. Padilla, *Southern California Gardens*, 115.

17. Padilla, *Southern California Gardens*, 150–56.

18. "Flowers, Flowers Beautiful Flowers," *South Pasadena Record*, October 27, 1911.

19. Cornell also designed the landscape surrounding the West India Gardens office. Marie Barnidge-McIntyre, "Ralph Dalton Cornell, FASLA," *Eden: Journal of the California Garden & Landscape Society* 17, no. 4 (Fall 2014), 4.

20. P. D. Barnhart, "Flower Show of the Pasadena Horticultural Society," *The Florist's Exchange*, November 19, 1911.

21. Fred's photograph appeared in the newspaper. West India Gardens, *The Avocado*, 1912.

22. "Avocado Has Fine Future," *Los Angeles Times*, November 5, 1911.

23. West India Gardens, *The Avocado*.

24. E. B. Rivers, "Marketing," CAA, AR 1 (1915–1916): 75–77; "Ford Employees Find Pay More Than Doubled," *The Detroit Times*, January 19, 1914.

25. Rivers, "Marketing," 75–77.

26. Popenoe, "Recollections," 5.

27. "Hard to Secure Date Palms Now for Great California Industry," *Los Angeles Times*, June 9, 1912.

28. "Los Angeles Woman Largest Date Grower," *Los Angeles Sunday Times*, July 21, 1912.

29. "Los Angeles Woman Largest Date Grower," *Los Angeles Sunday Times*.

30. Rosengarten, *Wilson Popenoe*, 13–18.

31. Philip J. Pauly, *Fruits and Plains: The Horticultural Transformation of America* (Cambridge, MA: Harvard University Press, 2007), 145.

32. Howard Seftel, "Government Regulation and the Rise of the Fruit Industry: The Entrepreneurial Attack on Fruit Pests, 1880–1920," *Business History Review* 59, no. 3 (Fall 1985): 369; Paul Popenoe and Roswell Hill Johnson, *Applied Eugenics* (New York: The Macmillan Company, 1918).

33. "National Plant Quarantine Law, Lately Passed, Now Takes Effect," *Times-Democrat* (New Orleans), September 22, 1912.

34. Hertrich, "Early Experiences," 159.

35. Wilson Popenoe, "Origin of the Name 'Fuerte,'" CAS, Y 26 (1941): 34.

36. "The Recent Freeze and the Avocado," *Monrovia Daily News*, March 21, 1913.

37. "The Recent Freeze and the Avocado," *Monrovia Daily News*.

38. Wilson later mentioned that the Fuerte "cost the West India Gardens five thousand dollars." Popenoe, "Reflections," 97.

39. "Orange and Lemon Land Located in a Proven District," *Long Beach Press*, March 8, 1913; "North Whittier Heights Orange and Lemon Land on Easy Payments," *The Whittier News*, February 22, 1913.

40. "Will Celebrate Formal Opening," *The Whittier News*, May 14, 1913; "From Grain Field to Citrus Empire," *The Whittier News*, September 20, 1913.

41. John Steven McGroarty, ed., *History of Los Angeles County* (Chicago: The American Historical Society Inc., 1923), 3:87.

42. "Scenic Drive for Whittier," *The Whittier News*, April 19, 1913.

43. "Rideout to Rideout Heights, Get Rightout and see the Sights," *The Whittier News*, April 10, 1913.

44. Esther Rideout, interviewed by Phyllis Pearce and Martha Russel, Whittier Public Library, September 22, 1976, localhistory.whittier library.org/collections/oral-histories.

45. Esther Rideout, interviewed by Phyllis Pearce and Martha Russel.

46. "Avocado Tree Is to Yield $2,500," *Santa Ana Daily Register*, December 4, 1912.

47. "Whittier Man Owns Most Valuable Tree in the World," *Monrovia Daily News*, March 14, 1914.

48. "Real Estate; Serves You Right," *The Whittier News*, October 29, 1919.

49. "Would Remove Freeze Fangs," *Los Angeles Times*, January 30, 1913.

50. Herbert J. Webber, "The Two Freezes of 1894–95 in Florida and What They Teach," *Yearbook of the United States Department of Agriculture 1896* (Washington, D.C.: Government Printing Office, 1897).

51. Ryerson, "Avocado Reminiscences," 71–75.

3 • Birth of an Industry

1. "Study Habits of Avocado Weevil," *Los Angeles Express*, August 14, 1913.

2. John Shepherd and Gary Bender, "A History of the Avocado Industry in California," CAS, Y 85 (2001): 29–50.

3. Seftel, "Government Regulation," 386–87.

4. Seftel, "Government Regulation," 387–88.

5. "The Centennial International Exhibition," *Illustrated Australian News*, August 15, 1888.

6. Wilson Popenoe, "Brazilian Expedition, 1913–1914," Office of Foreign Seed and Plant Introduction, USDA. babel.hathitrust.org/cgi/pt?id=ucl.31175035218547&seq=15.

7. Popenoe, "Recollections," chap. 2, p. 2.

8. Popenoe, "Recollections," chap. 2, p. 1. Wilson erroneously recalls the date of the tree's transplantation as 1908. "President Warmly Welcomed Within California Borders; Fresh at End of a Hard Day," *San Francisco Chronicle*, May 8, 1903.

9. "Naturalists Bring Jaca, Pitomba, and Imbu Home From Brazil After Thrilling Tropic Hunt," *The Washington Times*, May 24, 1914.

10. Theodore Roosevelt, *Through the Brazilian Wilderness* (NY: Charles Scribner's Sons, 1914; repr., Greenwood Press, 1969), 272.

11. Clayton S. Ellsworth, "Theodore Roosevelt's Country Life Commission," *Agricultural History* 34 (October 1960): 155–72.

12. Rosengarten, *Wilson Popenoe*, 33.

13. "San Francisco Hotel Man Is Pioneer in New Industry," *Monrovia Daily News*, September 8, 1914.
14. "Citrus Fruits' Great Future," *Los Angeles Times*, November 12, 1914.
15. "Citrus Fruits' Great Future."
16. Rosengarten, *Wilson Popenoe*, 33.
17. David Fairchild, "Reminiscences of Early Plant Introduction Work in South Florida," *Proceedings of the Florida State Historical Society* 51 (1938): 11–13.
18. H. J. Webber, "New Horticultural and Agricultural Terms," *Science* 28 (1903): 501–3; Jane Maienschein, *Whole View of Life? Embryos, Cloning, and Stem Cells* (Cambridge, MA: Harvard University Press, 2003), 120.
19. Wilson Popenoe to Fred Popenoe and Marion Popenoe, February 2, 1915; February 5, 1915; February 12, 1915; February 25, 1915, 16:254; F. O. Popenoe, "Varieties of the Avocado," CAA, AR 1 (1915–1916), 44–69.
20. Wilson Popenoe to Fred Popenoe, January 4, 1915; January 31, 1915; March 19, 1915, 16:254; Popenoe, "Recollections," chap. 2, p. 6.
21. Wilson Popenoe to Fred Popenoe, January 22, 1915, 16:254.

4 • Roots

1. F. O. Popenoe, "Our Association," CAA, AR 11 (1925–1926): 44–48.
2. "Pear Growers to Organize," *Los Angeles Express*, May 10, 1915; "Join Forces to Promote New Industry," *The Whittier News*, May 15, 1915; Popenoe, "Our Association."
3. "Report of the Organization of the California Ahuacate Association," CAA, Y 18 (1933): 109–18; "General Discussion," CAA, AR 1 (1915–1916): 81–91.
4. "For Benefit of Avocado Market, Growers of Fine Fruit Form Organization," *Los Angeles Times*, May 15, 1915.
5. Wilson Popenoe to Fred Popenoe and Marion Popenoe, May 5, 1915; May 20, 1915, 16:254.
6. Fred did not name Killick in his article. Popenoe, "Our Association," 44.
7. Alma Whitaker, Sugar and Spice, *Los Angeles Times*, June 5, 1927.
8. "W. A. Spinks on Board of Avocado Society," *Monrovia Daily News*, June 2, 1915; W. A. Spinks, "A Wonderfully Interesting and Promising New Industry," *Monrovia Daily News*, June 19, 1915.
9. "Productions of St. Thomas," *The New England Farmer*, October 5, 1831; "The Brazilian Empire," *The New York Daily Herald*, June 4, 1854;

"The Traveler in Cuba, Life in Havana," *Monongahela Valley Republican*, March 18, 1853.

10. Thomas J. Murrey, *Valuable Cooking Receipts* (New York: George W. Harlan, c. 1880), 58; "Terrapin Tom a Suicide," *The New York Times*, May 23, 1900.

11. Thomas J. Murrey, *Murrey's Salads and Sauces* (New York: Charles T. Dillingham, 1884), 45.

12. Maria Parloa, *Miss Parloa's Kitchen Companion* (New York: The Clover Publishing Co., 1887), 435–36.

13. Anna M. Paris, "The Avocado, or Alligator Pear," *The American Magazine [Frank Leslie's Popular Monthly]* 31 (January 1891), 54.

14. Stella Burke May, "Each According to His Like," *The Boston Cooking-School Magazine* 19 (August–September 1914): 138.

15. Willa Cather, *The Song of the Lark* (Boston: Houghton Mifflin Company, 1915), 334.

16. May, "Each According to His Like," 138.

17. *Los Angeles Times Cook Book No. 2* (Los Angeles: The Times-Mirror Company, 1905).

18. "'The Times' New School of Domestic Science," *Los Angeles Times*, November 10, 1912.

19. "How to Cook as the Spanish Do," *Los Angeles Times*, February 13, 1913.

20. "A La Espanola. Cooks Chicken Spanish Style," *Los Angeles Times*, February 14, 1913.

21. "Progress at the Times School of Domestic Science," *Los Angeles Times*, April 20 and 22, 1913.

22. "A La Espanola. Cooks Chicken Spanish Style," *Los Angeles Times*.

23. "Filibusters from Los Angeles Depart for the Mexico Border," *Los Angeles Times*, March 12, 1913.

24. "Pitiful Suffering in Sonoratown," *Covina Argus*, November 22, 1913.

25. Bertha Haffner-Ginger, *California Mexican-Spanish Cook Book* (Los Angeles: Citizen Print Shop, 1914).

26. Haffner-Ginger, *California Mexican-Spanish Cook Book*.

27. "See Big Money in Avocados," *Los Angeles Times*, October 24, 1915.

28. C. P. Taft, "Things to Be Expected," CAA, AR 1 (1915–1916): 73–75.

29. "Pomological Experts Wonder at Rare Fruit," *Los Angeles Times*, August 26, 1915.

30. "Milk Tester Finds Fat In Alligator Pear," *Oakland Tribune*, October 7, 1915; "Tests Fruit Like Milk," *Los Angeles Times*, October 8, 1915.

31. "Warns of Citrus Peril, Advises Avocado as Measure of Relief," *Oakland Tribune*, August 8, 1915.

32. Burton, "Avocados Made to Order."

33. Popenoe, "Southern California Field Notes."

34. "William Hertrich, In Appreciation."

35. "Epochal: Big Things for New Industry," *Los Angeles Times*, October 16, 1915.

36. "General Discussion," CAA, AR 1 (1915–1916): 83.

5 • The Fuerte's Rise

1. Advertisement, CAA, AR 1 (1915–1916), 102.

2. Margaret Stewart, "My Experience in Growing Avocados," CAA, AR 3 (1917–1918): 63–66.

3. Edwin G. Hart, "The Association and Its Purposes," CAA, AR 1 (1915–1916): 7–9.

4. Professor Ira J. Condit, "New Items of Interest," CAA, AR 1 (1915–1916): 10–21.

5. "Avocado Growers' Meeting," *California Cultivator*, October 28, 1915, 114.

6. "For Benefit of Avocado Market."

7. "Horticultural Society," *Daily Independent* (Santa Barbara), November 9, 1891.

8. Charles Ranhofer, *The Epicurean* (New York: C. Ranhofer, 1900), 355.

9. "For Benefit of Avocado Market."

10. "Will Raise Alligator Pears," *Los Angeles Times*, May 25, 1912.

11. "Preface," CAA, AR 1 (1915–1916): 5.

12. "The California Avocado Association Is Issuing in Folder Form the Following Suggestions for Preparing the Avocado for the Table," CAA, AR 1 (1915–1916): 91–93.

13. "Preface," CAA, AR 1 (1915–1916): 5–6.

14. A. D. Shamel, "Individual Tree Records," CAA, AR 1 (1915–1916): 42–43.

15. Popenoe, "Varieties of the Avocado."

16. H. J. Webber, "Station Work for the Avocado," CAA, AR 1 (1915–1916): 69–72.

17. "Avocado Varieties Will Be Standardized," *Monrovia Daily News*, April 5, 1916.

18. Rosengarten, *Wilson Popenoe*, 40.

19. Collins, *The Avocado, a Salad Fruit from the Tropics*, 11–13.

20. Amanda J. Landon, "Domestication and Significance of *Persea americana*, the Avocado, in Mesoamerica," *Nebraska Anthropologist* 47 (2009): 65.

21. Pedro Cieza de Léon, *The Travels of Pedro de Cieza de Léon, 1532–50*, ed. Clements R. Markham (London: Hakluyt Society, 1864), 16.

22. Richard Hakluyt, *The Principal Navigations, Voyages, Traffiques, and Discoveries of the English Nation*, vol. 9 (Glasgow: James MacLehose and Sons, 1904), 384.

23. Wilson Popenoe, George A. Zentmyer, and Eugenio Schieber, "The Avocado Has Many Names," CAS, Y 81 (1997): 155–62.

24. "Avocado Growers Discuss the New Industry, Thousand Planters of Salad Fruit of Tropics in Annual Session," *Los Angeles Evening Express*, May 19, 1917.

25. Thomas Shedden, "How Shall We Eliminate the Misnomer 'Alligator Pear'?" CAA, AR 3 (1917–1918): 41–44.

26. Victor Hirtzler, "The Avocado for the Table," CAA, AR 3 (1917–1918): 51–54.

27. "Circular on Varieties," CAA, AR 3 (1917–1918): 101–4.

28. T. U. Barber, "Special Report of Directors on Avocado Varieties," CAA, AR 3 (1917–1918): 99–101.

29. William H. Sallmon, "The California Avocado Association: Its History and Progress," CAA, AR 4 (1918–1919): 44–50.

30. Charles H. Harris and Louis R. Sadler, *The Archaeologist Was a Spy: Sylvanus G. Morley and the Office of Naval Intelligence* (Albuquerque: University of New Mexico Press, 2009), 136; File 20944-362, RG 38, National Archives; File 20996-1, RG 38, National Archives.

31. "Entertain Explorer Popenoe At Dinner In Riverside," *The California Citrograph*, April 1918, 125.

32. "Vista Locals," *The Times-Advocate* (Escondido), April 6, 1917; "Vista Vitagraphs," *The Times-Advocate*, May 16, 1918.

33. Charles Sheldon to Wilson Popenoe, March 4, 1918; March 19, 1918; March 27, 1918, RG 38, National Archives.

34. Popenoe, "Atlixco"; Rosengarten, *Wilson Popenoe*, 54; Popenoe, "Recollections," chap. 4, p. 1.

35. Wilson Popenoe, "Mexico Field Notes," December 18, 1918, University of California, Riverside, Citrus Research and Agricultural Experiment Station records, University Archives, UC Riverside, Popenoe, "Atlixco."

36. Popenoe, "Atlixco"; Popenoe, "Recollections," chap. 4, p. 4.

37. Popenoe, "Summary of Research at Dirección de Estudios Biológicos," August 3, 1918, University of California, Riverside, Citrus Research and Agricultural Experiment Station records, University Archives, UC Riverside.

38. Wilson Popenoe, "Reflections," 101; Wilson Popenoe, *Manual of Tropical and Subtropical Fruits* (New York: The Macmillan Company, 1920), 18. Paul and Betty Popenoe later named their home at 2503 N. Marengo Avenue in Altadena "Ahuacatlán." Invitations, cards, etc., 33:15, WPFP, HI.

39. Rémi Siméon, *Dictionnaire de la Langue Nahuatl ou Mexiaine* (Paris: Imprimerie Nationale, 1885).

40. Popenoe, "Summary of Research," 9.

41. Merilee Grindle, *In the Shadow of Quetzalcoatl: Zelia Nuttall and the Search for Mexico's Ancient Civilizations* (Cambridge, MA: The Belknap Press, 2023), 87; Popenoe, "Recollections," chap. 4, pp. 11–12.

42. Popenoe, Zentmyer, and Schieber, "The Avocado Has Many Names."

43. Popenoe, "Recollections," chap. 4, p. 11; Popenoe, "Atlixco."

44. Popenoe, "Summary of Research," 4–5.

45. Popenoe, "Mexico Field Notes," December 18, 1918.

46. Popenoe, "Mexico Field Notes," December 19, 1918.

47. Wilson Popenoe to Fred Popenoe, December 31, 1918, 16:256, WPFP, HI.

48. Popenoe, "Mexico Field Notes," January 1, 1919; Wilson Popenoe to Fred Popenoe and Marion Popenoe, December 18, 1918, 16:256, WPFP, HI.

6 • Mission Avocado

1. Wilson Popenoe, "The Avocados of Mexico: A Preliminary Report," CAA, AR 4 (1918–1919): 58–74.

2. "New Variety of Alligator Pears," *Punta Gorda Press*, April 10, 1919.

3. "Sees Future for Guatemalan Avocado Here," *The Fort Myers Press*, April 4, 1919; "Avocado Expert Coming to Fort Myers," *The Fort Myers Press*, March 5, 1919.

4. Wilson Popenoe to Fred Popenoe and Marion Popenoe, March 27, 1919, 16:257, WPFP, HI.

5. Wilson Popenoe to Fred Popenoe and Marion Popenoe, May 1, 1919, 16:258, WPFP, HI.

6. Wilson Popenoe to Fred Popenoe and Marion Popenoe, May 25, 1918, 16:256, WPFP, HI.

7. Wilson Popenoe to Fred Popenoe and Marion Popenoe, July 16, 1919, 16:258, WPFP, HI.

8. Wilson Popenoe to Fred Popenoe and Marion Popenoe, August 29, 1919; September 1, 1919, 16:258, WPFP, HI.

9. David L. Browman, "Spying by American Archaeologists in World War I," *Bulletin of the History of Archaeology* 21, no. 2 (2011): 10–17.

10. "Deep Waters for Bankrupt," *Los Angeles Times*, August 26, 1914.

11. Wilson Popenoe to Fred Popenoe and Marion Popenoe, July 16, 1919; September 18, 1919, 16:258, WPFP, HI.

12. "Vista Items," *The Times-Advocate*, July 11, 1919; "More Water for Vista," *The Times-Advocate*, August 15, 1919.

13. "Noted Plant Man Buys Altadena Gardens," *Pasadena Post*, December 2, 1919.

14. "Rudolph Schindler: Popenoe Cabin (Coachella, Calif.)," R. M. Schindler papers, 1904–1954, Architecture and Design Collection, Art, Design and & Architecture Museum, University of California, Santa Barbara.

15. Jill Lepore, "Fixed: The Rise of Marriage Therapy, and Other Dreams of Human Betterment," *The New Yorker*, March 22, 2010; Wendy Kline, "The Surprising History of Marriage Counseling," PBS American Experience, October 19, 2018.

16. Popenoe, *Manual of Tropical and Subtropical Fruits*, 15–16; Wilson Popenoe, trans., "Padre Cobo on the Avocado," CAA, Y 18 (1933): 120–21.

17. L. B. Scott, "Work of the California Nurserymen's Bud Selection Association," CAA, AR 5 (1919–1920): 71–73.

18. "Avocado Men Select Five Commercial Varieties," *The California Citrograph*, June 1920, 260.

19. Agnes McNally, "The CAA and Its Bud Department," CAA, AR 5 (1919–1920), 41.

20. "Minutes of the 5th Annual Meeting of the California Avocado Association," CAA, AR 6 (1920–1921), 11.

21. "Minutes of the 5th Annual Meeting," 10.

22. "Saturday 2p.m.," CAA, AR 5 (1919–1920), 52.

23. Wilson Popenoe, "Letter from Ecuador," CAA, AR 6 (1920–1921): 76–81.

24. Commander Fred F. Rogers to Wilson Popenoe, August 4, 1920, RG 38, National Archives; Wilson Popenoe to Fred F. Rogers, February 25, 1921, RG 38, National Archives.

25. "Avocado Growers Decide on Marketing Plan," *The California Citrograph*, December 1921, 48–49.

26. William Hertrich, "Effect of the Recent Cold Weather on the Different Varieties of Avocados in Different Localities," CAA, AR 7 (1921–1922): 16–27.

27. Wilson Popenoe, "Avocados of the Chota Valley, Ecuador," CAA, AR 7 (1921–1922): 35–39.

28. Ernest Braunton, "Avocado Growers Discuss Problems," *Los Angeles Times*, May 28, 1922.

29. *Rideout Avocado Nurseries* [catalog], 1921, www.biodiversitylibrary.org.

30. "Exhibits at Semi-Annual Meeting," CAA, AR 8 (1922–1923), 9.

31. A. B. Stout, "Clocking the Avocado: A Study in Cross Pollination," *Los Angeles Times*, July 8, 1923.

32. B. S. Nirody, "Investigations in Avocado Breeding," CAA, AR 7 (1921–1922): 65–78.

33. A. B. Stout, "A Study in Cross-Pollination of Avocados in Southern California," CAA, AR 8 (1922–1923): 29–45.

34. Stout, "A Study in Cross-Pollination," 42.

35. Editor, *Los Angeles Times*, "Clocking the Avocado."

7 • Calavo

1. *The Edgewater Beach Hotel Salad Book* described the French dressing of the day as a version of the "early Roman Jus Simplex, or the early Grecian Sharp Sauce, composed of oil, wine and liquamen, or oil, vinegar and garum with a little honey added." By 1931, "a simple French dressing made with lemon or lime" was advised, "never mayonnaise, which is too oily to be used with the fruit, very oily in itself." Arnold Shircliffe, *The Edgewater Beach Hotel Salad Book* (Chicago: Hotel Monthly Press, 1928), xiv; Christine Frederick, "Take Advantage of Avocados in May," *San Francisco Examiner*, May 24, 1931.

2. Rosengarten, *Wilson Popenoe*, 90.

3. Rosengarten, *Wilson Popenoe*, 91–99; Wilson Popenoe to Fred Popenoe, November 17, 1923, 17:262, WPFP, HI.

4. CAA, AR 8 (1922–23); Rahno Mabel MacCurdy, *The History of the California Fruit Growers Exchange* (Los Angeles: G. Rice & Sons Printers, 1925), 13–14.

5. J. Eliot Coit, "President's Address," CAA, AR 9 (1923–1924): 37.

6. Coit, "President's Address," 37.

7. J. Eliot Coit, "Birthday Pains of a Co-op," CAS, Y 58 (1974–1975): 54–56; "California Avocado Association, Field Day—Hewes Park, Orange County," CAA, AR 10 (1924–1925): 9–13.

8. George B. Hodgkin, "First Annual Report, California Avocado Growers Exchange," CAA, AR 10 (1924–1925): 62–68.

9. "State Avocado Association to Hold Meeting at Carlsbad," *The Times-Advocate*, September 18, 1925; E. C. Dutton, "President's Address," CAA, AR 11 (1925–1926), 103.

10. "Health Apostle Eats Fruit While on Long Hike," *Colton Daily Courier*, June 25, 1925.

11. "Avocados Are Touted as Real Staff of Life," *Oroville Daily Register*, June 26, 1925; "Hiking Health Exponent Visitor in Bakersfield," *The Bakersfield Californian*, July 23, 1925.

12. Lyra Kilston, "Philip Lovell: The Eccentric Health Guru Behind Neutra's Lovell Health House," PBS SoCal, March 19, 2019; Lyra Kilston, *Sun Seekers: The Cure of California* (Los Angeles: Atelier Éditions, 2019); Perry J. Ashley, ed., "American Newspaper Journalists, 1926–1950," *Dictionary of Literary Biography* 29 (Gale Research Inc., 1984).

13. Philip Lovell, Care of the Body, *Los Angeles Times*, August 9, 1925.

14. Arthur Millier, "A New Art," *Los Angeles Times*, January 2, 1929.

15. George B. Hodgkin, "Calavo," CAA, AR 11 (1925–1926), 43.

16. "The Eleventh Annual Meeting of the California Avocado Association," CAA, AR 11 (1925–1926), 59.

17. "The World Is My Campus: Knowles A. Ryerson," interviewed by Joann A. Larkey, University of California, Davis, Library, Special Collections, 1977.

18. W. C. Tesche, "Meet 'Calavo, California's Butter Fruit,'" *Los Angeles Times*, March 7, 1926.

19. Popenoe, "Our Association."

20. "Many Varieties of the Avocado Recommended," *The Whittier News*, June 14, 1926.

21. H. B. Griswold, "The Hass Avocado," CAA, Y 30 (1945): 27–31.

22. "The Hass Mother Tree," CAS, Y 57 (1973–1974): 16–17.

23. "Avocados Sent out by Carload," *Los Angeles Times*, December 18, 1926.

8 • Envisioning an Empire

1. "Calavo Packing House Only One in Whole World," *The Whittier News*, May 4, 1929.

2. "Calavo Packing House Only One," *The Whittier News*.

3. John P. Mills, "Avocado Culture Attracts Many to Encinitas District," *Los Angeles Evening Express*, March 16, 1929; Edwin G. Hart, "$7212 from 3 Acres of Avocados," *Los Angeles Evening Express*, March 16, 1929.

4. "Avocado Show Opened with Radio Address by Governor Young," *The Whittier News*, May 7, 1929.

5. "Prizes Awarded for Best Fruit Displayed at Big Avocado Show," *The Whittier News*, May 8, 1929.

6. "On the Air," *Los Angeles Times*, July 21, 1929; "On the Air," *Los Angeles Times*, August 11, 1929.

7. Alma Whitaker, Sugar and Spice, *Los Angeles Times*, June 1, 1930.

8. Bruce Buttles, "The Fruit Was Sold: Avocado 'Co-op' Did the 'Impossible,'" *Los Angeles Times*, April 12, 1931.

9. Paul K. Wilson, "New Outlets for Avocados," *Los Angeles Times*, December 21, 1930.

10. Buttles, "The Fruit Was Sold."

11. Richard F. Eaton, "Calavo By-Products," CAA, Y 17 (1932): 107–8.

12. Louis Gassner Inc., "And Now the Untrimmed Coat Event, 'To Glorify a Limited Income,'" *San Francisco Examiner*, March 29, 1931.

13. Schiller's United Dress Stores, "A Fascinating Collection of Lovely New Fall Frocks," *The Yonkers Statesman*, August 24, 1928; Livingston Brothers, "At the Smartest Daytime Affairs One Meets Flat Crepe Frocks in the Lovely New Dusty Pastels," *San Francisco Examiner*, March 16, 1930; "Henry Morgan & Co. Limited, A Prelude to Spring Fashions," *The Gazette* (Montreal), March 10, 1930.

14. C. A. Schroeder, "Recollections of Avocado History at U.C.L.A.," CAS, Y 76 (1992): 77–83; Robert W. Hodgson, "The Division of Subtropical Horticulture and the Avocado Industry Plans and Prospects," CAA, Y 15 (1930): 25–29.

15. "Ten-Year Avocado Experiment Begun by UCLA," *The Calavo News* 12, no. 1 (January–February 1938): 1.

16. "New Calavo Seedling Plan Is Approved, Report Says," *Pasadena Post*, July 3, 1932.

17. "Hey Hix," *Pasadena Post*, October 6, 1932; "Thieves Interfere," *Pasadena Post*, February 6, 1933.

18. Leigh Crosby, "Marketing of Avocados," CAA, Y 19 (1934): 68–75.

19. Christine Frederick, "Enter the Aristocratic Avocado," *San Francisco Examiner*, May 24, 1931.

20. Christine Frederick, *Selling Mrs. Consumer* (New York: The Business Bourse, 1929), 123, 128.

21. Frederick, "Enter the Aristocratic Avocado."

22. Frederick, *Selling Mrs. Consumer*; Florence Finch Kelly, "Woman's Hand in the Market Place," *The New York Times*, August 25, 1929.

23. Crosby, "Marketing of Avocados."

24. "Avocado Tariff Proposed Today," *Pasadena Post*, May 20, 1929.

25. George B. Hodgkin to Wilson Popenoe, September 1, 1934, 10: 153, WPFP, HI.

26. "Roosevelts Enjoy Calavos in Salad," *The Times-Advocate*, February 13, 1935.

27. Christine Frederick, "Take Advantage of Avocados in May," *San Francisco Examiner*, May 12, 1935.

28. "1935 Avocado Returns Will Reach Million," *The Whittier News*, May 16, 1935.

29. "Calavo Secures Unity in Florida," *The Times-Advocate*, July 30, 1935.

30. "Avocados Grown for Entire Land," *Riverside Daily Press*, December 28, 1935.

31. Rudolph G. Hass, avocado, U.S. Plant Patent 139, filed April 17, 1935, and issued August 27, 1935.

32. "New Type Avocado Developed by Hass," *Santa Ana Register*, August 1, 1935.

33. "Miscellaneous, for Sale," *The Whittier News*, August 1, 1935.

34. "California Avocado Society 1973 Award of Honor: Harold Hazzard Brokaw," CAS, Y 57 (1973–1974), 8.

35. "1935 Calavo Sales Equal 11 Years," *The Times-Advocate*, January 7, 1936.

36. Marion F. Sawyer, "Calavos, Once Salad Fruit Only, Now Available for Other Ways of Serving," *Detroit Free Press*, January 10, 1936.

37. "Calavos Can Be Turned to Various Tasty Uses; California Fruit Delicacy Now Available at Reasonable Prices in Stores," *The Pittsburgh Press*, January 24, 1936.

38. George B. Hodgkin, "Marketing Avocados After the Freeze," CAA, Y 21 (1937): 77–80.

39. Hodgkin, "Marketing Avocados After the Freeze," 78.

40. Hodgkin, "Marketing Avocados After the Freeze," 79.

41. "The Avocado Wins American Favor," *Housekeepers' Chat*, USDA Radio Service, March 5, 1937.

42. "Local Calavo Growers Hold Annual Meet," *Daily Times-Advocate* (Escondido), January 13, 1938.

9 • Mother Tree

1. A. D. Shamel, "The Parent Fuerte Avocado Tree," CAA, Y 21 (1936): 86–92.
2. Shamel, "The Parent Fuerte Avocado Tree."
3. The address had changed since Wilson's visit nearly twenty years earlier.
4. Shamel, "The Parent Fuerte Avocado Tree."
5. "Avocado Growers to Visit Mexico," CAA, Y 22 (1937): 251.
6. "Avocado Growers to Visit Mexico."
7. "Local Growers Plan Mexico Event," *The Weekly Times-Advocate* (Escondido), October 29, 1937.
8. Edward Frank Allen, "Louis Adamic's Picture of Guatemala," *The New York Times*, October 3, 1937.
9. Louis Adamic, *The House in Antigua: A Restoration* (New York: Harper & Brothers, 1937), 218–19.
10. Rosengarten, *Wilson Popenoe*, 109.
11. Ruth Billheimer, "Peck Pasadena Home Attracts Wide Interest," *Chicago Tribune*, May 7, 1939; "Certificate of Appropriateness," 1100 South Grand Avenue, Historic Preservation Commission, City of Pasadena, June 19, 2018.
12. "Calavo Outlines Details of Trip to Mexico," *The Tustin News*, January 28, 1938; "Association Members and Friends Who Generously Responded with Donations to the Voluntary Fund for the Le Blanc Commemoration," CAA, Y 23 (1938): 64.
13. "Message from Señor Alejandro Le Blanc," CAA, Y 23 (1938): 37–38.
14. "Calavo Outlines Details."
15. Dr. H. J. Webber, "Honoring the Parent Tree of the Fuerte Avocado," CAA, Y 23 (1938): 49–53.
16. Webber, "Honoring the Parent Tree," 48–50.
17. Webber, "Honoring the Parent Tree," 52; Carter Barrett, "Parent Fuerte Avocado Tree at Atlixco," CAA, Y 23 (1938): 62–63.
18. Jorge Labra, "La ingenua condecoración a un aguacate," *Diario de Yucatán*, republished in Opinion Ajenas, *La Opinión*, May 9, 1938. Translation by Lucía Mier y Terán Romero.
19. Labra, "La ingenua condecoración a un aguacate."
20. A. D. Shamel, "Avocado Studies in Mexico in 1938," CAA, Y 23 (1938): 67–85.
21. Shamel, "Avocado Studies in Mexico."

22. Shamel, "Avocado Studies in Mexico."
23. "Se suicido el dueño del aguacate padre," *La Opinión*, June 22, 1938; "Original Avocado Grower Kills Self," *Hollywood Citizen-News*, June 22, 1938; "Owner of Original Avocado Tree Dies," *The San Bernardino County Sun*, June 23, 1938.
24. "The Avocado Institute," CAA, Y 23 (1938): 173; "Avocado Aid Rewarded," *Los Angeles Times*, May 7, 1939.

10 · Wild Avocado

1. Bonnie Miller, "Food on Display: Design Techniques of the Food Exhibits of the New York World's Fair of 1939–40," *Food, Culture, and Society* 24 (2021): 257.
2. Grace Turner, "Streamline Your Dinner Parties," *Los Angeles Times*, November 19, 1939.
3. Crosby Gaige, *New York World's Fair Cook Book: The American Kitchen* (New York: Doubleday, Doran & Company, 1939), 261.
4. Pierre Franey, 60-Minute Gourmet, *The New York Times*, July 25, 1979.
5. William T. Horne, "Pests and Diseases—Latest Developments in Avocado Disease Control," CAA, Y 18 (1933): 28–33.
6. W. T. Horne, *Avocado Diseases in California*, Bulletin 595 (Berkeley: University of California College of Agriculture, 1934).
7. Kenneth Smoyer, "Avocado Tree Decline," CAA, Y 25 (1940): 50–51.
8. Rosengarten, *Wilson Popenoe*, 125, 128.
9. "Report of the Committee on Varieties," CAS, Y 29 (1944): 12–16.
10. "Report of the Variety Committee on Avocados," CAS, Y 30 (1945): 12–16.
11. Coit, "Mexican Explorations of 1948."
12. "Mamma Fuerte Nears Death," *The Calavo News*, October–December 1942; "California Avocado Society Plants Tree in Mexico City," *Los Angeles Times*, April 14, 1948.
13. Carter Barrett, "The 1948 Pilgrimage to Mexico," CAS, Y 33 (1948): 28–40; Coit, "Mexican Explorations," 59–62.
14. "Avocado Society Changes Name," *The Calavo News* 15, no. 2 (June 1941); Carter Barrett, "Presentation Ceremonies at Antigua, Guatemala," CAS, Y 31 (1946): 100–102.
15. H. B. Griswold, "Primitive Avocados of Central America and Mexico," CAS, Y 31 (1946): 103–5.

16. Wilson Popenoe and Louis O. Williams, "The Expedition to Mexico of October 1947," CAS, Y 32 (1947): 22–28.

17. "Transcript of Original Notes on Avocado Varieties of Which Budwood Was Obtained," 1947–1948, 33:3, WPFP, HI.

18. Popenoe and Williams, "The Expedition to Mexico of October 1947."

19. Popenoe and Williams, "The Expedition to Mexico of October 1947."

20. "Sentimental Journey," *The Whittier News*, December 4, 1947; "Mexico Film Here Monday," *The Whittier News*, January 15, 1948.

21. "California Avocado Society 1948 Pilgrimage to Mexico," *Los Angeles Times*, March 28, 1948.

22. Barrett, "The 1948 Pilgrimage to Mexico," 28–40.

23. "Record Order," *Weekly Times-Advocate*, April 9, 1948.

24. Barrett, "The 1948 Pilgrimage to Mexico," 28–40.

25. Catherine Vézina, *Diplomacía migratoria: Una historia transnacional del Programa Bracero, 1947–1952* (México: Secretaría de Relacionas Exteriores, Acervo Histórico Diplomático: Centro de Investigación y Docencia Económicas, 2017), 181.

26. Barrett, "The 1948 Pilgrimage to Mexico," 30–32.

27. Barrett, "The 1948 Pilgrimage to Mexico," 32–40.

28. Barrett, "The 1948 Pilgrimage to Mexico," 40.

29. Popenoe and Williams, "Mexican Explorations of 1948."

30. William C. Cooper and Norman Maxwell, "The Search for Avocado Varieties Adapted to the Rio Grande Valley," *Proceedings of the Rio Grande Valley Historical Society* 10 (1956): 126–33.

31. Cooper and Maxwell, "The Search for Avocado Varieties Adapted to the Rio Grande Valley." The society changed its name to the Rio Grande Valley Horticultural Society.

32. Coit, "Mexican Explorations of 1948."

33. Coit, "Mexican Explorations of 1948."

34. William C. Cooper, "The Texas Avocado Society," CAS, Y 33 (1948): 137–38.

35. "Avocado Production Is Pushed," *The Brownsville Herald*, December 31, 1948; "Hoblitzelle Ranch Does Wide Experimental Farming," *The Brownsville Herald*, Dec. 31, 1950.

36. Popenoe and Williams, "Mexican Explorations of 1948," 58.

37. Wilson Popenoe, "Notes from Honduras," *Proceedings of the Florida State Horticultural Society* 64 (1951), 255–57.

38. E. C. Dutton, "President's Address," CAA, Y 12 (1928), 79.

39. Maria de la Luz Martin Carbajal, "The Historical Formation of the Innovation System of the Avocado Industry in Michoacán," *Tzintzun: Journal of Historical Studies*, no. 63 (January 2016).

40. Hamilton P. Traub and T. R. Robinson, "Improvement of the Avocado," CAA, Y 23 (1938): 131.

41. Coit, "Mexican Explorations of 1948," 62.

42. Harlan Griswold, "Report on the Committee on Foreign Explorations," CAS, Y 35 (1950): 28 30.

43. Griswold, "Report on the Committee on Foreign Explorations."

44. Griswold, "Report on the Committee on Foreign Explorations."

11 • Believers

1. Helen Bauer and Roberta Logerman, *The Avocado Cookbook* (Garden City, NY: Doubleday & Company, 1967).

2. "Postal Employee for 30 Years Dies at Fallbrook," *Los Angeles Times*, October 26, 1952.

3. S. J. Richards, P. W. Moore, F. T. Bingham, T. W. Embleton, and C. K. Labanauskas, "Avocado Irrigation and Nitrogen Fertilization Plots at the Citrus Experiment Station," CAS, Y 42 (1958), 25–29.

4. Ben Faber, author interview, January 18, 2021.

5. "Distribution of Varieties to Calavo Growers," CAS, Y 43 (1959): 17.

6. Berthold Orphie Bergh, "Avocado Breeding in California," *Proceedings of the Florida State Horticultural Society* 70 (1957): 284–90.

7. Loren J. Mead, "Variety Improvement Program," CAS, Y 42 (1958): 56.

8. "Certificate of Fictitious Name," *The Whittier News*, March 18, 1922.

9. "For Sale: Miscellaneous," *The Whittier News*, December 20, 1926.

10. "California Avocado Society 1973 Award of Honor."

11. "Avocado Industry Taking Major Part in Southland Role as Agriculture Area," *The Whittier News*, December 1, 1948.

12. Hugh T. Walker, "Report of the President," CAS, Y 43 (1959): 11.

13. "Report of the President," CAS, Y 42 (1958): 11.

14. "Farm Adviser Takes Office," *Los Angeles Daily Times*, January 4, 1918.

15. R. G. Platt, "A Day with a Farm Advisor," CAS, Y 45 (1961): 23–25.

16. Marvin P. Miller, "What About Avocados in Riverside County?" CAS, Y 43 (1959): 31–32; Hunter Johnson Jr., "The Avocado Situation in Los Angeles County," CAS, Y 43 (1959): 27–28.

17. "Ten Named to Avocado Board," *Daily Times-Advocate*, November 4, 1961.

18. "Minutes 44th Annual Meeting," CAS, Y 42 (1958): 12.

19. Clyde B. Markeson, *Economic Aspects of Marketing Florida Avocados* (Washington, D.C.: Farmer Cooperative Service, 1963).

20. Hyunok Lee, Julian M. Alston, Hoy F. Carman, and William Sutton, *Mandated Marketing Programs for California Commodities* (Davis: Giannini Foundation of Agricultural Economics, 1996).

21. Ellen Brokaw, author interview, May 12, 2021.

22. Duncan Abbott, email correspondence with the authors, January 26, 2024.

23. "California Avocado Society Membership List—1958," CAS, Y 42 (1958): 122.

24. Walter Reuther, ed., "A Review of Avocado Research at the University of California, Riverside," CAS, Y 45 (1961): 45–52; William F. Catlin, "President's Report," CAS, Y 46 (1962): 8.

25. Reuther, "A Review of Avocado Research."

26. C. A. Schroeder, "Growth and Development of the Avocado Fruit," CAS, Y 42 (1958): 114–18.

27. "Crop Testing Station Set for Irvine Ranch," *Los Angeles Times*, December 2, 1954; "Building at Tustin Farm Field Station Started," *Los Angeles Times*, December 18, 1956.

28. "Work to Start in Spring on UC Farm Unit," *Los Angeles Times*, January 9, 1955.

29. "Superfund Site: El Toro Marine Corps Air Station," U.S. Environmental Protection Agency, accessed August 23, 2024, cumulis.epa.gov /supercpad/cursites/csitinfo.cfm?id=0902770.

30. "James Irvine II Turns Ranch into Agricultural Treasure," Irvine Historical Society, accessed January 8, 2024, irvinehistory.org/wp-content /uploads/2020/10/James-Irine-II-turns-Irvine-into-Agriculture-Treasure .pdf; Darren L. Haver, author interview, August 17, 2023.

31. "Vistas for the Future: Planner William Pereira," *Time* 82, no. 10, September 6, 1963.

32. "Jimmy Utt a Guest at UCI," *Tustin News*, June 25, 1964.

33. A. M. Boyce, "Listing and Description of Avocado Projects at the University of California Citrus Experiment Station," CAS, Y 40 (1956): 113–19.

34. Wilson Popenoe, "Avocados in Spain—and Elsewhere," CAS, Y 43 (1959): 55–66.

35. "Report of the President," CAS, Y 42 (1958): 11.

36. Hank Brokaw, "In Memoriam, Dr. George Zentmyer," CAS, Y 86 (2002): 46.

37. George Zentmyer, W. A. Thorn, A. O. Paulus, and R. M. Burnes, "Hot-Water Treatment of Avocado Seed," CAS, Y 42 (1958): 108–10.

38. George Zentmyer, "Description of Project," c. 1981, personal papers shared with the authors by Jane Fernald, Zentmyer's daughter, on October 23, 2023.

39. George A. Zentmyer, "Collections for Phytophthora Root Rot Resistance in Mexico and the Caribbean," CAS, Y 45 (1961): 59–62; "Report of the Foreign Exploration Committee," CAS, Y 46 (1962): 12.

40. Florida Lime & Avocado Growers, Inc. v. Paul, 373 U.S. 132 (1963).

41. Bauer and Logerman, *The Avocado Cookbook*; Email correspondence with author from Alexis Percle, archivist, LBJ Presidential Library and Museum, March 6, 2024.

42. "4 County Avocado Handlers Help Form Marketing Group," *Ventura County Star-Free Press*, September 27, 1970.

43. "Avocado Growers, Ask the Pro!" *Daily Times-Advocate*, August 9, 1970.

44. Frank Gilkerson, "Avocado Marketing Methods: The Commercial Association," CAS, Y 46 (1962): 33.

45. Edward F. Frolich and Robert G. Platt, "Use of the Etiolation Technique in Rooting Avocado Cuttings," CAS, Y 55 (1971–1972): 97–109.

46. "Crystal Balls No Help Here," *Ventura County Star-Free Press*, February 27, 1970.

47. W. B. Storey, "What Kind of Fruit Is the Avocado?" CAS, Y 57 (1973–1974): 70–71.

48. Robert C. Rock, "Expansion in the California Avocado Industry," CAS, Y 58 (1974–1975): 36–41.

12 • The Battle

1. Craig Claiborne, "Food Columnist Finds County an Avocado Heaven," *Ventura County Star-Free Press*, February 28, 1979.

2. J. M. Kotzé, J. N. Moll, and J. M. Darvas, "Root Rot Control in South Africa: Past, Present and Future," *South African Growers' Association Yearbook* 10 (1987): 89–91.

3. Eugenio Schieber and G. A. Zentmyer, "Collecting Perseas in Central America and Mexico," CAS, Y 56 (1972–1973): 94–101.

4. Douglass Sullivan-Gonzalez, *The Black Christ of Esquipulas: Religion and Identity in Guatemala* (Lincoln: University of Nebraska Press, 2016).

5. Kathy Barton, "Q&A: George Zentmyer, Plant Pathologist," *California Agriculture* 50, no. 6 (November 1, 1996): 38.

6. Donald A. Cooksey, *George A. Zentmyer 1913–2003: Biographical Memoirs* (National Academy of Sciences, 2014).

7. Eugenio Schieber and G. A. Zentmyer, "Hunting for Persea steyermarkii in the Mountains of Guatemala," CAS, Y 62 (1978): 67–71.

8. Eugenio Schieber and G. A. Zentmyer, "The Quetzal and the Persea," CAS, Y 63 (1979): 34–40; Schieber and Zentmyer, "Collecting Perseas in Central America and Mexico."

9. Laura L. Jefferson, "Collecting Avocados in Mexico," CAS, Y 57 (1973–1974): 148–52.

10. Schieber and Zentmyer, "Collecting Perseas in Central America and Mexico"; Eugenio Schieber and G. A. Zentmyer, "Collecting Persea schiedeana in Guatemala," CAS, Y 61 (1977): 91–94.

11. George A. Zentmyer, "Eugenio Schieber," CAS, Y 77 (1993): 53–56.

12. George A. Zentmyer, Eugenio Schieber, and Fred B. Guillemet, "History of the Martin Grande Rootstock," CAS, Y 72 (1988): 121–25.

13. "Genocide in Guatemala," Holocaust Museum Houston, accessed August 21, 2024, hmh.org/library/research/genocide-in-guatemala-guide.

14. Eugenio Schieber and George Zentmyer, "Persea Exploration in Middle America: An Interview and Discussion," CAS, Y 67 (1983): 93–103.

15. E. Schieber and G. A. Zentmyer, "Exploring for Persea on Volcano Quetzaltepeque, Guatemala," CAS, Y 65 (1981): 57–63.

16. Matthew Caire-Pérez, "A Different Shade of Green: Efraím Hernández, Chapingo, and Mexico's Green Revolution, 1950–1967" (PhD diss., University of Oklahoma, 2016).

17. Ana Bárcenas and Charlie Campos, *Diego Rivera en Chapingo | Capilla Riveriana*, Universidad Autónoma Chapingo, 2015, video, 24:39.

18. Grace Kuipers, "Revolution, Renewable: Subsoil Political Ecologies in Rivera's *Song of the Earth*," *react/review: a responsive journal for art & architecture* 1 (2021): 15–23.

19. "Ing Salvador Sánchez Colín," accessed August 21, 2024, www.bejucos .net/historia/html/hist16.html; *Documental: Ing. Salvador Sánchez Colín*, Ilustre y Benemérita Sociedad Mexicana de Geografía y Estadística del Estado de México, August 2, 2015. youtu.be/EhHhq6ifQgs ?si=F3WmTnnhUCKdgtsR, accessed September 7, 2023. Translation by Tamara and Ricardo Zúñiga; Celia Hare, "Mexico Studying U.S. Citrus Deal," *Valley Evening Monitor* (McAllen, Texas), March 19, 1944.

20. "Minutes of the Meeting of November 7, 1940," Committee on Inter-American Cooperation in Agricultural Education, USDA, WPFP, HI.

21. Neil Foley, *Mexicans in the Making of America* (Cambridge, MA: The Belknap Press, 2014).

22. Foley, *Mexicans in the Making of America*.

23. Mynatt Smith, "City of Palms," *Valley Evening Monitor* (McAllen, Texas), March 26, 1944.

24. C. D. Gustafson, "Summary of Our Trip to Mexico," CAS, Y 52 (1968): 173–76.

25. Coit, "Mexican Explorations of 1948"; Elwood E. Trask, "Observations on the Avocado Industry in Mexico," CAS, Y 33 (1948): 50–53.

26. Salvador Sánchez Colín, Pedro Mijares Oviedo, Luis López-López, and Alejandro F. Barrientos-Priego, "Historia del aguacate en México," *CICTAMEX Yearbook 1998–2001*: 171–87; Rob Brokaw, author interview, March 28, 2023.

27. Salvador Sánchez Colín and Eulogio De La Cruz Torres, "The Avocado Breeding and Selection Program at CICTAMEX," *Proceedings of the Second World Avocado Congress* (1992): 501–4.

28. Takashi Turu, "Avocados South of the Border," CAS, Y 53 (1969): 31–37; Takashi Turu, "The Aguacate in Mexico," CAS, Y 52 (1968): 169–72.

29. Gustafson, "Summary of Our Trip to Mexico."

30. Gustafson, "Summary of Our Trip to Mexico."

31. "Meet Sr. Salvador Sanchez Colin," CAS, Y 56 (1972): 11.

32. Turu, "Avocados South of the Border."

33. Turu, "The Aguacate in Mexico."

34. Turu, "Avocados South of the Border."

35. Don Gustafson, "1976 World Avocado Production," CAS, Y 60 (1976): 74–90.

36. "Industry Statistical Data," California Avocado Commission, accessed August 23, 2024, www.californiaavocadogrowers.com/industry/industry -statistical-data.

37. Wally Smith, "New Irrigation Boosts County Avocado Crop," *Ventura County Star-Free Press*, February 23, 1975.

38. C. Don Gustafson, "History and Present Trends of Drip Irrigation," CAS, Y 63 (1979): 47–49.

13 • The Breeders

1. B. O. Bergh, "The Avocado and Human Nutrition. II: Avocados and Your Heart," *Proceedings of the Second World Avocado Congress* (1992): 37–47.
2. Mary Lu Arpaia and John A. Menge, "Enhancement of Avocado Productivity. Plant Improvement: Selection and Evaluation of Improved Varieties and Rootstocks" (Seminario Internacional de Paltos, Quillota, Chile, September 29–October 1, 2004).
3. Robert W. Hodgson, "The University's Research Program on the Avocado," CAA, Y 21 (1937): 228–33.
4. Bergh, "Avocado Breeding in California."
5. B. O. Bergh, "Avocado Breeding and Selection," *Proceedings of the First International Tropical Fruit Short Course: The Avocado*, ed. J. W. Sauls, R. L. Phillips, and L. K. Jackson (Gainesville: Florida Cooperative Extension Service, 1976).
6. Gary S. Bender, "Avocado Flowering and Pollination," in *Avocado Production in California: A Cultural Handbook for Growers, Book One*, 2nd ed., ed. Gary S. Bender (University of California Cooperative Extension, San Diego County, and the California Avocado Society, 2013), 33–44.
7. M. L. Arpaia, A. E. Fetscher, and R. Hofshi, "Avocado Flowering Basics," UC Riverside Avocado Variety Collection, accessed January 11, 2024, avocado.ucr.edu/avocado-flowering-basics.
8. F. F. Halma, "Avocado Rootstock Experiments—A 10-Year Report," CAS, Y 38 (1953–1954): 79–86; "Obituary: Walter E. Lammerts," *The Sacramento Bee*, June 11, 1996.
9. Dr. Walter E. Lammerts, "The Avocado Breeding Project," CAS, Y 30 (1945): 74–80.
10. "Report of Research Station Committee," CAS, Y 43 (1959), 23.
11. Bob Bergh and Don Gustafson, "Fuerte Fruit Set as Influenced by Cross-Pollination," CAS, Y 42 (1958): 64–66.
12. "Teague Avocado Just One of Several Under Study in Search for Perfection," *Ventura County Star-Free Press*, July 6, 1974.
13. Bergh, "Avocado Breeding and Selection."
14. B. O. Bergh, "Breeding Avocados at C.R.C.," CAS, Y 45 (1961): 67–74.
15. "Teague Avocado Just One of Several Under Study."
16. Gray E. Martin, author interview, July 24, 2023.
17. "Teague Avocado Just One of Several Under Study."

18. Wilson Popenoe, "A New Avocado of the Mexican Race," CAS, Y 48 (1964): 56–57.

19. Zentmyer, "Description of Project."

20. Jack S. Shepherd, "Wilson Popenoe . . . Vaya Con Dios," CAS, Y 59 (1975–1976): 10.

21. *Proceedings of the First International Tropical Fruit Short Course: The Avocado*, eds. J. W. Sauls, R. L. Phillips, and L. K. Jackson (Gainesville: Florida Cooperative Extension Service, 1976); "Avocado Star in Tropical Fruit Course," *Sentinel Star* (Orlando, Florida), October 28, 1976.

22. Miriam Silberstein, "In the Memory of Bob Bergh," August 19, 2021, www.avocadosource.com/obituaries/BobBergh.htm.

23. Bergh, "Avocado Breeding and Selection."

24. B. O. Bergh, and R. H. Whitsell, "Three New Patented Avocados," CAS, Y 66 (1982): 51–56.

25. Mary Lu Arpaia, author interview, June 2, 2021.

26. Greg Alder, "What Happened to the Gwen Avocado?" *The Yard Posts*, November 4, 2022, gregalder.com/yardposts/what-happened-to-the-gwen-avocado.

27. W. H. Brokaw, "Clonal Rootstocks: Personal Observations and a Peek into the Future," CAS, Y 66 (1982): 81–92.

28. "Plastic Tubes: New Avocado Idea," *Ventura County Star-Free Press*, February 27, 1970.

29. Bob Bergh and Gray Martin, "The Gwen Avocado," CAS, Y 72 (1988): 195–207.

30. Tom Pfingsten, "Fallbrook: Avocado Festival Builds on Tradition," *The San Diego Union-Tribune*, April 18, 2009.

31. B. O. Bergh and Rudolph G. Hass, "Resolutions," CAS, Y 75 (1991): 14.

32. Gordon Dillow, "Family Tree: Hass' 1st Avocado Seedling Still Stands and Bears Fruit," *Los Angeles Times*, March 29, 1992.

33. D. M. Obenland, S. Collin, B. E. Mackey, J. Sievert, K. Field, and M. Arpaia, "Determinants of Flavor Acceptability During the Maturation of Navel Oranges," *Postharvest Biology and Technology* 55, no. 2 (May 1, 2009): 156–63.

34. M. L. Arpaia, G. S. Bender, and G. Witney, "Avocado Clonal Rootstock Trial," CAS, Y 74 (1990): 27–34; M. L. Arpaia and I. Eaks, "Avocado Fruit Quality as Influenced by Preharvest Cultural Practices," CAS, Y 74 (1990): 35–42; M. L. Arpaia, D. Faubian, F. G. Mitchell

and G. Mayer, "The Use of Controlled Atmosphere For Long Term Storage of 'Hass' Avocados," CAS, Y 74 (1990): 43–48; J. L. Meyer, M. L. Arpaia, M. V. Yates, E. Takele, G. Bender, and G. Witney, "Irrigation and Fertilization of Avocados Research Findings," CAS, Y 74 (1990): 71–83; E. Takele, J. L. Meyer, M. L. Arpaia, M. V. Yates, G. Bender, and G. Witney, "Irrigation and Fertilization Management of Avocados Economic Analysis Progress Report," CAS, Y 74 (1990): 85–98.

35. Daniel H. Janzen and Paul S. Martin, "Neotropical Anachronisms: The Fruits the Gomphotheres Ate," *Science* 215, no. 4528 (January 1982): 19–27.

36. B. N. Wolstenholme and A. W. Whiley, "Ecophysiology of the Avocado (*Persea americana* Mill.) Tree as a Basis for Pre-Harvest Management," *Revista Chapingo Serie Horticultura* 5 (1999): 77–88.

37. Marion Popenoe de Hatch, author interview, January 29, 2024.

38. Seung-Koo Lee, "A Review and Background of the Avocado Maturity Standard," CAS, Y 65 (1981): 100–109.

39. M. L. Arpaia, D. Boreham, and R. Hofshi, "Development of a New Method for Measuring Minimum Maturity of Avocados," CAS, Y 85 (2001): 153–78.

40. S. K. Lee and C. W. Coggins Jr., "Dry Weight Method for Determination of Avocado Fruit Maturity," CAS, Y 66 (1982): 67–70.

41. Lee, "A Review and Background of the Avocado Maturity Standard."

42. Arpaia, Boreham, and Hofshi, "Development of a New Method."

43. Nada el Sawy, "Paying Respects to Avocado's Ancestral Timber," *Oakland Tribune*, October 18, 2003.

14 • The Avocado Wars

1. Carole Sugarman, "Face Off at the Border," *The Washington Post*, January 20, 1998.

2. "'Love of Avocados' Takes to Airways," *Palo Alto Times*, March 31, 1978, 3; Elizabeth Magill, "Let's Win One for the Dippers," *The County Telegram Tribune* (San Luis Obispo, Calif.), January 27, 1993.

3. Marc Lacey, "Is 'Agent X' a Mole in the Avocado War?" *Los Angeles Times*, June 28, 1996.

4. Rebecca S. Weiner, "Importing Avocados Bugs Growers," *Los Angeles Times*, December 25, 1995.

5. David R. Baker, "Growers Fear Lifting a Ban on Avocados from Mexico," *Los Angeles Times*, August 20, 1995.

6. Michael A. Browne, "Avocados of the Americas . . . Caution: Merging Traffic Ahead," CAS, Y 78 (1994): 53–58.

7. Stanford, "Mexico's *Empresario* in Export Agriculture."

8. Sugarman, "Face Off at the Border."

9. Ramón Paz-Vega, email correspondence with author, November 12, 2023.

10. Lois Stanford and Julie A. Hogeland, "Designing Organizations for a Globalized World: Calavo's Transition from Cooperative to Corporation," *American Journal of Agricultural Economics* 86, no. 5 (December 2004): 1269–75.

11. Robert W. Hodgson, "The Avocado in the Lower Rio Grande Valley," CAA, AR 10 (1924–1925): 41–43.

12. Ramón Paz-Vega, author interview, March 9, 2023.

13. Associated Press, "Welcome Back, Avocado," *The Courier* (Waterloo, IA), November 9, 1997.

14. Rick Bayless, author interview, January 26, 2024.

15. Vicenta T. de Rubio, *Cocina Michoacana* (Zamora: Imprenta Moderna, 1896).

16. Carlos Illsley, "Review of the Mexican Avocado Industry in 1991," *Proceedings of the Second World Avocado Congress* (1992): 633–37.

17. Ramón Paz-Vega, author interview, March 9, 2023.

18. Lucy La Rosa and David A. Shirk, "New Policy Brief: The New Generation—Mexico's Emerging Organized Crime Threat," Justice in Mexico, March 19, 2018.

19. Sánchez Colín and De La Cruz Torres, "The Avocado Breeding and Selection Program at CICTAMEX."

20. Sánchez Colín and De La Cruz Torres, "The Avocado Breeding and Selection Program."

21. Lois Stanford, "Mexico's *Empresario* in Export Agriculture: Examining the Avocado Industry of Michoacán," paper presented at the Latin American Studies Association, Chicago, IL, September 24–26, 1998.

22. Edgar Aragón, "Market Failures and Free Trade: Hass Avocados in Mexico," in *Export Pioneers in Latin America*, ed. Charles Sabel, Eduardo Fernández-Arias, Ricardo Hausmann, Andrés Rodríguez-Clare, and Ernesto Stein (Inter-American Development Bank, 2012), 147–76.

23. Edgar Aragón, Anne Fouquet, and Marcia Campos, *The Emergence of Successful Export Activities in Mexico: Three Case Studies* (Inter-American Development Bank, February 2009).

24. Aragón, "Market Failures and Free Trade."

25. Illsley, "Review of the Mexican Avocado Industry in 1991."

26. John Ross, "Behind the Death of 'Irangate' Courier," *San Francisco Examiner*, March 21, 1989.

27. Ramón Paz-Vega, "Mexican Avocados: Threat or Opportunity for California?" CAS, Y 73 (1989): 87–106.

28. Mark Affleck, "World Avocado Market: A Brief Review," *Proceedings of the Second World Avocado Congress* (1992): 621–24.

29. Donna Roberts and David Orden, "Determinants of Technical Barriers to Trade: The Case of US Phytosanitary Restrictions on Mexican Avocados, 1972–1995," paper presented at the Understanding Technical Barriers to Agricultural Trade Conference, Tucson, AZ, 1995.

30. "Mexican Tomatoes and Avocados," *Rural Migration News* 2, no. 4 (October 1996), migration.ucdavis.edu/rmn/more.php?id=159.

31. Roberts and Orden, "Determinants of Technical Barriers to Trade."

32. David Clark Scott, "Mexico's Avocado Growers Grumble Over Unlikely Beachhead—Alaska," *The Christian Science Monitor*, November 9, 1992.

33. H. Leonard Francis, "Mexico—Is It Really What We Hear?" CAS, Y 77 (1993): 59–65.

34. Steve Waterstrat, "Avocado Growers to Be Recognized," *North County Times* (Escondido, California), December 6, 1997.

35. "Calavo Growers, Inc.," file 000-33385, Form 10-K, United States Securities and Exchange Commission, 2002, www.sec.gov/Archives/edgar/data/1133470/000095014803000098/v87183e10vk.htm.

36. USDA, *Importation of 'Hass' Avocado Fruit (Persea Americana cv. Hass) from Mexico: A Risk Assessment*, June 2003.

37. Luque, Bazan, and Kinser, "The Story Behind the Avocado."

15 • Cartel

1. Rick Bayless, author interview, January 26, 2024.

2. Juan Andrés Muñoz, "Secret Behind 'Mexican' State Dinner at the White House," CNN, May 26, 2010.

3. "Remarks at a State Dinner Honoring Presidente Felipe de Jesús Calderón Hinojosa of Mexico," The American Presidency Project, May 19, 2010, www.presidency.ucsb.edu/documents/remarks-state-dinner-honoring-president-felipe-de-jesus-calderon-hinojosa-mexico.

4. Muñoz, "Secret Behind 'Mexican' State Dinner."

5. Rick Bayless, author interview, January 26, 2024.

6. Gabriel Hernandez and Mark Ford, *Mexico Avocado Annual: Mexico Avocado Production to Increase* (USDA Foreign Agricultural Service, December 1, 2009).

7. Gabriel Hernandez, *Mexico Avocado Annual 2003* (USDA Foreign Agricultural Service, November 14, 2003); Hoy F. Carman, "The Story Behind Avocados' Rise to Prominence in the United States," *ARE Update* 22, no. 5 (2019): 9–11.

8. Aragón, "Market Failures and Free Trade."

9. Brett McNeil, "Holy Guacamole—What a Drug Bust; Cocaine Hidden in Buckets of Dip," *Chicago Tribune*, September 23, 2003.

10. CNN Wire Staff, "U.S., Mexican Presidents Say Key Issues Must Be Tackled Together," CNN, May 20, 2010.

11. Carmen Boullosa and Mike Wallace, *A Narco History: How the United States and Mexico Jointly Created the "Mexican Drug War"* (New York: OR Books, 2015).

12. Lulu Garcia-Navarro, "Mexico's Drug Wars Leave Rising Death Toll," *Morning Edition*, NPR, September 21, 2006.

13. David A. Shirk, author interview, January 15, 2024.

14. David T. Courtwright, "A Century of American Narcotic Policy," in *Treating Drug Problems, Volume 2: Commissioned Papers on Historical, Institutional, and Economic Contexts of Drug Treatment*, ed. D. R. Gerstein and H. J. Harwood (Washington, D.C.: National Academies Press, 1992).

15. Boullosa and Wallace, *A Narco History.*

16. Boullosa and Wallace, *A Narco History.*

17. Boullosa and Wallace, *A Narco History.*

18. Guadalupe Correa-Cabrera, *Los Zetas Inc.* (Austin: University of Texas Press, 2017).

19. Romain Le-Cour-Grandmaison and Paul Frissard Martinez, "Violent and Vibrant: Mexico's Avocado Boom and Organized Crime," Global Initiative Against Transnational Organized Crime, January 5, 2024, globalinitiative.net/analysis/mexicos-avocado-boom-and-organized -crime.

20. La Rosa and Shirk, "New Policy Brief: The New Generation."

21. José Reveles, "Social and Economic Damage Caused by the War Against Drugs in Mexico," in *Transnational Organized Crime: Analysis of a Global Challenge to Democracy*, ed. Heinrich-Böll-Stiftung and Regine Schönenberg (Bielefeld: transcript Verlag, 2013), 149–60.

22. Marco Lara Klahr, "Extortion in Everyday Life in Mexico," in

Transnational Organized Crime: Analysis of a Global Challenge to Democracy, ed. Heinrich-Böll-Stiftung and Regine Schönenberg (Bielefeld: transcript Verlag, 2013), 161–68.

23. Damien Cave and Karla Zabludovsky, "Navy Officer's Killing Escalates Fight for Mexican State," *The New York Times*, July 30, 2013.

24. Correa-Cabrera, *Los Zetas Inc.*

25. Leovigildo González, "Arrollan y matan a sexagenario en Uruapan," *Quadratín Michoacán*, May 16, 2016, www.quadratin.com.mx/justicia /Arrollan-y-matan-a-sexagenario-en-Uruapan.

26. Display advertisements, *Diario ABC de Michoacán*, May 18, 2013, www.calameo.com/read/0016550948678145f7ec6, 2–3.

27. Jan-Albert Hootsen, author interview, December 13, 2023.

28. Jan-Albert Hootsen, "Blood Avocado: The Dark Side of Your Guacamole," *Vocativ*, November 18, 2013, accessed October 22, 2024, web .archive.org/web/20180405025625/https://www.vocativ.com/under world/crime/avocado/index.html.

29. José de Córdoba, "The Violent Gang Wars Behind Your Super Bowl Guacamole," *The Wall Street Journal*, last updated January 31, 2014, www.wsj.com/articles/SB10001424052702303277704579349283584 121344.

30. Richard Marosi, Marisa Gerber, and Tracy Wilkinson, "Pope Makes Stand at the Front Line of Mexico's Drug War," *Los Angeles Times*, February 17, 2016; Laura Tillman, "Families Yearn to Hear Francis Speak of 'Los 43,'" *Los Angeles Times*, February 17, 2016.

31. *Rotten: The Avocado War*, directed by Lucy Kennedy (2019, Zero Point Zero, Netflix Worldwide Entertainment).

32. Manuel A. Abascel to James G. Hall, November 16, 2023, U.S. Department of Justice; "Calvo Growers Inc.," file 000-33385, Form 10-K, United States Securities and Exchange Commission, 2023.

33. Kate Linthicum, "Inside the Bloody Cartel War for Mexico's Multi-billion Dollar Avocado Industry," *Los Angeles Times*, November 21, 2019.

34. Mark Stevenson, "US Suspends Mexican Avocado Imports on Eve of Super Bowl," Associated Press, February 13, 2022.

35. "Tijuana Accountability Review Board," U.S. Department of State, July 26, 2021, www.state.gov/tijuana-accountability-review-board.

36. Angeles Bretón, "Súper Bowl 22. El aguacates de Puebla se usará en el guacamole gringo," *El Universal Puebla*, February 9, 2022, www.eluniversalpuebla.com.mx/estado/super-bowl-2022-el-aguacate -de-puebla-se-usara-en-el-guacamole-gringo.

37. Jesús Noé Suárez, "El origen del aguacate no se encuentra en Michoacán sino en Puebla, revela estudio," *El Sol de Puebla*, January 14, 2022; Sánchez Colín, Mijares Oviedo, López-López, Barrientos-Priego, "Historia del Aguacate en México."

38. "#ConferenciaPresidente | Jueves 3 de noviembre de 2022," Gobierno de México, November 3, 2022, video, 2:52:07, www.youtube.com /watch?v=LwglGoa6XaM.

39. Brooke DiPalma, "Why Rising Avocado Prices Won't Be a Big Deal for Chipotle," *Yahoo Finance*, June 26, 2024; Marina Alejandra Martínez, "Michoacán Perdió De 3 A 4 Millones De Dólares Diarios Por Veto EU Al Aguacate," Changoonga.com, June 27, 2024.

40. Weekly Newsline, California Avocado Society, June 20, 2024.

41. California Avocado Commission, "California Avocado Commission Calls on USDA to Maintain Direct Oversight of Mexico Avocado Export Program," news release, June 26, 2024.

42. La-Cour-Grandmaison and Martinez, "Violent and Vibrant."

43. "Remarks by President Obama and President Calderón of Mexico at Joint Press Availability," the White House Office of the Press Secretary, May 19, 2020, obamawhitehouse.archives.gov/realitycheck/the-press -office/remarks-president-obama-and-president-calder-n-mexico-joint -press-availability.

44. Ramón Paz-Vega, author interview, March 9, 2023.

16 • Icon

1. Alyse Whitney, "This Avocado Toast Cocktail Is My New Favorite Brunch Drink," *Bon Appétit*, March 13, 2018, www.bonappetit.com /story/avocado-toast-cocktail.

2. "Avocados and BFFS | #AvocadoHair | Avocados From Mexico," Avocados From Mexico, February 6, 2018, video, 2:15, www.youtube.com /watch?v=a05H7uJyKt8.

3. Michelle Castillo, "The Most Talked About Super Bowl Advertiser Online Was Avocados From Mexico," CNBC, last updated February 5, 2018, www.cnbc.com/2018/02/05/the-most-talked-about-super-bowl -ad-online-was-about-avocados-.html.

4. Lou Rotell, author interview, June 14, 2024; Erica Cheng, "Texas Grocery Chain Breaks Guinness World Record with Massive Avocado Display," *Chron*, May 6, 2024, www.chron.com/food/article/texas -avocados-world-record-broken-19441526.php.

5. Seth Motel, "2010, Hispanics in the United States Statistical Portrait," Pew Research Center, February 21, 2012, www.pewresearch

.org/hispanic/2012/02/21/2010-statistical-information-on-hispanics
-in-united-states/#hispanic-population-by-nativity-2000-and-2010.

6. Carey Funk and Mark Hugo Lopez, "A Brief Statistical Portrait of U.S. Hispanics," Pew Research Center, June 14, 2022, www.pew research.org/science/2022/06/14/a-brief-statistical-portrait-of-u-s-hispanics.

7. Lauren Rothman, "Avocado Stout Is the Beer Nobody Asked For," *VICE*, November 5, 2018, www.vice.com/en/article/ev3g74/avocado -stout-is-the-beer-nobody-asked-for; Raisa Bruner, "Lattes in Avocados Are Inevitably Here to Combine Two Millennial Favorites," *Time*, May 22, 2017, time.com/4789145/avocado-latte-australia; Tim Nelson, "California Is Obsessed with This Avocado Beer," *myrecipes*, last updated September 13, 2019, www.myrecipes.com/news/avocado -beer-here-california; Angel Kilmister, "An All-Avocado Restaurant Was on 'Shark Tank' Last Night—Here's How It Did," *VICE*, February 12, 2018, www.vice.com/en/article/d3w7bz/an-all-avocado -restaurant-was-on-shark-tank-last-nighttheres-how-it-did.

8. Erin Ailworth, "Super Bowl Means 'Avocado Hand' Is Back—With a Vengeance," *The Wall Street Journal*, January 28, 2020, www.wsj.com /articles/super-bowl-means-guacamoleand-a-spike-in-avocado-related -knife-injuries-11580230243.

9. "Sesame Street: 'Do the Guacamole' Song, Elmo the Musical," Sesame Street, September 19, 2012, video, 1:35, www.youtube.com /watch?v=HgXfLe4l5aA; Munchies Staff, "2017 Was a Strange Year for Avocados," *VICE*, December 12, 2017, www.vice.com/en/article /mb9exx/2017-was-a-strange-year-for-avocados.

10. Emiliano Escobedo, author interview, July 12, 2023; Emiliano Escobedo, "Mexico Marketing Report," World Avocado Congress 2011, Cairns, Australia, September 5–9, 2011.

11. Sam Levin, "Millionaire Tells Millennials: If You Want a House, Stop Buying Avocado Toast," *The Guardian*, May 15, 2017.

12. Ralph M. Pinkerton, "California Avocado Advisory Board," CAS, Y 46 (1962): 15–16.

13. Mark Affleck, "So Long, Ralph Pinkerton," CAS, Y 87 (2004–2005): 27–28.

14. Affleck, "So Long, Ralph Pinkerton"; Suzanne Hendrich, "George M. Briggs (1919–1989)," *The Journal of Nutrition*, 127, no. 12 (December 1997): 2267–69.

15. *The Avocado Bravo*, revised edition, California Avocado Advisory Board, Newport Beach, Calif., 1975.

16. Salvador Dalí, *Dalí: Les Diners de Gala*, trans. J. Peter Moore (Cologne: Taschen, 2016).

17. "Leather Takes on New Look in Designer's Deft Hands," *The Evansville Courier*, July 19, 1956.

18. David Nash, "The True Story of CW Stockwell and the Famous Beverly Hills Hotel Wallpaper," *Architectural Digest*, March 19, 2019, www.architecturaldigest.com/story/cw-stockwell-famous-beverly-hills -hotel-wallpaper-martinique.

19. "History of Appliance Innovation," GE Appliances, accessed August 22, 2024, geappliancesco.com/innovation-history.

20. "'Love of Avocados' Takes to Airways," *Palo Alto Times*, March 31, 1978.

21. Jack Shepherd, "Recognition of the 75th Anniversary: Commemoration and Commitment," CAS, Y 74 (1990): 151–57.

22. Pamela G. Hollie, "Rise in Avocado Use Aids Coast Investors," *The New York Times*, December 23, 1978.

23. Ralph M. Pinkerton, "The End of the Tunnel," CAS, Y 65 (1981): 37–46.

24. Dick Roraback, "Niikura: If You Knew Sushi Like . . ." *Los Angeles Times*, November 25, 1979.

25. Patt Morrison, "Eat Like a Local—Have a California Roll, a French Dip and a Moscow Mule, All Invented in L.A.," *Los Angeles Times*, July 12, 2022.

26. Miguel Barcenas, author interview, November 21, 2023.

27. S. K. Lee and C. W. Coggins Jr., "Feasibility of Marketing Soft Avocado Fruit," CAS, Y 66 (1982): 57–62.

28. Victor Tokar, "The History of Commercial Avocado Ripening," CAS, Y 90 (2007): 77–85.

29. Jessica Weber, "UCR on the Silver Screen," *UCR Magazine*, Summer 2023, www.ucr.edu/magazine/summer-2023/ucr-on-the-silver -screen.

30. Charlene Rainey, Mark Affleck, Kari Bretschger, and Roslyn B. Alfin-Slater, PhD, "The California Avocado: A New Look." *Nutrition Today* 29, no. 3 (May 1994): 23–27.

31. Richard Simon, "Avocado Aid Measure May Spark Dispute," *Los Angeles Times*, October 23, 2000.

32. Charley Wolk, author interview, July 24, 2023.

33. Hass Avocado Board, *One World One Strategy*, 2003/2004,

hassavocadoboard.com/wp-content/uploads/2019/03/hass-avocado
-board-financials-annual-report-2003-4.pdf.

34. United States v. United Foods Inc., 533 U.S. 405 (2001).

35. "State Audit Questions Expenditures at California Avocado Commission," *The Produce News*, January 15, 2009.

36. Hass Avocado Board, *Finer Focus = Clearer Direction*, 2007/2008, hassavocadoboard.com/wp-content/uploads/2019/03/hass-avocado
-board-financials-annual-report-2007-8.pdf.

17 • Avocados From Mexico

1. "Pearl Jam's Eddie Vedder and Jeff Ament Sit Down with Bill Simmons," *The Bill Simmons Podcast*, May 3, 2024.

2. Emiliano Escobedo, author interviews, December 21, 2022, and July 12, 2023.

3. Associated Press, "Pepper, Avocado Recall," *Odessa American*, July 18, 2008.

4. Emiliano Escobedo, author interview, December 14, 2023.

5. Dr. Gary W. Williams and Dan Hanselka, *The U.S. Economic Benefits of Hass Avocado Imports from Mexico: 2022 Update* (College Station: Agribusiness Food and Consumer Economics Research Center, September 2022).

6. Alvaro Luque, author interview, May 23, 2023.

7. Billy Yost, "Alvaro Luque Knew When the Time Was Ripe," *Hispanic Executive*, August 17, 2020.

8. Federal Tax Form 990, Department of Treasury Internal Revenue Service, Avocados From Mexico, Tax Year ending June 30, 2023, accessed via ProPublica Nonprofit Explorer, projects.propublica.org/nonprofits
/organizations/463082698/202343359349300214/full.

9. Hass Avocado Board 2012 Annual Report, hassavocadoboard.com
/inside-hab/reports-evaluations.

10. Li Wang, Peter L. Bordi, Jennifer A. Fleming, Alison M. Hill, and Penny M. Kris-Etherton, "Effect of a Moderate Fat Diet with and Without Avocados on Lipoprotein Particle Number, Size and Subclasses in Overweight and Obese Adults: A Randomized, Controlled Trial," *Journal of the American Heart Association* 4, no. 1, January 7, 2015.

11. "Superfoods or Superhype?" *The Nutrition Source*, Harvard T.H. Chan School of Public Health. nutritionsource.hsph.harvard.edu
/superfoods/, accessed September 8, 2024.

12. Lorena S. Pacheco, Yanping Li, Eric B. Rimm, JoAnn E. Manson, Qi Sun, Kathryn Rexrode, Frank B. Hu, Marta Guasch-Ferré, "Avocado Consumption and Risk of Cardiovascular Disease in US Adults," *Journal of the American Heart Association* 11, no. 7, March 30, 2022.

13. Pati Jinich, author interview, January 10, 2024.

18 • Global Avocado

1. "Chile Verde Guacamole," Pati Jinich, accessed August 22, 2024, patijinich.com/chile-verde-guacamole.

2. Stefan Lovgren, "Cinco de Mayo: How a Mexican Holiday Became a Party in the USA," *National Geographic*, May 5, 2006; updated May 4, 2023.

3. "Industry Statistical Data"; Magaña, Van Rijswick, Salinas, and Piggot, "Global Avocado Update 2024"; Weekly Newsline, California Avocado Society, December 28, 2023, and August 22, 2024.

4. Jason Cole and Ken Melban, "Re: Importation of Mexican Avocados into the United States," September 23, 2024, accessed October 14, 2024, www.californiaavocadogrowers.com.

5. Lucero Hernandez, APHIS public affairs specialist, email correspondence with author, October 17, 2024.

6. Calavo Growers Inc., "2022 Annual Report," accessed January 14, 2024, ir.calavo.com/static-files/6e332a44-dbe0-4ef3-ae82-e636daacb265.

7. Calavo Growers Inc., "2023 Annual Report," accessed June 12, 2024, ir.calavo.com/static-files/14a32c2f-f7f0-402d-9cea-70ad649d476d.

8. Author email with Lea Boyd, California Avocado Society, September 4, 2024.

9. FAS Staff, *Avocado Annual: Mexico* (USDA Foreign Agricultural Service, April 5, 2024).

10. FAS Staff, *Avocado Annual: Mexico*; Alejandro Gavito, email correspondence with the author, January 26, 2024.

11. "Chavez Wins First Election in County Under New Law," *Ventura County Star-Free Press*, September 6, 1975.

12. Miriam Pawel, *The Crusades of Cesar Chavez, A Biography* (New York: Bloomsbury Publishing, 2014); Ventura County Cultural Heritage Board Staff, *Ventura County Historical Landmarks & Points of Interest*, third edition (Ventura County Cultural Heritage Board, May 2016).

13. "The Story of Consuelo," Farm Worker Justice, accessed July 10, 2023, www.farmworkerjustice.org/stories-from-the-field/consuelo.

14. Consuelo Mendez, author interview, July 10, 2023. Translation by Consuelo Fernández and Olivia Pickens.

15. Angel Serrano García, author interview, September 11, 2023. Translation by Tamara Zúñiga.

16. Ernesto Veloz, author interview, November 3, 2022.

17. Nancy Rivera Brooks, "PUC Links 5 Deaths to Lax Safety by Edison," *Los Angeles Times*, September 18, 2001; Tyler Hayden, "Farm Worker Fatally Electrocuted," *Santa Barbara Independent*, November 5, 2010; "Accident Report Details," U.S. Department of Labor Occupational Safety and Health Administration, accessed August 22, 2024, www.osha.gov.

18. Shreyasi Majumdar, Sarah McLaren, Sarah Sorensen, and Brad Siebert, "Carbon and Water Footprinting of Avocado Production in New Zealand," in *Adaptive Strategies for Future Farming*, ed. C. L. Christensen, R. Singh, and D. J. Horne (Farmed Landscapes Research Centre, 2022).

19. "Marvel—Trademark Details," Justia Trademarks, accessed January 16, 2024, trademarks.justia.com/882/75/marvel-88275447.html.

20. Holly Ober, "UC Riverside and Eurosemillas partner to bring the next generation of avocados to market," University of California, Riverside, June 9, 2020, news.ucr.edu/articles/2020/06/09/uc-riverside-and -eurosemillas-partner-bring-next-generation-avocados-market.

21. Srinivas Rao, Zenlin Wu, Yu Lifan, Global Avocado Congress, July 7, 2022; ATO Guangzhou, *2022 Fresh Avocado Report* (Foreign Agricultural Service, November 14, 2022).

22. Wayne Prowse, "Australian Avocado Exports and Imports," Avocados Australia Limited, August 17, 2023, avocado.org.au/wp-content /uploads/2022/08/AV-FY-2023-annual.pdf.

23. 2022 Fresh Avocado Report, People's Republic of China, Global Agricultural Information Network, USDA Foreign Agricultural Service, November 14, 2022.

24. Éric Imbert, Lead Researcher, CIRAD French Agricultural Research for International Development, Keynote Address, World Avocado Congress, Auckland, New Zealand, April 3, 2023.

25. David Magaña, author interview, July 15, 2024.

26. Majumdar et al., "Carbon and Water Footprinting."

27. Viridiana Hernández Fernández, "Avocados Are a 'Green Gold' Export for Mexico, but Growing Them Is Harming Forests and Waters," *The Conversation*, May 29, 2024, theconversation.com/avocados

-are-a-green-gold-export-for-mexico-but-growing-them-is-harming
-forests-and-waters-226458.

28. "Unholy Guacamole: Deforestation, Water Capture, and Violence Behind Mexico's Avocado Exports to the U.S. and Other Major Markets," Climate Rights International, November 2023, cri.org/reports/unholy-guacamole.

29. Eugenio Y. Arima, Audrey Denvir, Kenneth R. Young, Antonio González-Rodríguez, and Felipe García-Oliva, "Modeling Avocado-Driven Deforestation in Michoacán, Mexico," *Environmental Research Letters* 17, no. 3 (February 23, 2022).

30. Simon Romero and Emiliano Rodríguez Mega, "Americans Love Avocados: It's Killing Mexico's Forests," *The New York Times*, November 28, 2023.

31. Cassandra Garrison, "Mexican Avocados Grown on Illegal Orchards Should Not Be Exported to U.S., Ambassador Says," *Reuters*, February 26, 2024.

32. Cassandra Garrison, "Mexico's Michoacán State Launches Avocado Certification Aimed at Curbing Deforestation," *Reuters*, August 28, 2024.

33. Max Schoening, author interview, March 7, 2024.

34. Brad Adams, author interview, March 6, 2024.

35. Joel Simon, *Endangered Mexico: An Environment on the Edge* (San Francisco: Sierra Club Books, 1997).

36. Correa-Cabrera, *Los Zetas Inc.*

37. Avocado Sustainability Center, Hass Avocado Board, accessed August 22, 2024, sustainability.hassavocadoboard.com.

38. Author telephone interview with John McGuigan, October 4, 2023.

39. EWG Science Team, "EWG's 2023 Shopper's Guide to Pesticides in Produce," Environmental Working Group, March 20, 2024, www.ewg.org/foodnews/summary.php#clean-fifteen.

40. Louise Gray, *Avocado Anxiety: And Other Stories About Where Your Food Comes From* (New York: Bloomsbury Publishing, 2023).

41. Patricia Manosalva, author interview, August 14, 2023.

42. Stefan Köhne, author interview, January 19, 2024.

Epilogue

1. Marion Popenoe de Hatch, author telephone interview, January 29, 2024.

2. Miguel Ángel Domínguez Ríos, "Historia del aguacate padre en

Atlixco: El origen de una variedad legendaria," *La Jornada de Oriente*, August 21, 2024.

3. Angelina Bueno, "Atlixco y el Aguacate," *Región Atlixco*, July 16, 2021.

4. Beatríz Zafra, interview with translator Olivia Pickens, August 9, 2023.

5. Tara Law, "Next-gen Avocado," *Time*, October 24, 2023, time.com /collection/best-inventions-2023/6324155/luna-ucr.

6. Avocado Variety Database, UC Riverside Avocado Variety Collection, accessed January 18, 2024, avocado.ucr.edu/avocado-variety-database; Greg Alder, "Avocado Variety Profiles," *The Yard Posts*, April 3, 2020, gregalder.com/yardposts/avocado-variety-profiles.

7. Consuelo Fernández Noguera and Kamille Garcia-Brucher, author interview, July 10, 2023.

8. Raquel Folgado, author interview, April 28, 2023.

9. Martha Rendón-Anaya, Alfonso Méndez-Bravo, Enrique Ibarra-Laclette, and Luis Herrera-Estrella, "The Avocado Genome Informs Deep Angiosperm Phylogeny, Highlights Introgressive Hybridization, and Reveals Pathogen-Influenced Gene Space Adaption," *PNAS* 116, no. 34 (August 6, 2019).

10. Onkar Nath, Stephen J. Fletcher, Alice Hayward, Lindsay M. Shaw, Ardashir Kharabian Masouleh, Agnelo Furtado, Robert J. Henry, and Neena Mitter, "A Haplotype Resolved Chromosomal Level Avocado Genome Allows Analysis of Novel Avocado Genes," *Horticulture Research* 9 (August 1, 2022).

11. "Happy Green Gucacamole—The Non-Browning Avocado. Dr. Jeff Touchman," *Talking Biotech with Dr. Kevin Folta*, June 17, 2023.

12. Miguel Gonzalez, author interview, May 4, 2024.

13. The BOLD Program, Hass Avocado Board, hassavocadoboard.com /bold-program/.

Additional Sources

Arellano, Gustavo. *Taco USA: How Mexican Food Conquered America.* Scribner, 2012.

Berners-Lee, Mike. *How Bad Are Bananas? The Carbon Footprint of Everything.* Greystone Books, 2011.

Chamovitz, Daniel. *What a Plant Knows: A Field Guide to the Senses.* Scientific American/Farrar, Straus and Giroux, 2017.

Charles, Jeffrey. "Searching for Gold in Guacamole: California Growers Market the Avocado, 1910–1994." In *Food Nations: Selling Taste in Consumer Societies.* Edited by Warren Belasco and Philip Scranton. Routledge, 2001.

Cohen, Rich. *The Fish That Ate the Whale: The Life and Times of America's Banana King.* Farrar, Straus and Giroux, 2012.

Ellstrand, Norman C. *Sex on the Kitchen Table: The Romance of Plants and Your Food.* University of Chicago Press, 2018.

Farmer, Jared. *Trees in Paradise: The Botanical Conquest of California.* Heyday, 2015.

Gonzales, Juan. *Harvest of Empire: A History of Latinos in America.* Penguin Books, 2011.

Hernandez, Kelly Lytle. *Bad Mexicans: Race, Empire, and Revolution in the Borderlands.* W. W. Norton & Company, 2022.

Holtz, Déborah, and Juan Carlos Mena. *Avocadomania.* Rizzoli, 2022.

Miller, Jeff. *Avocado: A Global History.* Reaktion Books Ltd., 2020.

Olsson, Tore C. *Agrarian Crossings: Reformers and the Remaking of the US and Mexican Countryside.* Princeton University Press, 2017.

Pilcher, Jeffrey M. *Planet Taco: A Global History of Mexican Food.* Oxford University Press, 2012.

Reisner, Marc. *Cadillac Desert: The American West and Its Disappearing Water.* Penguin Books, 2017.

Schaffer, Bruce, B. Nigel Wolstenholme, and Anthony W. Whiley. *The Avocado: Botany Production and Uses*, 2nd ed. CAB International, 2013.

Starr, Kevin. *Americans and the California Dream, 1850–1915.* Oxford University Press, 1973.

Starr, Kevin. *Inventing the Dream: California Through the Progressive Era.* Oxford University Press, 1985.

Stone, Daniel Evan. *The Food Explorer: The True Adventures of the Globe-Trotting Botanist Who Transformed What America Eats.* Dutton, 2018.

Acknowledgments

Green Gold began with a question: Why are avocados everywhere? To find the answer, we called on dozens of experts, talked with avocado growers from around the world, and explored archives throughout the country. Many people shared their passion for avocados, and all contributed to the collective enthusiasm underlying the fruit's rise to fame.

We were inspired by those who let us follow them through the orchards, especially Mary Lu Arpaia, Eric Focht, Patricia Manosalva, Rob Brokaw, Consuelo Fernández Noguera, Kamille Garcia-Brucher, Tim Bliss, Carl Stucky, and Robert Abbott.

We also thank Ben Faber, Ramón Paz-Vega, Ellen Brokaw, Steve Barnard, Rob Wedin, Wendy and Tim MacMurray, Duncan Abbott, Scott Van Der Kar, Ben Van Der Kar, Marvin Ota, Charley Wolk, Bob Lucy, Gray E. Martin, Consuelo Mendez, Alvaro Luque, Rick Bayless, Pati Jinich, Neil Foley, Jane Zentmyer Fernald, Raquel Folgado, Arnon Dag, Matias Purcell, Angel Serrano García, Ernesto Veloz, Matthew Elvena, Amber Newsome, Max Schoening, Brad Adams, Miguel Gonzalez, Billy and Will Carleton, and Stefan Köhne for sharing their time and expertise with us. Speaking with Marion Popenoe de Hatch from her home in Guatemala was a special privilege.

The California Avocado Society and its members were indispensable resources, along with the staff at Brokaw Nursery and the Hass Avocado Board, especially Emiliano Escobedo, Nikki Ford, Gina Widjaja, Alejandro Gavito, and John McGuigan. Special thanks to Sean Bettles of Rincon Farms for sharing the treasure trove of CAS yearbooks.

While we could not include everyone who played a role in the avocado's story, we appreciate those who answered our calls and provided resources, including Miguel Barcenas, Gary S. Bender, Rick Shade, Terry Splane, Jan DeLyser, John Krist, David A. Shirk, Jan-Albert Hootsen, Lea Boyd, Lou Rotell, David Magaña, Éric Imbert, Beatríz Zafra, Claudia Asensio, David M. Obenland, Tom Frew, Alison Kendall, Darren L. Haver, and Zachariah Rutledge. Greg Alder's California gardening newsletter and the late Reuben Hofshi's avocadosource.com archive were helpful references. We learned from all who contributed to this project, and we take responsibility for any mistakes or misinterpretations.

Leora Siegel and Donna Herendeen of the Lenhardt Library of the Chicago Botanic Garden shared their archives, insights, and enthusiasm. We thank them and the Los Angeles Public Library; the Huntington Library, Art Museum, and Botanical Gardens; the California Avocado Society; UC Riverside; Lindsay Martinez of Calavo Growers; and Ramón Paz-Vega for sharing the images featured in the book. Mike Hall created the beautiful map. Allison Saltzman generously offered direction and feedback. Thanks also to the librarians of Jones Library, Amherst, who processed our many interlibrary loan orders.

Lucía Mier y Terán Romero, Tamara Zúñiga, Ricardo Zúñiga, Consuelo Fernández Noguera, Nan Pickens, and Olivia Pickens expertly translated Spanish documents and conversations. Olivia also interviewed and connected us to key sources in Mexico. Carly Weinberger provided valuable research assistance early in the project.

We are indebted to the Hunt Institute for Botanical Documentation at Carnegie Mellon University for digitizing the Wilson Popenoe papers, without which this story could not have been told.

Jessica Geiser, management librarian at Special Collections and University Archives, UC Riverside, assisted us in research related to Calavo and the Fuerte mother tree.

Special thanks to Patrick Spence for tracking down Wilson Popenoe's correspondence at the National Archives and sharing his expertise on all things geographical.

We were privileged to work with the team at Counterpoint Press. Our editor, Dan López, thoughtfully guided us to a completed manuscript, and associate production editor tracy danes helped create a book reflecting its subject's personality. Executive editor Dan Smetanka saw potential in the humble avocado's story. Lena Moses-Schmitt and Rachel Fershleiser enthusiastically spread the word, Lily Philpott developed and coordinated events, and Farjana Yasmin created the eye-catching cover design. Copy editor Jordan Koluch, proofreader Marie Landau, and indexer Matthew MacLellan contributed their expertise. Thanks also to our agent Stacey Glick of Dystel, Goderich & Bourret, whose love of avocados and belief in our story launched the project.

Green Gold honors the memory of Monica Comer Parsons, who many years ago saw something in two awkward sixth graders that caused her to say, "You two should write a book together." Monique is grateful to David Wecker for suggesting the topic and offering love and support and to Ruth Wecker for sharing Neil Foley's indispensable book. Thanks also to Louis, Isidora, Monty, Karen, and Jan. Monique dedicates *Green Gold* with love to Teddy, Ruth, and Jules, who brighten her days and tolerate her avocado anecdotes.

Sarah is forever grateful to her parents, Steven Allaback and Patty Manuras, for passing on their love of books, writing, and avocados. Katy and Mark Allaback provided support and encouragement throughout the avocado book's remarkable journey.

Green Gold benefited significantly from Caleb Carr's tips on content, agents, and publicity. Ethan Carr championed the book from the very beginning and gave Sarah the time and place to write. Her greatest debt is to Marion Carr, the catalyst for the revision that launched the book. Marion's insights, social connections, editorial contributions, and unwavering faith in the project were essential in bringing *Green Gold* to fruition.

Index

Page numbers in italics refer to images.
Page numbers followed by "i" refer to pages in the insert.

SARAH ALLABACK, a historian specializing in architectural history and landscape preservation, has worked for the National Park Service, Monticello, and the Library of American Landscape History. Her books and articles explore the lives of designers who shaped the American landscape. Allaback is a graduate of Princeton University and MIT, where she earned her doctorate in architecture, art, and environmental studies. She grew up in Carpinteria, California, and lives in Amherst, Massachusetts.

© Kelly Feldmiller

MONIQUE F. PARSONS is a journalist and award-winning audio producer whose work has aired on NPR and public radio stations nationwide. She is a graduate of Princeton University, Northwestern University's Medill School of Journalism, and Harvard Divinity School. A native of Carpinteria, California, where her family grows organic avocados, Parsons lives in suburban Chicago.